Turning Points in Twentieth-Century Irish History

Editor

THOMAS E. HACHEY

IRISH ACADEMIC PRESS
DUBLIN • PORTLAND, OR

First published in 2011 by Irish Academic Press

2 Brookside
Dundrum Road
Dublin 14, Ireland

920 NE 58th Avenue, Suite 300
Portland, Oregon,
97213-3786, USA

This edition © 2011 Irish Academic Press
Chapters © 2011 individual contributors

www.iap.ie

British Library Cataloguing in Publication Data
An entry can be found on request

Turning points in twentieth century Irish history.
1. Ireland—History—20th century. 2. Ireland—Social
conditions—20th century.
I. Hachey, Thomas E.
941.5'082-dc22

978 0 7165 3121 0 (cloth)
978 0 7165 3122 7 (paper)

Library of Congress Cataloging-in-Publication Data
An entry can be found on request

Printed by Good News Digital Books, Ongar, Essex

Contents

Notes on Contributors

Mike Cronin is Academic Director of Boston College – Ireland, and has written widely on aspects of Irish history. His publications include: *The Blueshirts and Irish Politics* (1997); *Sport and Nationalism in Ireland* (co-editor) (1999); *A History of Ireland* (2001); *Wearing the Green: A History of St Patrick's Day* (2002); and *The Gaelic Athletic Association, 1884–2009* (co-editor) (2009).

Enda Delaney teaches history at the University of Edinburgh. He has written widely on Irish migration, including: *Demography, State and Society: Irish Migration to Britain, 1921–1971* (2000); *Irish Emigration Since 1921* (2002); and *The Irish in Post-War Britain* (2007). He is working on a book on *Ireland and Modernity*, for publication by Oxford University Press in 2013.

Anne Dolan is Lecturer in Modern Irish History at Trinity College Dublin. Her more recent publications include: *Commemorating the Irish Civil War: History and Memory, 1923–2000* (2003); *'No Surrender Here!' The Civil War Papers of Ernie O'Malley* (co-editor) (2007); and *Reinterpreting Emmet: Essays on the Life and Legacy of Robert Emmet* (co-editor) (2007).

Diarmaid Ferriter is Professor of Modern Irish History at University College Dublin. His major works include: *A Nation of Extremes: The Pioneers in Twentieth-Century Ireland* (1999); *Lovers of Liberty? Local Government in Twentieth-Century Ireland* (2001); *The Transformation of Ireland, 1900–2000* (2004); *Judging Dev: A Reassessment of the Life and Legacy of Éamon de Valera* (2007); and *Occasions of Sin: Sex and Society in Modern Ireland* (2009).

Louise Fuller holds a faculty appointment in the Department of History at the National University of Ireland, Maynooth. Her publications include: *Irish Catholicism since 1950: The Undoing of a Culture* (Dublin, 2002); and *Irish and Catholic? Towards an Understanding of Identity* (co-editor)(Dublin, 2006).

Tom Garvin is an Honorary Research Fellow at the Institute for British–Irish Studies and was Professor of Politics at University College Dublin from 1991 to 2008. His books include: *Nationalist Revolutionaries in Ireland* (1987); *The Birth of Irish Democracy* (1996); *Preventing the Future: Why Was Ireland So Poor for So Long?* (2004); and *Judging Lemass: The Measure of the Man* (2009).

Thomas E. Hachey is University Professor of History and Executive Director of the Centre for Irish Programmes at Boston College. Among his publications are: *The Problem of Partition: Peril to World Peace* (editor) (1972); *Britain and Irish Separatism: From the Fenians to the Free State, 1867–1922* (1977); *Perspectives on Irish Nationalism* (co-editor) (1989); and *The Irish Experience Since 1800: A Concise History* (co-author) (2010, 3rd edn).

The late **Peter Hart** was Canada Research Chair in Irish Studies at Memorial University of Newfoundland. He wrote extensively on the Irish Republican Army: *The IRA and Its Enemies, Violence and Community in Cork, 1916–23* (1998); *British Intelligence in Ireland, 1920–21: The Final Reports* (2002); *The IRA at War, 1916–1923* (2003); and *Mick: The Real Michael Collins* (2006).

Thomas Hennessey holds the rank of Reader in the Department of History and American Studies at Canterbury Christ Church University. His publications include: *A History of Northern Ireland* (1996); and *Dividing Ireland: World War I and Partition* (1998).

Jason Knirck is Associate Professor of History at Central Washington University. He is the author of *Imagining Ireland's Independence: The Debates over the Anglo-Irish Treaty of 1921* (2006); and *Women of the Dáil: Gender, Republicanism and the Anglo-Irish Treaty* (2006).

Maria Luddy is Professor of Modern Irish History at the University of Warwick. Her numerous publications include: *Hanna Sheehy Skeffington* (1995); *Women and Philanthropy in Nineteenth-Century Ireland* (1995); *Female Activists: Irish Women and Change, 1900–1960* (co-editor) (2001); and *Prostitution and Irish Society, 1800–1940* (2007).

Gillian McIntosh is Leverhulme Research Fellow in the School of History and Anthropology, Queen's University Belfast. Her publications include *The Force of Culture: Unionist Identities in Twentieth-Century Ireland* (1999); *Belfast City Hall: One Hundred Years* (2006); and a co-edited volume entitled *Irish Women at War: The Twentieth Century* (2010).

Acknowledgements

I am indebted to a number of people for their help and support in the preparation of this book, Alissa Condon foremost among them. Alissa brought to this project excellent editorial abilities and a strong familiarity with twentieth-century Irish historiography. She was of particular help in identifying content issues that might have proven difficult for some readers.

It was also my good fortune to be the beneficiary of generous assistance given primarily by Joan Reilly, together with Michael J. Burns, Jane Hachey and Lauren Hoehlein, all of whom read and proofed the revised texts. Irish Academic Press editor Lisa Hyde provided her experienced counsel in all stages of the production, even to the extent of identifying and selecting the distinctive cover for the book. Her splendid in-house editor, Aonghus Meaney and proofreader, Geraldine Brady ensured that the final manuscript would ultimately reflect creditably upon publisher and contributors alike. I do, of course, assume full responsibility for any and all errors that may have eluded such corporate scrutiny.

Mike Cronin, a talented colleague who helped in the initial planning of the lecture series and book, was an invaluable resource. Mike offered prudential guidance at successive stages in the planning and implementation of the project and I owe him much for his willing and persistent spirit.

I wish to thank the President, Provost and Dean of the College of Arts and Sciences at Boston College whose support for the Centre for Irish Programmes' lecture series in Irish Studies enables the university to promote published collections of this kind. Virtually all of the chapters contained in this volume were first presented in an earlier iteration at either the Center's headquarters in Connolly House on the university's main campus in Chestnut Hill, Massachusetts, or at the Dublin house in St. Stephen's Green.

Lastly, I am grateful for the professionalism of a diverse and distinguished group of co-contributors, for the engaging and stimulating company of my Irish Studies and Department of History colleagues, and for the indispensable asset that a great university library system does render. Scholarship is especially well served at Boston College by the work of University Librarian Dr. Thomas Wall, Burns Librarian Dr. Robert O'Neill, Archives and Manuscripts Librarian David Horn, and Circulation Manager and Irish Collections specialist Kathleen Williams.

Introduction

History embraces a layered fabric of both the readily identifiable and subliminally obscure factors that help shape human experience. And Ireland's history, no different from that of any other nation, has been in part a welter of events, decisions and missed opportunities that offer insights regarding the causes, character and consequences of transformative change. But there also exists a multiplicity of more eclectic dimensions to the historical process that can further enrich our understanding of the broader narrative. It was, therefore, this more holistic approach to interpreting the past that prompted the diversity of the essays to follow. It is not that the 'turning points' referenced in these chapters represent anything more than a finite sampling of the agents of change in Irish life. Our 'turning points' are not necessarily those historical developments or happenings that were catalysts for new beginnings or for cataclysmic changes. There are foundational aspects that are particular to every nation's history, whether it be Britain's Glorious Revolution of 1688, America's Declaration of Independence in 1776 or the establishment of the People's Republic of China in 1949. But such events are not our central focus here. For example, included in this collection of essays is a reassessment of the 1916 Rising by Peter Hart, and Maria Luddy's use of women's history as a means of understanding women's activism in the new state. The former would certainly be included in the category of seismic change, but not the latter. Yet both, or so we argue, are equally important. The year 1916 may very well have had an indelible impact upon the struggle for Irish independence, but the way in which women were employed had a clear impact on gender relations, household incomes and societal ideas of equality. It is the aim of this book to illustrate how the twists and turns of history do reflect and define the past in the social, political, economic, religious and other aspects of the national experience.

In affirming how Irish history has turned on numerous axes, some quite apart from the political history of the nation and the contested identities that exist on the island, we further acknowledge how the ways in which Irish history is researched and written have profoundly changed in recent decades. It is in itself yet another turning point that this collection acknowledges. Ireland was by no means alone in having most of the history written about it up to the 1970s concentrate almost exclusively on the high politics of the nation. Vociferous arguments typified the revisionist debate of the 1980s and '90s, in which traditional interpretations were soundly challenged. Contentious disputes often centred on the ways in which national histories were produced, especially pertinent given the inconclusive nature of the Irish revolution and the continuing link of the six counties of Northern Ireland with the United Kingdom. The national (or nationalist) school defended the received wisdom that included the orthodox treatment of Ireland's historical experience, while the revisionist school demanded a reassessment of the role that all traditions had played in the nation's history. Perhaps intensifying the tenor of that dialogue was the fact that those arguments were being advanced against the backdrop of the enduring violence in Northern Ireland. And there were the often hostile exchanges over what was being debated and commemorated in 1995, the 150th anniversary of the start of the Famine, and 1998, the 200th anniversary of the 1798 rebellion.[1]

The ubiquitous influence of those debates extends even to the work of Irish poets, writers and clerics, and to popular films like *Michael Collins* and *The Wind That Shakes the Barley*. Reviews of such productions, especially in the popular press, often elicited a nationalist spin that eclipsed any artistic criticism. Whatever the passions aroused by that debate, it represented a timely and essential corrective. Revisionists challenged the dominant nationalist history of Ireland, and in the context of the sectarian strife throughout the North, offered a series of more nuanced and rounded histories of the island that sought to bring other communities and narratives in from the cold. And their impact within the Irish Republic was equally reformative. The reanalysis of Ireland's histories, as demanded by revisionism, was part of a socio-political rethinking of what it meant to be Irish in all its forms, and the more inclusive character of that debate during the 1980s and '90s undoubtedly helped inform the spirit of the peace process that came to fruition with the signing of the Belfast Agreement in 1998.

However salutary a legacy revisionism might represent, it did contain at least one notable shortcoming. The favoured form of history that it celebrated was essentially political. Compounding that affinity was the creation of the National Archives in 1988. Until that date Ireland had not been in conformity with the increasing number of countries with a thirty-year rule governing the release of government archives, and researchers had been severely handicapped by their inability to access official sources. The opening of the Irish government archives released a wealth of riches to a new generation of historians who could undertake pioneer work or test theses published prior to the availability of such documents. The overwhelming dominance of political history, already the principal medium within the discipline for Irish academics, together with graduate and undergraduate students, became still more entrenched in the aftermath of these developments. As Tom Garvin noted in 1996, the creation of the National Archive and its rapid release of a vast amount of material changed the manner in which Irish history was researched and also defined its own research agenda.[2] That epic circumstance would shortly result in having much of Irish history dominated by the archive from the moment of its creation, now little more than two decades ago.

And what have been the implications of that imbalance? Until almost the dawn of the twenty-first century, Irish historiography remained predominantly political in focus. And that predilection would endure despite the fact that historians elsewhere were turning away from political history and embracing what was euphemistically labelled the 'new' history. Even as most of Ireland's revisionist battles were being fought in the field of political history, now substantially enriched by the sheer volume of archival accounts, a different tack was taken in other countries where the interest in social history morphed almost seamlessly into what would hence be known as the 'new history'. It began with a gravitation toward cultural history, and proceeded to the adoption of theories from literature and elsewhere that first introduced postmodernism and poststructuralist debates to history during the 1980s and '90s when such discourse was largely absent in Ireland. With politics the focus of research now reinforced by the new archival facility on Bishop Street in Dublin, there was no time for, and little interest in, methodological or theoretical innovation.

Pervasive change has accompanied the start of a new century in a very notable way. There continues to be solid and important scholarship undertaken with a classically traditional approach to Irish history, but there has also emerged more diverse approaches to the subject that are indicative of the new methodologies. Each of the topics contained in the chapters of this book represent various kinds of turning points in history. And at another level, the manner in which some of these essays are written, as well as the elements that they analyze, is indicative of a turning point in the practice of historical research and writing in the post-revisionist age.

Gillian McIntosh examines how civic portraits were employed as political tools in late nineteenth-century Belfast and explains how they embodied the aspirations, values and agendas of local political elites. Anne Dolan shifts the focus on IRA-inflicted deaths between 1919 and 1923 from *who* was killed to *how* they were killed, explaining that by choosing to kill in a particular way the IRA altered the terms of war in Ireland. Maria Luddy identifies the ways in which women activists drew political power from the specific language of the 1916 Proclamation and the 1922 Constitution. Enda Delaney looks at modernity – as distinct from modernization – in 1960s Ireland. His 'bottom up' analysis helps illustrate how grassroot social and political forces often have been overlooked in the rush to highlight the policies of Lemass, Whitaker and other members of the political elite. Mike Cronin discusses President John F. Kennedy's 1963 visit to Ireland through the vehicle of spectacle, and illustrates how the visit did not symbolize 'Lemass modernism' but rather spoke to an Ireland that was quickly passing away. And Tom Garvin's nuanced reading of the process of secularization draws on his knowledge of development theory and utilizes revelatory sociological surveys in providing an insightful analysis of the decline of the church's influence in both Irish society and politics.

The other chapters may appear to assess what many readers might judge to be more clear-cut, or at least more commonly recognized, historical turning points. These include the essay by the late Peter Hart who revisits the Easter Rising within the broader matrix of the era in terms of both Irish and European social history, and invites the reader to consider the role of circumstantial forces that may challenge more conventional perceptions of how the Rising impacted Ireland's revolutionary legacy. My own chapter on Irish neutrality reviews the manner in which that policy has been understood or employed over the past seventy or more years, and explores its meaning and sustainability in the world of the twenty-first century. Jason Knirck offers an informative account of the women of the Irish revolutionary period, explaining how the means by which they gained influence ironically became the facilitator for their political demise. Louise Fuller provides an historiographical portrayal of the Irish Catholic narrative in the twentieth century, while Diarmaid Ferriter examines Dublin Archbishop John McQuaid's long and controversial career and argues that Ireland had outgrown McQuaid's leadership even before his episcopal tenure had drawn to a close. The book concludes with an essay by Thomas Hennessey on the origins of the peace process. Given his own involvement in and proximity to that process, Hennessey's judgment that the Belfast Agreement of 1998 was the most significant political development in the history of Ireland since partition is certainly worthy of serious reflection. He was, as Dean Acheson famously titled his own autobiography, 'Present at the Creation ...'

In its entirety, *Turning Points in Twentieth-Century Irish History* offers a fresh way of viewing the Irish historical experience. It builds on recent historiographical, albeit conventional, approaches to Irish history, as well as on theoretical approaches embraced by the new scholarship that steps outside, or at least reconfigures, the study of Ireland's past, often in ways not wedded to traditional political history. Both help to complete framing the questions and issues that specialists in the discipline must continue to address. While the basic idea of a turning point in Irish history will always be contested, with battle lines drawn over what should be included and excluded, what we offer here is a selectively chosen and intentionally balanced collection of essays that focus on periods, events and movements that transformed Ireland.

Thomas E. Hachey
Higgins Beach
Scarborough
Maine
24 July 2010

CHAPTER ONE

What Did the Easter Rising Really Change?

PETER HART

The 1916 Easter Rising was a 'turning point' in Irish history. The Irish Revolution started there, along with the Irish Republican Army and modern republicanism. A whole new phalanx of national leaders was propelled into the political arena, which they would dominate for decades. Dublin Castle was discredited, home rule became impossible and partition became inevitable. The Proclamation of the Republic is seen as a kind of foundational document for the independent Irish state, and the commemoration of the event has just been revived as the centrepiece of the state calendar. As Yeats wrote, 1916 utterly changed the currents of Irish history etc.

Or so it is said.

Why was the Rising so important? After all, only a thousand or so people were involved, it was largely confined to Dublin, it lasted less than a week and it was doomed to military failure. A death toll of fewer than 500 also seems modest by wider contemporary standards: it took a lot more killing than that to constitute a turning point in the Great War.[1]

The answer, according to the standard – and very familiar – storyline, is that the combination of rebellion and official repression caused a massive shift in nationalist public opinion that laid the basis for revolution and independence. Fighting bravely and dying by firing squad made the rebels heroes and martyrs, Sinn Féin exploded in popularity by association, the 'moderate' Irish Party was discredited and the course was set for a republic. In academic terms it has been described as a 'cultural trigger point'.[2] In nationalist or republican terms, it was a kind of consciousness-raising exercise with guns, a revelation of sacred truth, even a miracle. Maybe the Rising wasn't sufficient on its own to cause the Sinn Féin electoral victory of 1918 or the semi-victorious War of Independence of 1918–21, but it was still absolutely necessary (and therefore justified).

The role of the Rising in determining Ireland's future is something historians have often accepted rather than investigated. In fact, the 1916 Rising exists as a sort of island in history, a pivotal event seemingly explainable only in the actors' own terms. Patrick Pearse, Seán MacDermott and the other Irish Republican Brotherhood leaders sought a blood sacrifice to save Ireland's soul or honour, and that's more or less what they got.

Where were the structural causes? The institutional or class interests? Can a few people just decide to change the course of history by sheer Al-Qaedaesque willpower?

For the purposes of this essay, however, the status of the Rising as an event unto itself, driven by personal choices and small-group ideologies, is useful. It makes it much easier to distinguish it from the larger flow of events going on around it. So while it is tricky to ask how differently things would have been if the Rising had never happened, we can certainly ask: what else had happened, what was happening and what might have happened anyway?

I

If we begin by asking what had already happened that might help explain events in 1916 and after, we must go back to the near-rebellion, or perhaps pseudo-rebellion, of two years before. It was the home rule crisis of 1913–14 that produced the first unionist challenge to the legitimacy of British rule, and the first armed resistance movement, the Ulster Volunteer Force. Given the government's acquiescence to paramilitarism, and the Irish Party's reliance on the Liberal alliance to deliver home rule, the logic of ethnic politics allowed more militant nationalists to seize the initiative and organize the countervailing Irish Volunteers. After 1913, therefore, any resolution of the problem would almost certainly require some kind of military confrontation. The Bachelor's Walk shootings by British soldiers in July 1914 could have turned into something much worse, and the outbreak of war in Europe did not really change the political equation beyond forcing a temporary truce. Unionists did not accept the home rule bill and the Ulster question was not yet settled. Most important of all, the Irish Volunteers split, giving the Irish Republican Brotherhood a vehicle for insurrection. The Easter rebellion could not have happened without these unprecedented decisions and events, which cast a long shadow over the whole following decade.[3]

The Rising may have been the mutant offspring of the home rule crisis and the Great War, but it cannot really be said to have been caused by either. They gave republican conspirators the opportunity to enact their fantasy, but Pearse and company were not actually motivated by or reacting to these events as such. They were not disappointed or frustrated by the absence of home rule self-government, nor did they care deeply about the war. Nevertheless, while they were scheming away in Parnell Square and Rathmines, the gravitational pull of total war was gradually pulling Irish politics off course, rebellion or no. As has been pointed out before, the centrality of 1916 to the Irish historical narrative often obscures those otherwise era-defining dates, 1914 and 1918.[4]

Ireland's fate was always ultimately decided in London and, thanks to the intensity and longevity of the war, British politics were changing. Various crises forced Prime Minister Asquith to bring British and Irish unionists into a coalition government in May 1915, which meant anti-nationalist hardliners like Andrew Bonar Law and Walter Long had a direct say in Irish policy. And this influence only increased, as December 1916 saw David Lloyd George replace Asquith as prime minister with Conservative backing. The Liberals – the party of home rule – split as a result and the Tory resurgence was capped by victory in the December 1918 general election (although Lloyd George remained premier at the head of a Conservative-dominated coalition). Thus, regardless of what Irish revolutionaries were doing, the government was growing increasingly anti-nationalist and pro-unionist.

On the other hand, the war also moved Ireland a long way down the list of British policy priorities – a slide that the Rising could only temporarily reverse. This, and the decline of the Liberal Party, meant that Irish self-government was no longer the main issue defining party politics in Britain – which, in turn, eventually opened up more room to reach a settlement with cross-party support. Thus, paradoxically, while John Redmond and Herbert Asquith couldn't cut a deal with the Conservative leadership in 1914 (or 1916), Michael Collins and David Lloyd George could in 1921.

The war also had a huge economic impact. Consumption and income taxes went up and up, and prices rose with them. For farmers and agribusiness in general – and thus the Irish economy – this created a boom. Agricultural product prices doubled between 1914 and 1917, and continued to rise through 1920, until falling back again in 1921 and after.[5] By the end of the war, branch banks were reporting record deposits.[6] The value of land increased accordingly. In the Limerick area, for example, the annual average sale price per acre of agricultural land ranged from £5.8 to £16.6 in the years 1903–13. In 1914–24, the comparable lowest and highest figures were £10.8 and £56.3.[7]

Nevertheless, this windfall notably bypassed those small farmers and would-be farmers living in the west and midlands – the 'land hungry' – and they were growing increasingly frustrated. Both the Land Commission and the Congested Districts Board slowed their operations once war was declared, so much less land was purchased for redistribution. Access to land was also becoming much more expensive: if Limerick is anything to go by, conacre rents tripled between 1913 and 1919.[8] The greatest beneficiaries of this situation were the big cattle ranchers, making a fortune in the wartime marketplace.

Another group hurt by inflation was the working class, whose wages barely kept pace with rising prices. For Irish consumers, the price of potatoes had doubled by 1919, while butter and pork rose even higher. Inflation raised wage demands, while wartime labour shortages and increasing government regulation tilted the balance of power from employers to unions, which gained new members by the hundreds and thousands. Most striking of all was the growth of the militant Irish Transport and General Workers' Union (ITGWU), which went from less than ten branches in April 1916 to over 200 in December 1918 and over 400 a year after that.[9] As elsewhere in the world, these circumstances eventually launched a strike wave. There were fifty-eight strikes in Ireland in 1914, sixty-two in 1915, seventy-five in 1916, 112 in 1917 and 228 in 1918. The number of strikers went from 5,900 to 68,000, and days lost from 290,000 to 736,000.[10] This upsurge promised a powerful new political presence: an Irish Labour Party. This new movement would be a vital component of the revolutionary coalition.

Another major change – albeit one of uncertain significance[11] – was the near-stoppage of emigration during the war. The annual migration rate per 1,000 people fell from 7.1 in 1913 to 4.6 in 1914 and then all the way down to 0.2 in 1918, before rebounding to 3.5 in 1920.[12] Of course it is impossible to know how many people would have left the country if there had been no war, and the emigration rate had been slowly declining for decades, but it seems fair to conclude that well over

100,000 young men and women were forced to stay when they otherwise would have left. This group would have added considerably to the pool of potential revolutionary recruits, as well as provided, perhaps, an extra element of frustration to be channelled into patriotic activism.

It is difficult to say how much social or economic opportunity affects political commitment, and the presence of so many would-be Americans, Australians or whatever must be set against the removal of tens of thousands of uniformed migrants to France and other war zones. However, emigration and military service did come together in a series of widely reported panics over conscription in 1914 and 1915.[13] Thousands of young men reportedly left Ireland for fear of being drafted (although official statistics do not show a big jump in the ratio of male to female migrants in 1914 and 1915), and the cutting off of this escape route undoubtedly fuelled anxiety over the question.

The war was increasingly unpopular in nationalist Ireland in 1915–16, where enthusiasm (especially in rural areas and outside Ulster) was never high to begin with. Voluntary recruitment among Catholics never came close to matching British standards, even among those with non-agricultural occupations, and enlistment rates plummeted as the war dragged on.[14] A trial survey by the newly established Department of Recruiting was conducted in Charleville, County Cork in late 1915, and the response is illuminating. Of the 204 men of military age who gave answers, 144 refused to enlist, thirty-one were unfit or had already been rejected and twenty-two declared themselves 'needed at home'. A variety of other reasons were given, including 'won't go until compelled'; 'would not fight for British monarchy' and 'nothing to fight for'. Fifty-eight men refused to say why, some of whom 'offered violence'.[15] It is hard to imagine anything like these results coming from England, Scotland or Wales. Outright opposition to the war was still scarce in 1915 and early 1916 but there was also much less patriotic engagement with it than in Protestant Ulster or Britain. Nationalist newspapers echoed and emphasized this mood, as Allied disasters and lack of progress filled their pages alongside complaints about government neglect and abuse.[16] As Chief Secretary Augustine Birrell put it, 'Irish criticism of the war and its chances were not of the optimistic cast that prevail in Britain. Every event and result was put in the balance, and weighed.'[17]

Partly as a result of these fears and grievances, the anti-Party, anti-war Irish Volunteers were gradually gaining members and energy through 1915 and 1916, up to the Rising. The organization was also becoming more hostile to Redmond and Dublin Castle and more openly separatist. This wasn't just nefarious IRB influence either. Eoin MacNeill, who opposed the Rising, was very much in the van of this increased militancy, as was evident in the pages of the weekly *Irish Volunteer*. In a July 1915 statement, for example, the Volunteer Executive pledged:

> ... resistance to any partition or dismemberment of Ireland which would exclude a part of the people of Ireland from the benefits of national autonomy ... resistance to any scheme of compulsory military service under any authority except a free National Government ... resistance to any scheme of taxation which may be imposed without the consent of the people of Ireland, and which may defeat all their hopes of national prosperity ...[18]

The basic expectation among active Volunteers was that Liberal home rule promises would be betrayed and the government would inevitably move against them. If so, the Volunteers were determined to defend themselves: they would fight rather than give up their arms. As Mac-Neill himself put it, just weeks before the Rising, 'Whether it is on equal terms, or two or five or twenty or forty to one, let them come against us and we will not shirk it.'[19] Some kind of battle was coming and, indeed, almost did happen in February 1916 when the army and the Dublin police planned a round-up of Volunteer leaders, followed by mass internment.[20] If the conspirators had waited, they'd have probably got their sacrificial confrontation, and with a lot more public support (as MacNeill pointed out).

What this meant was that the Irish Party was faced with enormous problems, even without the Rising. Grievances piled up that it could not address, alienating sections of the electorate. John Redmond had committed himself to backing a long, unpopular war. The party's three great achievements – land reform, home rule and leverage with the Liberal government – were blocked indefinitely or slipping away.

II

The home rule crisis, the war and their cumulative consequences meant that some later events would occur, Rising or no. The first of these was the failed attempt to negotiate a home rule deal in the spring and summer of 1916. Once the rebellion had been quashed in early May, Liberal and Irish Party thoughts turned to the idea of completing the suspended political settlement, to match coercion with conciliation in the traditional British manner. Prime Minister Herbert Asquith told then-Minister of Munitions David Lloyd George to explore the options and, in a remarkable feat of deal-making, he managed to craft an agreement between Redmond and Edward Carson, the Ulster Unionist Party leader. A Dublin parliament would be set up as soon as possible, but its writ would not run in the six north-eastern counties of present-day Northern Ireland. Two key issues were creatively fudged, however: the permanence of partition and the extent of cabinet backing for the deal. Such ambiguities were always present when Lloyd George dealt with Irish politicians, but both Carson and Redmond went ahead in good faith and sold the deal to their followers as reciprocal sacrifices.

Before the agreement could be implemented, however, Walter Long, a senior Conservative minister (and habitual trouble-maker) and Lord Lansdowne, a southern unionist peer, seized upon these inevitable gray areas to lead a wreaking campaign from inside the government. Threatening to break up the coalition, they were able to get the proposals amended to make partition permanent. Redmond furiously rejected this and, as the obstructionists had hoped, the deal fell through in July. This failed negotiation was the last real opportunity for a consensual nationalist–unionist compromise backed by all the key Irish players.[21]

Lloyd George and Carson were angry at how their efforts had been sabotaged, but by far the biggest loser was John Redmond. He looked weak, gullible and a failure, and by the time the talks had ended, he had spent most of his political capital in both London and Ireland. The Catholic hierarchy had not spoken out on the Rising itself (they couldn't agree on what to say), and they also remained officially silent on the Lloyd George scheme, but were deeply opposed in private. Particularly galling was the idea of a Protestant-dominated northern Executive. Cardinal Logue said that 'it would be infinitely better to remain as we are for 50 years to come, under English rule, than to accept these proposals'.[22]

This deep-seated objection to partition – and rejection of those who advocated it, even at the price of home rule – was widespread in nationalist Ireland, and probably much more important in radicalizing public opinion than any feelings for or against rebellion. A survey of the three national newspapers in the months after the Rising suggests that concerns about executions and internment in the early weeks in May quickly gave way to the old questions and drama over home rule. Whereas two-thirds of *Irish Independent* editorials were devoted to the Rising and its repression in May, this fell to 11 per cent in June. Self-government and the fate of Ulster were the subjects in 21 per cent of editorials in May, and fully 88 per cent in June. Letters to the editor followed the same pattern, with the percentage of those dealing with the Rising falling from 45 per cent to 12 per cent, while home rule went from occupying one-fifth to nearly four-fifths of the letter columns. And, while their political perspectives differed, both the *Freeman's Journal* and the *Irish Times* followed the same pattern. Police reports reveal a similar shift, with the home rule talks becoming the country's principal political preoccupation in June and July.[23] The fact that Redmond was willing to agree to the exclusion of six northern counties and then lost home rule anyway produced both relief and anger. As Patrick Maume put it, 'the Irish Party accepted partition without receiving its prize; now, accusing the government of treachery, it convicted itself of folly'.[24]

The same sources also suggest that the Easter rebels were often given credit for forcing the government's hand in re-starting home rule negotiations – and it is fair to say that they would indeed not have taken place in the spring of 1916 if there had been no insurrection. However, it should also be pointed out that some such process was bound to occur sooner or later, simply because the issue was unresolved and a home rule bill was actually on the statute books, subject only to a Suspensory Act, which had to be renewed in September 1915. Any political crisis, or the end of the war, would have revived it, and the government's desire to mollify American opinion might well have reintroduced the question regardless (as with the Irish Convention of 1917–18).

The second crisis to follow the Rising was the land war that erupted in western Ireland in 1917–18, largely out of frustration with the slow-down in land transfers and redistribution, coupled with the Congested Districts Board's decision to let untenanted land to graziers.[25] This agitation followed the usual script of cattle drives, vandalism, riots and land seizures, only this time the campaign was conducted largely under the aegis of local Sinn Féin clubs and leaders (rather than the United Irish League), thereby providing the first concrete opportunity for the reorganized and re-launched movement to assert a kind of national leadership. It proved to be a major boost to party fortunes. If we plot the number of new members joining Sinn Féin per county per capita between December 1917 and March 1918 against the incidence of agrarian 'outrages' over the same period, we find an impressive correlation coefficient of 0.66, the strongest result of any variable tested (out of over 100). Moreover, the result is still 0.42 if we compare the same agrarian violence with new Sinn Féiners recruited between July 1917 and December of the same year, suggesting (as does other evidence) a lesser but still significant agrarian element to the earlier phase of expansion as well.[26]

After March 1918, the imminent threat of military conscription expanded insurgency ranks. Once the British government had introduced the necessary legislation, every sector of nationalist opinion was actively united against it, from the Catholic Church to Irish-based trade unions. So much so that the government ultimately backed off, although not before the political damage was done. Sinn Féin and the Volunteers were handed an unparalleled propaganda victory, the government – and the concept of devolved home rule – lost all credibility, and the Irish Party lost any chance of recovering ground lost to their new political rivals. It was this national mobilization that set the stage for the overwhelming republican victory at the polls in the December general election. Conscription presented by far the biggest crisis for nationalist Ireland between 1914 and 1918 and by far the biggest opportunity for the republican movement, and it would have happened regardless of rebellion.

One of the key players in both the anti-conscription campaign and in the election was the revived labour movement. It independently organized protest rallies and an impressive one-day general strike on 23 April, a clear demonstration of what could be done if the government attempted to impose its will. In electoral terms, the Labour Party played a crucial role by not taking part, and instead throwing its weight behind self-determination, i.e. Sinn Féin.[27] There would have been no republican landslide if this potentially powerful rival had taken the field.

It would be impossible to weigh precisely the different variables that produced the rise of Sinn Féin and its popular and electoral triumph, but the failure to achieve a home rule settlement in 1914, 1916 and after, the renewal of land agitation, the parallel rise of the trade union movement, and the threat of conscription were all highly influential.

One final thing the Rising didn't change was Ulster unionist opinion. It has often been said that joint nationalist–unionist involvement in the war effort opened a window for compromise or co-operation, but that the Rising (in combination with the Ulster Division's losses on the Somme in July 1916) closed it again with a bang. The rebellion helped drive the Protestant North and the Catholic South further apart, and made partition more likely – an ironic result given the aims of the rebels.

This idea is false. The Rising did allow unionist writers and politicians to paint all nationalists as untrustworthy or separatists at heart, and the idea of self-government as dangerous to the UK's national security. However, the reality was that no matter what nationalists said or did, northern unionists were never going to change their minds about home rule. As noted, wartime changes to British politics helped reconcile some Conservatives to home rule, but only if permanent partition came with it. And some form of partition was clearly going to be part of any Irish settlement from 1914 onwards. The Rising was again irrelevant in this regard.

If we step back and look at the whole period 1914 to 1918, therefore, the three great challenges facing Irish nationalists since the 1870s were still their three top priorities after the Rising: land, self-government and British coercion. The war certainly changed a lot of things, but much remained the same.

III

So what *did* the Rising change? The most important direct outcome was within the Volunteers themselves. Previously, there had been debate and tension between the offensive-minded IRB faction – the war party – and the defensive-minded majority led by Eoin MacNeill. The two sides were not so far apart in many ways, but they disagreed fundamentally on matters of strategy. MacNeill, J.J. O'Connell and others thought they could not prevail without nationalist public opinion on their side, and that would only happen if they were fighting against active British repression. Moreover, having an army-in-being deterred the government from enacting conscription or other anti-nationalist measures. Also, time was on their side: the longer they waited, the more formidable the organization would become.

IRB militants, on the other hand, feared that if they didn't act, they might lose the Volunteers and their arms to police pre-emption. Public opinion would follow where they led: it could be inspired and guided by their example of heroic self-sacrifice. And the war offered a possibly final opportunity. Home rule might follow, which would change the political landscape, and German arms were on offer – along with a possible place at the peace conference if the Allies lost or were forced to negotiate. Finally, while the Brotherhood was influential and held key staff positions, they were not actually in control of the organization. Thus, part of the purpose of the Rising was to turn the Volunteers into a genuinely revolutionary, republican movement.

It was in this last respect that the rebellion proved to be an unqualified success. It destroyed the power of the MacNeillites and, when the organization was revived in 1917, its Executive and headquarters were firmly under IRB control. The old struggle for power was far from over (many members would drop out rather than follow the militants' lead) but the events of 1916 did lay the basis for the emergence of the IRA in 1920.

Easter Week also achieved another general Volunteer goal, which was to be taken seriously by the Irish public. Where once they were derided as radical geeks playing soldiers, the battle for Dublin ensured they would be at least respected as patriotic men. Of course, a similar change in attitude also took place within the government. Dublin Castle regularly buzzed with rumours of further planned insurrections, and was also most conscious of the widespread belief (enshrined in the *Report of the Royal Commission on the Rebellion*) that the pre-Rising administration had been far too tolerant of seditious rhetoric and paramilitary posturing. Republican speeches, not to mention drilling, waving the tricolour or singing the Soldier's Song, were no longer to be ignored, leading to numerous arrests, riots and trials from late 1916 onwards. Imprisonment meant further protests, leading in turn to hunger strikes, and repeated defeats for a Dublin Castle regime trying to avoid major controversy. Just as the Irish Party had always warned, this cycle of confrontation and grievance only enhanced the status of those involved, and was inevitably seen as an attack on nationalist free speech.[28] The new atmosphere undoubtedly gave New Sinn Féin extra political traction. Some such combination of crackdown and popular backlash was probably inevitable given the slowly increasing tension between the authorities and separatists in 1915 and 1916, but the Rising did create a new and much more favourable political landscape for republican activists to operate in.

Many of the activists who took over the Volunteers – people such as Michael Collins and Harry Boland – were also key players in the re-launch of Sinn Féin in 1917, which got a lot of its new energy and leadership from veterans of the Rising. Participation and incarceration gave them a tremendous aura of patriotic celebrity: exactly the quality most lacking in the increasingly decrepit Irish Party.

So was the Rising necessary to produce this new generation of leaders? Would the genius of Éamon de Valera and Michael Collins not have emerged otherwise? In fact, the revolution's deep talent pool was there before the Rising. It drew on the Gaelic League, the Gaelic Athletic Association, Sinn Féin, the Volunteers, the IRB and their assorted projects and newspapers. These Gaels made up a political counter-culture and were very aware of their status as an alternate nationalist leadership. All they needed was an opportunity – political, not military – and that would likely have appeared somewhere along the line regardless.

For Collins and company to rise to the top, old leaders had first to be killed or pushed aside. Among the former was the unusual but effective partnership of earthy James Connolly, mystical Patrick Pearse, loveable Joe Plunkett and canny Seán MacDermott. Among the latter, the Rising ruined or cramped the careers of such pioneers as Bulmer Hobson. Many were lost who might have done as well or better as their successors: Collins' cousin, Jack Hurley, for example.[29] It isn't at all clear that the replacements were superior to the originals. The downside of the automatic authority granted to Rising veterans was that it promoted some people beyond their abilities and allowed incompetents to assume responsible positions. Without the rebellion, a more meritocratic leadership might have emerged.

It wasn't just these ex-fighters and ex-prisoners who made the difference in 1917 and 1918 though – there were also a large number of brand new activists, young men and women in whom the Rising and its martyrs produced a quasi- or actual religious experience (often during the many requiem masses held for dead rebels in the summer of 1916). In such people, it awakened a personal commitment to the cause of Irish freedom as defined in the 1916 Proclamation.

Many of these converts went on to play important roles in the movement: the kind of true believers any movement needs to collect money, get out the vote, rally the troops and do the dirty work. Liam Lynch of Fermoy in north Cork is a perfect example of such a case. He was a staunch Irish Party man until 1916, when a local family, the Kents, became martyrs, with one killed in action and one executed. Lynch was a different man after that, and wound up as chief of staff of the IRA in the Civil War: a man who refused to give in.[30] This is the sense in which Patrick Pearse's prophesied 'miracle' definitely occurred: not in the population at large but among the few thousand who actually made the revolution possible.

There was a direct line of descent, then, between the two risings of 1916 and 1920, with a minority of militants forcing the pace, and with the IRB behind the scenes. There was the same fear that violence was needed to stop politics as usual and sacrilegious compromise, and the same belief that popular opinion would follow, but that a democratic mandate wasn't needed.[31] And, of course, much the same could be said of the anti-Treaty IRA in the Civil War of 1922–3. It didn't start the war in the same way as in 1916 or 1919–20, and the IRB was no longer at work, but they firmly believed themselves to be acting in the name and spirit of the Easter Rising and its sacred dead.

Another crucial shift that took place in 1916 was financial. Irish-American money began to pour into Ireland again – only not to the Irish Party, but to the officially non-partisan Irish National Aid and Volunteer Dependents' Fund. As the omnibus title suggests, these were once two separate organizations that amalgamated in August, and quickly fell under the sway of the IRB. Michael Collins was appointed secretary in early 1917.

The National Aid handled large sums of money (over £140,000 between 1916 and 1919), much of it from abroad and almost all of it going to republican families and ex-prisoners.[32] Hundreds of future revolutionaries were thereby subsidized, boosting morale and making their activism financially viable. And that was only the start. American dollars would pour in again to fund Sinn Féin, fight conscription and float the whole revolution after 1918. The Irish Party – formerly the primary recipients of transatlantic largesse – suffered badly by comparison. It was often noted during elections how many more cars and trains and everything else their opponents could afford.

There is no doubt that it was sympathy for the rebels and their families that prompted these initial donations, and that we can take the fact that they rose considerably in the late summer of 1916, and in 1917, as a growth in at least implied support for their cause. The publicity campaign certainly became more explicitly republican over time, so donors would presumably have been alerted to the fact that theirs was a political act. On the other hand, nationalist tradition had long legitimated – or even demanded – support for 'physical force' prisoners, even by those who rejected violence or radical aims, so we cannot assume donors shared their aims.

The timing and circumstances of how and when money was given also suggest an alternative conclusion. Prior to 19 August 1916, the Irish National Aid (INA) had collected £13,415 while the Volunteer Dependents' Fund (VDF) garnered £4,459.[33] The former was the more respectable and bourgeois body, connected to the Irish Party. The latter had numerous IRB members and connections, including Kathleen Clarke, widow of Thomas, the first signatory of the Easter Proclamation. The INA's greater success in the immediate post-Rising period no doubt reflects its access to middle-class (and clerical) funds, but it also may well indicate where the balance of opinion lay with regard to the rebellion.

It was only after the funds were amalgamated – and, crucially, after the home rule talks had finally failed – that the real money began to roll in: £2,000 a week in the last months of 1916; £5–6,000 per week in January 1917; over £7,000 the first week in May and over £10,000 the first week in July.[34] Greater organization played a role, as did the combination of contested by-elections and renewed repression in early 1917. Nevertheless, INA records reveal that numerous bishops, archbishops and cardinals in the United States, Australia and New Zealand played a key role in generating ever-larger donations. It seems reasonable to suggest that it was the revival of the struggle over home rule and partition that triggered the real financial avalanche, not the Rising.

IV

What did the Easter rebels achieve? The short answer is: power. Veterans of the Rising dominated nationalist politics within two years of their bloody protest, negotiated an Anglo-Irish settlement within six years and ran their new country for the next five decades. And they did it their way – Pearse's way – through armed struggle, fighting for a united and utterly sovereign republic.

They were quite right that the only way to get there was to use force, but they were very wrong in thinking that they could generate enough violence to overcome their political and military foes, or that their people would back them all the way. Nationalist public opinion turned solidly against *pur laine* republicanism in 1922 and backed the twenty-six-county Free State dominion instead, as adequate to its needs. The Ulster Unionist party and its allies (including much of the Conservative Party) were not going to accept inclusion in a Catholic-majority state without a fight. And the British government and political class saw such a republic as a threat to its national interest. The Ireland of the 1916 Proclamation was far beyond the gunmen's reach.

Violence was also irrelevant to the old Sinn Féin agenda of building a new political coalition and a mass separatist party and forcing negotiations with the government. That kind of radical mobilization had happened before, after all, over Catholic civil rights, land reform and home rule, and while the government usually tried to suppress such movements, they never needed guns to survive and make their various breakthroughs.[35] The political upheavals of 1916–18 mostly grew out of the crises and circumstances left over from 1914, or generated by the Great War. They dictated the fall of the Irish Party, the rise of a more radical successor, and framed the ultimate political solution. The Easter Rising just got a lot more people killed in the process.

CHAPTER TWO

Ending War in a 'Sportsmanlike Manner': The Milestone of Revolution, 1919–23

ANNE DOLAN

There were five bullets in Kitty Carroll's body when it was found in April 1921. Her hands were tied behind her back; 'Spies and Informers Beware, Convicted IRA' was written on the calling card pinned to her breast. Either the bullet to the head or heart had certainly killed her. The other three, one through her cheek, were just fired for good measure.[1]

Kitty Carroll had been distilling *poitín* in her home in Aghnameena, County Monaghan. She had been caught by the IRA; she was fined by a republican court, but still she refused to stop. The British Military Court of Inquiry that investigated her death declared that 'she was probably suspected of disclosing information to the Police with regard to local Sinn Féin activities'.[2] The Military Court of Inquiry was possibly right. Maybe she was a threat to the local IRA, maybe she had written letters to the Royal Irish Constabulary informing on these IRA men who seemed intent on hounding her out of business; maybe her letters had led to arrests and executions. But Kitty Carroll was, as the Court of Inquiry politely put it, 'a woman of feeble intellect'.[3] She was a 40-year-old spinster who lived with her indigent parents and her deranged brother on a couple of acres of meagre Monaghan land. She was, as one member of the 3rd Battalion Monaghan IRA admitted, 'by any standards a half-wit'.[4]

However, the Court of Inquiry never found out that Kitty Carroll had been pestering one of the local IRA volunteers; that she had some notion that one of them might marry her; that perhaps some fumbled promise on a dark evening had not been kept in the cold light of day when the once amorous volunteer no longer liked what he saw.[5] There was no way that the Court of Inquiry could pronounce on that. And so the problems mount. Five months after IRA General Headquarters prohibited the shooting of female spies, we have the body of a woman shot five times.[6] She might be a spy, she might not; there might be some personal grievance, there might not. And then, of course, she is a Protestant as well.

At present there seem to be two ways to respond to this kind of information. There is the old conventional, nationalist, republican, call it what you like, way: that while this may have been an unfortunate case, spying is still spying, and, as one IRA man admitted, 'there was only one punishment – death'.[7] This is the way that produced the notion of the 'four glorious years', the noble struggle for the cause that recounts stories of brave men doing brave deeds for the freedom of Ireland; that portrays it all as a struggle of good against evil, just as any other veteran or partisan does in any other war. The other way likes to think that it is a little more sophisticated. It plots and charts and counts; it sounds more scientific. In its most recent guise, Kitty Carroll might be called to bear witness to the sectarianism of 1919–21. But in truth her death has limited appeal to either side. It is far too embarrassing to the former and just a little too complicated for the latter. Both extremes of interpretation seem to have their own preferred kinds of killings – spies and informers and secret service men on one side; Protestants, landowners and ex-servicemen on the other. The patriot dead are marched out and met by the massacred, murdered minorities; British brutality is increasingly trumped by the savagery of the IRA. Neither interpretation makes much allowance for the fact that it was all a little more complicated than that.

The purpose of raising Kitty Carroll's case, the purpose of this essay, is to begin to suggest a slightly different approach, to shift the emphasis from *who* was killed to *how* they were killed, because by choosing to kill in a particular way the IRA changed the terms of war in Ireland. My chosen milestone in Irish history is therefore awkward and unpleasant, but it has ramifications far beyond the sleepless nights and the troubled consciences of the men who had to kill. It has festered under the quite sanitized surface of Irish nationalism; it has agitated historians since. How do you reconcile the details of the deaths of 1919–23 with the need for a myth of independence? Might pride in the past be undermined by the notion that the lauded 'fight for freedom' may have been little more than a sequence of 'dirty deeds'? Do the details make hypocrites of those who established the state? How do you tell subsequent paramilitaries to stop when the archives in London and Dublin reveal the kind of war, the kind of killing, which was once considered necessary – maybe even acceptable – to achieve independence years before?

The more details one discovers about killings the more difficult it becomes to ignore these questions, the more difficult it becomes to fit individual cases into a neat pattern, to call them casualties and to draw conclusions about the efficacy of one type of war or another. There is a certain comfort, perhaps convenience, in keeping the bodies at arm's length, in tabulating them and counting them and moving on to the finer points of something else. To whose benefit is it to know how many times Kitty Carroll was shot, to know where the five bullets entered her body, to know that she was left in a field, that she was labelled a spy? Is it enough just to say that she was killed? Yet the details of Kitty Carroll's death reveal that she was killed in a particular way, in a way that denoted she was an enemy of the new order, in a way that let everyone else in Aghnameena know not to do what she had done. Her dead body was marked with the wounds of a spy, and the way she was killed would forever condemn her as such. My milestone in Irish history then is this decision to execute or assassinate, to kill in this kind of way, to change war in Ireland, to turn every street, every field, and every front room into a battlefield, to change war into terror because now you could never really be sure where war was.

After four years of seeing every kind of brutality and battlefield, it would be foolish to imagine that the British forces were squeamish about a few assassinations in Ireland. But there is something in their response, in their propaganda, which suggests that the Irish had offended against their own acute etiquette of war. As it was publicly reiterated what was happening in Ireland was crime and murder, and it certainly was not war. A handbill issued by the director of Irish propaganda in the British Army directed at 'Members of the IRA' explains something of this, and is worth quoting at length:

> Read this and if you still decide to be led astray by your leaders in the belief that you are 'Soldiers', and entitled to be treated as soldiers, you have yourselves to blame. Only armed forces who fulfil certain conditions can avail themselves of the rights conferred by the laws and customs of war. These conditions are:

1. They must be commanded by a person responsible for his subordinates. 2. They must wear a fixed distinctive sign or uniform RECOGNISABLE AT A DISTANCE. 3. They must carry arms openly. 4. They must conduct their operations in accordance with the Laws and customs of war. These laws and customs of war were not drawn up by England for the purpose of fighting the IRA. They were drawn up by all the great nations including America, in order that war between white men should be carried out in a sportsmanlike manner, and not like fights between savage tribes. Your leaders will tell you that you are 'Soldiers' belonging to an Army. They will tell you that you cannot wear [a] uniform and come out into the open and fight, because the English are too strong for you, but yet they tell you that if you are captured you are entitled to be treated as 'prisoners of war' under the Laws of war. Your leaders are only lying to you for their own ends. They rarely get captured. They know that a man dressed in civilian clothes who tries to kill other persons whether soldiers, police or civilians, is nothing more than a common murderer.[8]

C.S. Foulkes produced many more handbills like this one. 'Is the IRA a murder gang?', 'The legality of guerrilla war', 'The belligerent status of the IRA', 'IRA justice', 'The Sinn Féin war on women': the list could go on.[9] All of these pamphlets and handbills made essentially the same argument again and again. What was happening in Ireland was not war; it was not going to be acknowledged as war because it was not playing by the rules. Even Foulkes' choice of language is striking: conducting war in 'a sportsmanlike manner, and not like fights between savage tribes'. While this might seem terribly inappropriate on several levels to us now, this mindset explains quite a lot about why this type of killing in Ireland marked such a very significant change. It shook British military and political attitudes, British public opinion, to the core. And you can see the confusion in some of the responses to it. Maurice Headlam, Treasury remembrancer in Dublin Castle, preferred to believe that the murders were being committed by what he called 'imported American gunmen who received £100 a head for their work'.[10] In other words, it was gangsterism, not war. There were more rational and realistic responses, but nonetheless of the same view. For instance, Lord Hugh Cecil, writing to the editor of *The Times*: 'Murder is not a legitimate political instrument; it is a cruel abomination, which deserves the gallows in this world and hell-fire in the next.'[11] There are many more statements of this kind from a predictable mixture of officials, and soldiers and politicians and newspapers. There is enough of a sense of outrage to denote that something significant had changed, something had altered the nature of war.

We can only understand this outrage by looking at the details, by looking at why this kind of killing was so shocking, so appalling to a sense of what was and was not 'sportsmanlike' according to the rules of war. There are many cases like Kitty Carroll's and they reveal this new intimate, local kind of killing. It is only in the details that one begins to see how this kind of killing was meant to terrify, how it was meant to deter and dissuade; how the fear of it became almost as potent as the act itself.

As historians we have been far more reticent than any of the IRA, than any of the British forces, in what we are prepared to examine and analyze. We have been extremely selective in what we have chosen to hear in combatants' testimonies. We have consistently failed to examine the killings in detail; we have never really examined the bodies of the dead in order to consider the nature of the war. In Kitty Carroll's case you can argue that she was killed because she was a Protestant; you can argue that she was killed because she was a nuisance to a man in Monaghan at a time when he had the weapon and the opportunity to kill her and get away with it. But to continue to try to find these kinds of reasons is to continue to polarize an historiography that already seems too partial to its own extremes. The way Kitty Carroll was killed has as much to tell us about the nature of the Irish war as any of the very many reasons that may have caused her death.

What follows are quite random examples from 1919–21 and from the Civil War which begin to suggest what I mean. These cases do say a lot about the type of people killed, but what should also be considered are the ways in which they were killed, and what the nature of these deaths can tell us about the kind of war, the kind of revolution, and why these deaths stand for a kind of milestone in terms of war in Ireland.

In October 1920 John Hawkes sold two watches that did not belong to him. He was caught by the IRA in Bantry and was put to work for them for two weeks. He fled to the local military barracks at the first opportunity believing his life to be in danger, and by this very action he made sure that it was. When the chance came he was grabbed outside the gates of Skibbereen Workhouse by a masked man, dragged along the road, knocked to the ground and shot through the head while his killer knelt on his chest to keep him still.[12]

Patrick Tuigin, a National Army soldier, was found 'lying across the avenue of Gurteen House' near Birr, County Offaly in October 1922. Dr Fleury, who examined his body, found one side of the face burned from the gunpowder. There was an entrance wound on his left cheek, with an exit wound behind the left ear; there were another two bullet wounds in the chest, and another in the stomach. He was thought to have been shot with dum-dum bullets, because of the nature of the wounds, because so much of his clothing was found inside his body. He was 26 years old, and he was on his way back from a day's leave spent with his wife.[13]

At a nursing home in Rahoon, County Mayo, Sergeants Gibbons and Gilmartin of the RIC were being treated for dropsy and influenza. On 24 February 1922 a group of young men in masks entered the nursing home and shot the two men in their beds. Gilmartin was shot in the chest and through the mouth; Gibbons was shot in the face, three times in the chest and through both hands which he had obviously held up in some vain defence of himself. Gilmartin was heard to say 'Oh God you are not going to do this'; he was then allowed to say an Act of Contrition before he was shot.[14]

In other cases the dead were meant to – and did – remain unknown. For instance, a body was found in a bag in Kilmaley churchyard in County Clare, fully clothed, legs tied together with a rope. There was a handkerchief, thought to have been a blindfold, tied round where his eyes should have been. The man had been dead for over four weeks; he was about 5 feet 8 inches tall; he had the clothes of what the medical examiner called 'a civilian of the labouring class'; he had a prayer book, some rosary beads and some decent boots, which the Civic Guard were going to keep in case someone might recognize them and claim him. There was a wound at the base of his neck and no longer any face. The coroner presumed he was young because the hair that was left was not grey.[15]

There were several other instances in which the face was attacked in this way. John Harrison, a farmer from Leitrim, was shot several times in April 1921, but his head was, as the report stated, 'battered in with some heavy instrument'. There was also a 'convicted spy' notice hung around his neck.[16] William Latimer, a 55-year-old farmer from Mohill, also in Leitrim, was killed the month before, having been taken from his house in the middle of the night and shot in the next field. Apart from the many bullet wounds which had certainly killed him, his head 'had been battered in with some sharp instrument'.[17] You could argue this was one of Leitrim's peculiar techniques when ridding the county of those considered to be 'Protestant loyalists', but a man named William Good was killed in a similar fashion in Timoleague the same month.[18] County Cork's distinction was that the blow to the head was enough to kill William Good; there was no need to use any bullets as the wasteful volunteers of Leitrim had done.

Some of the bodies do reveal other circumstances of death – William Elliot, a 22-year-old farmer from Ballinalee, County Longford, was found in a bog in January 1922. He had fallen in from a kneeling position; his hands were still clasped in prayer. There was £9 in notes and some papers left beside his body.[19] Francis Elliott was taken from his home in Roscommon, taken from his wife and five children, and shot two miles away from his house. He had been, as the report said, 'riddled with bullets', but had been allowed, as condemned men can, to wear a blindfold.[20] Christy O'Sullivan had been allowed to write his mother a note. He was 23, an ex-British soldier, and he had just got married to a woman called Madge. On 27 May 1921 he was taken by car to the outskirts of Cork city and shot through the head. The police found the note. 'Dear Mother, look after my Madge. I am going before my God. Christy.'[21] There was no time for any more than that. In Monaghan in March 1921 two men were found dead at Aghabog with white strips of paper pinned to the front of their coats, marking their hearts as targets. Two or three weeks before, one of these men, Frank McPhillips, had been tied to the railings of Aghabog chapel with his coat turned back to front on him and the word 'informer' chalked across his chest. McPhillips was about 20 years old and the sole source of income for his widowed mother and his sisters.[22] They were the reason he had not fled after this first attack.

So what do these details tell us? Most of these people were shot in or about the head; most were shot more than once, when more than once was not necessary; most were labelled in some fashion; most were certainly unarmed. All were killed in a close, intimate way, probably by someone from the same area, possibly, in some cases, by people they may have even known. They were effectively executions. The repetition of this shot to the head was significant, not only in making sure that the person died, but also in denoting a spy's death. The wound is significant, in much the same way as the bodies with the bludgeoned faces: not only dead but disfigured as well. Most of the victims were given no chance to escape, no chance to put up a fight. Arguably, that was the only way to make sure of killing them. A war fought largely by itinerant bands of young men with a limited supply of arms, by squads of gunmen slipping in and out of crowds, was never going to cherish each and every paragraph of the Geneva Convention. If you wanted to kill you had to take your opportunity as it presented itself; you stood close, you fired repeatedly to make sure, and you had to make sure because your weapons may have been poor, because your ammunition may have been faulty, because you had orders and your orders had to be carried out. You fired erratically because you were badly trained; because you were nervous, because you may never have done anything like this before. You took the time to write a label, to place it on the body, when all instinct must have told you to run away; you labelled the body because that way you made it political. You called them a spy and you made a political statement out of an execution, out of an assassination; you salved your conscience that killing a 40-year-old woman or a farmer in his fifties was an act of war not a cold-blooded murder. You had to shoot them in the head and label them a spy and that was enough now to make it seem like war. You left the body to be found on the side of the road, to be a warning to everyone else. By leaving out the details of death, historians miss the shock of it; the threat of it, in many cases the point of it.

Because it was meant to, this kind of killing quite naturally bred fear and callousness in those who witnessed and watched: don't look, don't get involved, because if you do you could be next. The slightest suspicion could mark you out – in Christy O'Sullivan's case suspicion of him was said to have grown from the fact that children on his street started calling him a spy once they had found out that he had been in the British Army. Of course, this cowardice or callousness is in some instances more understandable than others. The congregation ran for their lives when Sergeant Mulhern was shot nine times in the head and neck in the porch of the chapel at Bandon.[23] Indeed, congregations fled from the scene of the many other cases of policemen attacked and killed on their way to or from Mass or service throughout 1920 and 1921. What is harder to understand, though, is a case like William Vanston. Shot in the street outside his home in Maryborough in County Laois in February 1921, the neighbours who had lived beside him, who had passed the time of day with him, who liked him or hated him or were maybe even indifferent to him, now refused to help his wife to carry his body in off the road. It was now safer for them if he died in the gutter without their help.[24] Presumably, John Connolly's dead body was left lying in a laneway in Bandon for ten days for similar reasons.[25] No one wanted to take the risk of going near him; propriety or impropriety be damned.

While it may seem like an inadequate, rather prim choice of word, propriety does have rather a lot to do with this. There is something gnawing away at the heart of the conflict; a sense that it simply isn't, what Foulkes called, war carried out in a 'sportsmanlike manner'. The three men who came to Thomas Bradfield's house in Bandon on 22 January 1921, who allegedly accepted his invitation to stay for dinner, and 'made themselves at home', waited until they had had their fill before they took Bradfield outside and shot him on the side of the road.[26] Maybe you could argue that befriending him, that eating his food, was tactically astute; maybe it made it easier to lure this man out on to the road when the time came to kill him, maybe he was less likely to put up a fight. But no matter how you approach this, there does seem to be something terribly inappropriate about it all. Assassination, execution, the elimination of spies: there is an inadequacy about these words when they are confronted with the chosen means and the methods of the killings. You can opt, like the British forces and the British government and the British propagandists, to call it murder – whatever words you choose it makes for an uneasy and unsettling definition of war. It makes for an uneasy and unsettling legacy for Irish nationalism, for the Irish state, but also for the men who took part.

Much has been written about the effects of killing on soldiers in conventional armies, in more conventional battle situations, particularly by Joanna Bourke and Samuel Hynes in the context of the Great War, the Second World War, Korea and Vietnam, but there is no real consideration of killing and its effects on a band of largely untrained young men in a guerrilla war.[27] Unlike many of the theatres of conflict in the Great War, for instance, where, Joanna Bourke has noted, 'many servicemen never saw "the enemy"', where often 'injuries were not even usually caused by another identifiable individual', killing in Ireland as we have seen from these very few examples in the 1919–23 period regularly took the form of executions and assassinations.[28] Kneeling on a man's chest to keep him still while you shot him in the head was a different kind of war. IRA men often stood close to their victims, watched their restraint or their panic, the expression on their faces as they died. In their chosen kind of guerrilla war there was little opportunity and fewer resources to fight any other way. Although there are points of comparison with Bourke's work on face-to-face killing from the Great War to Vietnam, the conditions in Ireland were still distinct; they were intimate because victim and killer sometimes knew each other. In one case an IRA man killed a policeman because he had once summonsed him for having no light on his bicycle.[29] The Irish case is distinct because 'the majority of the Irish revolution's victims did not die in military combat', because most died, as Peter Hart has suggested, 'while defenceless [or] … alone'.[30] One has to take account of the fact that sheer physical proximity to the victim brought its own type of brutality to the killing. This was face-to-face killing where the battlefield was a bedroom or a laneway or wherever you could take your chance, where combat took the form of assassination, where the army was nothing more than a band of very young men without uniforms or, often, the training to use the weapons in their hands.

By choosing to kill in this way, this kind of war required or rather created a certain kind of combatant. And in some ways this is a type of milestone in itself. It was not now a question of being able to line up in an impeccable uniform, to drill in formation, to salute, to have buttons and boots and brasses shined. These men needed to be able to kill and kill at will, to kill without conscience, to satisfy themselves that these executions were now legitimate acts in their chosen war. Indeed, Seamus Robinson, who was involved in the first killings at Solo-headbeg in January 1919, had to rationalize it thus: 'to kill a couple of policemen for the country's sake and leave it at that by running away would be so wanton, as to approximate too closely to murder'.[31] For him the only thing to do now that this kind of killing had started was carry on. Like men in other wars, the reactions of those who killed varied from pleasure to indifference, from enjoyment to regret. What sets this war apart in Irish terms is that it brought all the consequences, all the traumas of modern combat, to bear on these men's lives. Some obviously coped better than others. For some it would define them for the rest of their lives.

John Horgan maintains that Bloody Sunday is the one day that many old IRA men fell 'silently defensive about'.[32] It was the apogee, if you will, of this kind of killing, this quick assassination, execution, murder that amounted to a new definition of war. Fourteen men whom the IRA said were spies were shot simultaneously at nine o'clock in the morning in their flats and boarding houses and hotels in Dublin. It was possibly the most shocking, most theatrical day in the revolution's calendar, and there is a palpable unease in the narrative which many of the participants in the killings of Bloody Sunday constructed around that morning's events.

The dull refrain that it needed to be done, that they had to be stopped, that they were all spies, that there were no mistakes, comes again and again with dreary repetition. Most is said about why it was done, about the rightness of it being done, about the care and attention that went into proving every case against each man, into proving each one to be what their brutal murders necessitated them to be – just vile English spies.[33] 'They were the murder gang. They were capable of murder certainly and there was a story that some had seen foreign service.'[34] They were the 'cream of British Military Intelligence'; spies 'disguised as civilians ... liable to the death penalty' like any others of their kind.[35] For many the dead must have been guilty because they supposed that 'the proof had to be a full 100% watertight before any action could be taken' by the IRA.[36] And the IRA could count on a degree of trust; they were 'good men and they wouldn't kill any innocent people'.[37] The killings may have been 'Dreadful! Horrible!', but the same person was sure: 'I have no doubt they deserved it.'[38] Enough people believed there was no smoke without fire.

But this retreat to explanations and justifications makes perfect sense. Although Todd Andrews revelled in the fact that the British press 'sucked Roget's Thesaurus dry to find words to denounce us. We were gunmen, terrorists, extremists, murderers, assassins, butchers, thugs', such bravado possibly came more easily to Andrews when writing his memoirs fifty-nine years after the event.[39] 'Murderer' was the word that seemed to rankle most, the only moniker that Michael Collins was ever said to resent.[40] Lloyd George may have pronounced that the fourteen dead 'got what they deserved, beaten by counterjumpers', Churchill may have thought them 'careless fellows' who 'ought to have taken precautions',[41] but nevertheless Collins still penned a remarkable defence of his actions in case the question of Bloody Sunday arose at the Treaty negotiations in London in December 1921.

> ... it was no more than a feeling such as I would have for a dangerous reptile. By their destruction the very air is made sweeter. That should be the future's judgment on this particular event. For myself, my conscience is clear. There is no crime in detecting and destroying in war-time, the spy and the informer. They have destroyed without trial. I have paid them back in their own coin.[42]

But it was easy for Collins to talk in terms of dangerous reptiles and sweeter air. He was elsewhere on Bloody Sunday morning. He was not pointing a gun at a man shivering in his bed. Whatever thoughts and images and descriptions of these fourteen dead men Collins cared to conjure with, the circumstances of the deaths, indeed the circumstances of any of the aforementioned deaths, would always undo his careful preparations. Shooting a detective on the street, on his way to or from Dublin Castle, even on his way to church, had become a relatively familiar type of brutality. At least the prey was armed, he had some chance, and as time went on he may have come to expect it: he often wore a 'steel waistcoat'; he sometimes walked different routes to his work. But some hierarchy of horror had been grossly breached on Bloody Sunday morning. It was one thing to gun down a man in cold blood in the street. It was quite another to barge into his bedroom, to shoot him where he lay, in front of his wife, within hearing of his child. That nine of the men killed wore only their pyjamas seemed to tip the scales of horror even further still; there was the added indignity of not even being properly dressed.[43] It was for these reasons that Larry Nugent was so insistent in his Bureau statement that it was not murder, that 'it was an act of war duly carried out under orders ... the life of every IRA man in Dublin was at stake';[44] why Frank Thornton kept insisting, even at lectures to army cadets in 1940, that 'that morning was one of the most critical ones in the history of our movement', that 'all jobs were executed' even when they were not.[45] 'The British Secret Service was wiped out on the 21st November 1920.'[46] That was the story and the brutality of the day meant that most of the men involved were going to stick to it.

A little over twelve hours before the shooting, most of the men involved still really knew nothing of what was to be done. They had that night to think about shooting a man in cold blood; a man they knew only as a name, maybe even an assumed name at that, at a certain address somewhere in the city. Some knew where to meet, where to collect their guns and ammunition, who would wait on guard, who would patrol the stairs, who would go with the intelligence officer and the Squad man to do the shooting in the room. Others knew less; just told where to go, to 'be ready for a job in the morning ... we weren't told what we were to do'.[47] For most, there was no real time to prepare, no time, the organizers might argue, to worry about right and wrong, about the fear of doing it and getting caught. In the same way that there had been no point in forcing men who believed only in a fair fight into the ranks of the Squad, this operation needed men whose scruples were not likely to take them unawares.[48] A conscience was all very well but, from a commanding officer's point of view, it was likely to ruin the chance of the killing and to get other men captured or killed in the attempt.

Some passed an uneasy night. Frank Saurin checked the location one more time;[49] Larry Nugent slept in the same bed with Éamon Fleming, both knowing the next day would be important but neither saying more than a few words.[50] Matty MacDonald knew it would be a big job so he played a game of cards and had a drink.[51] Todd Andrews went to Mass, played football, read a book. Apart from suffering a slight concussion at his match, and attending a meeting about the next day's killing, it was like any other given Saturday for the 19-year-old. He slept well. He had been to confession; he was in a state of grace like so very many more that night, all supposedly made ready for their own deaths mixed with some sort of guarantee of forgiveness in advance.[52] It was only in the morning that Andrews began to feel unease. He was, as he said, 'unattuned to assassination'. He was 'very excited by the assignment but the prospect of killing a man in cold blood was alien to our ideas of how a war should be conducted'.[53] The 17-year-old Charles Dalton was equally concerned. 'Outwardly we were calm and collected, even jesting with each other. But inwardly I felt that the others were as I was – palpitating with anxiety.' He described waiting to enter the house as 'the longest five minutes of my life. Or were they the shortest? I cannot tell, but they were tense and dreadful.'[54] It would be easy to say that Dalton wrote this partly for effect in his memoirs, as by this point he was a veteran of several other killings. Alternatively it could be taken that this was no ordinary shooting, that at least the teenager was not yet fully inured to what was about to be done. Indeed Matty MacDonald remembered that 'Charlie Dalton couldn't sleep that night of Bloody Sunday. He thought he could hear the gurgling of the officers' blood and he kept awake all night until we told him a tap was running somewhere.'[55] There was still that much of the child in him that could be fooled; wanting to hear the lie because it was so much better than putting up with the truth.

Charles Dalton wrote in his memoir that when it was over 'I started to run. I could no longer control my overpowering need to run, to fly, to leave far behind me those threatening streets.' Later he 'thought over our morning's work, and offered up a prayer for the fallen'.[56] Matty MacDonald told Ernie O'Malley that 'Charlie Dalton was very nervous. We went to the Capitol [Theatre] to ease his mind.'[57] 'I got the wind up rightly' was all Dalton admitted when O'Malley asked.[58] Yet for one who was blooded in the ways of the Squad, for one who was so afraid himself, Dalton made no allowance for those who had never been asked to kill or see killing like this before. He complained that 'in some instances the excuses put forward for the non-carrying out of instructions were not considered very satisfactory; in particular, those received from the Commandant of the 1st Battalion regarding two addresses they should have visited on the North Circular Road.'[59] Todd Andrews knew all about this kind of suspicion. 'I felt that, short of actual death, I would be unable to persuade my comrades in the Company or in the Battalion that I had not faked an accident to avoid the mission. This, of course, was nonsense but I felt that I could not live with myself if I failed for any reason to turn up.'[60] Some men in K Company of the 3rd Battalion quickly began to regret that they had. Larry Nugent found it difficult to get any information about what had happened on Bloody Sunday from any of them. 'The men would not talk. Three men of K Company never returned to duty after the operation.'[61] Twice in his Bureau statement Nugent stated that 'the men did not like this operation, but orders were orders and had to be obeyed.'[62] It was 'outside the ordinary scope of the soldier' and some reacted to the pressure better than others.[63] And this kind of pressure was not just part of this particular day; it was used elsewhere by the IRA leadership – in Monaghan, at its most extreme instance, men were chosen to kill on the basis of keeping them loyal, keeping 'our weak ones right', because by having them kill they could then never talk without incriminating themselves.[64]

But unsteady nerves and shaking beginners' hands explained why so many of the wounded survived on Bloody Sunday and on so many other days.[65] Even the dead were sometimes shot in unusual places or too many times, in parts of the body where a wound would never kill. The shootings were by nature often hurried and frenetic; the likelihood of failure was high. In one case a man had to have his gun taken away because his hand shook too much to fire.[66] Others of course were exhilarated about the thought of their first kill, and were overheard discussing it as they rushed from the scene.[67] Joe McGuinness was so frustrated that the man he was meant to shoot was not at home that he threw his gun in the canal.[68] Pat McCrea was proud that he had driven a car for one of the killings in Baggot Street. But his wife, under the impression that he had been fishing, put him out of the house when he joked about how plentiful the morning's catch had been. He spent Bloody Sunday night in St Anne's Park, but he still could not fathom why she was so perturbed.[69] He possibly no longer knew how to be. He needed someone to be outraged on his behalf.

Todd Andrews was certainly outraged with the behaviour of the men from the Squad that day. 'There were only women and children in the rest of the house but that did not prevent the pair from the squad behaving like Black and Tans.'[70] Joe Dolan started a fire, whether by intention or accident, which took the rest of the men a half an hour to put out.[71] What Andrews failed to mention in his book was that Joe Dolan beat the half-naked woman who was in Captain Noble's bed and stole all of her rings.[72] Naturally Dolan remained silent about it in his Bureau statement too. But then Joe Dolan had shot the porter of the Wicklow Hotel one morning and then went back there in the afternoon to eat his lunch.[73] The men of the Squad had learned to be callous. Their training was brutal and short, as Vinny Byrne explained: 'First of all, the men selected for squad work were brought on a few jobs and shown how they were carried out; secondly, each man had to prove his mettle, and was detailed to do an actual job' himself.[74] Each member of the Squad then killed in what Joe Leonard called strict rotation.[75] They quickly became proud of being known as an elite; as paid, young, full-time gunmen; they enjoyed being feared in London as 'gangs of tough youngsters', as 'wild young men'.[76] Obsessive to the point of fetishism about revolvers, they had their favourite weapons and squabbled between killings about who was the best shot, about which was better, the Webley, the Mauser or the Colt. There were 'staunch supporters' of the 'Peter the Painter', a lighter Mauser that was easier to conceal under your clothes.[77] Charles Dalton had a holster made for himself, a holster made out of a mail sack, but a holster nonetheless.[78] 'Tom Keogh,' it was said, 'never moved without his gun.'[79] He was dead by the age of 23. They all carried .45s not .38s. It had taken Detective Inspector Smith, the first detective to be assassinated in July 1919, two weeks to die from his wounds from a .38, so a .45 would be the weapon of choice after that.[80] They always brought a revolver as well as an automatic – the revolver in case the automatic ever stuck, as they had learned that it had many times on the Germans during the war.[81]

Many of them were still teenagers when they were asked to join with consciences more likely to overlook things older men might not condone. Mick White ate one of the dead men's breakfasts on Bloody Sunday morning.[82] Vinny Byrne recorded how he enjoyed 'plugging' British soldiers but he still filled his pockets with liquorice like any child would when he took part in a raid of the B&I stores.[83] Byrne was 19 when he went to kill a man in a house in Upper Mount Street on

Bloody Sunday morning. It was noted with astonishment 'how quickly and with what devotion these young men got down to their jobs. Anything they lacked in age and experience, they made up in enthusiasm.'[84] These men may have had a conscience but, as one commentator in *Blackwood's Magazine* put it, they had certainly come to terms with it.[85] Byrne may have had qualms about being put in charge of older, more experienced men like Tom Ennis on Bloody Sunday morning, but he could only feel pity for the 'old' medical officer sent with him who did not know what to do with a gun.[86]

For Joe Dolan, it was a simple matter: 'We had to learn to kill in cold blood and we got used to it.'[87] It is difficult to read statements from men like Byrne and Dolan and Leonard and so many others without concluding that these men took pleasure from the one thing that they had become very good at. Byrne said, 'It was the joy of my life when I was handed a .45 revolver and six rounds.'[88] And it was a joy some of them never learned to replace.

But this kind of killing took its toll. Liam Tobin had a nervous breakdown before Bloody Sunday could be carried out as he planned.[89] He had become, according to David Neligan, 'gaunt, cynical, with tragic eyes, he looked like a man who had seen the inside of hell'.[90] Bernard Byrne spoke of the agony of the drivers who had time to think in their cars of what was being done; he mentioned three who 'became nerve cases as a result of their work'.[91] Others turned to drink to make things bearable enough. When he was released after the truce, Éamon Broy was 'disagreeably surprised to see many fine and highly strung young Irish Volunteers, who had been teetotallers when I last met them, drinking whiskey neat. It was bound to have a bad effect on them especially after the long struggle they had endured.'[92] Harry Colley confirmed this, admitting that 'there was heavy drinking in Dublin. Charlie Dalton never drank till the truce. Reaction from strain.'[93] George White went further and suggested that by April 1921 there were serious breaches of discipline in the Squad because of drink; that Collins wanted to replace Tom Keogh with the abstemious Paddy Daly. 'The attitude of HQ Squad was definitely disobedient and they cut up rather rough.'[94] White is supported by a series of letters dating from the previous month from the O/C Fingal. He complained of a disturbance at a dance in Portrane asylum. When five men, led by Joe Dolan, refused to leave they were bundled into a padded cell. For the twenty minutes they were inside they slashed at the walls and door with knives. Michael Lynch wrote to Headquarters because, as he said,

if the newspapers got hold of it a grave scandal [would ensue] ...
I make this report not to bring trouble on the heads of the men
concerned (who are all attached to the staff of the Dr/Intell) but
because I believe they were more than drunk. They were stark
mad for at least a half an hour. I candidly believe that the present
strains on their nerves is too much for them and has left them in
such a condition that the taste of whiskey leaves them violent
lunatics, and would strongly urge – after watching them for about
three hours – that they be given a rest from all arduous duty.[95]

The hospital attendants were blamed in an 'attempt to cloak up the
whole affair' and Dolan continued as before.[96] Major General Russell
reported to the army inquiry in May 1924 that 'the very nature of their
work' before the truce 'left [these men] anything but normal ... if such
a disease as shell-shock existed in the IRA ... the first place to look for
it would be amongst these men.'[97] From the end of 1923, the new Free
State government was already worried enough to keep note of how
many army men were involved in serious crimes.[98] The record of
events in Oriel House, the actions of the Dublin Brigade in Kerry during the Civil War, the fact that Collins himself thought of sending many
of his Squad away seems to suggest that many of these men no longer
knew how to stop.[99]

By choosing to kill, by choosing to kill in a particularly brutal kind
of way, the new state had to cope with the consequences. How do you
preach law and order when for the last three years you have counselled
your best fighting men to kill; how do you get men to stop killing when
it is, possibly, the one thing that they are good at, when it is, for some,
the only thing that they now really enjoy, the only thing that sets them
apart from everybody else? These were questions the first government
faced when it tried to impose law and order on a country that had
become quite comfortable with a type of lawlessness, that had come to
take the cover or the excuse of revolution for granted. These were questions faced at the time of the army mutiny, at the time of Kevin O'Higgins' assassination, even still in the rumbling threat of a coup in 1931,
each instance inspired by those who had seen the worst of 1919–23.

Choosing to kill in this kind of way may not have been a milestone
in itself: the Phoenix Park murders of 1882 suggest themselves an
obvious precedent, just as there are other deaths before and after
Cavendish and Burke which might suggest themselves as examples. But
what is a milestone is the decision to turn this kind of killing into the

basis for war, to use it repeatedly, to extend the reach of war and terror from conventional exchanges to homes and beds and fields and front rooms. It is a milestone in Irish history because the decision had consequences far beyond itself, far beyond the young, possibly frightened gunman, far beyond Kitty Carroll, or any of the rest. Tom Barry referred to it as going down into the mire to find your freedom. It was no longer, as Foulkes said, 'war … in a sportsmanlike manner'. It is a milestone in Irish history, because this kind of killing marked a point at which there was now no turning back.

CHAPTER THREE

Women's Political Rhetoric and the Irish Revolution

JASON KNIRCK

The independent Irish state, its political system, and its foreign policy all stemmed from the Anglo-Irish Treaty of 1921, making the Treaty undoubtedly one of the most significant documents in Irish history. The Treaty also had another impact less emphasized by historians: its role in the near-banishment of women from parliamentary activity. Women, often working through the female nationalist organization Cumann na mBan, were tremendously active during the revolution, assisting the IRA, raising money and promoting awareness of the cause. Six women were elected as Dáil deputies in 1921 and took a leading role in the Second Dáil's debates over the Treaty. During this period, many active political women were relatives of male revolutionaries, with some of the most prominent related to men who had sacrificed their lives for the cause. This frequently invoked connection between women and the dead, highlighted by the women themselves in order to augment their political legitimacy, was successful during the revolution, resulting in greater visibility and authority for political women such as Mary MacSwiney, Kate O'Callaghan, Kathleen Clarke and Margaret Pearse. They continued to employ this rhetorical strategy throughout the Treaty debates and Civil War, but it received a much rockier reception. Seeking to discredit female anti-Treatyites and republicanism in general, pro-Treatyites seized upon the women's invocation of the dead as a vulnerable point in the republican argument, and began to character-ize it – and its advocates – as irrational, emotional, backward-looking and unsuited for political debate. Thus, the means by which women gained political authority during the revolution were the same means by which they lost it during the Treaty debates and Civil War. Women therefore emerged from the revolution with a much less secure political place than they held in the years leading up to the revolution.

Variations on this pattern are evident in many revolutions.[1] In post-revolutionary Ireland, though, the goal was not just to marginalize women, but also to marginalize a male-dominated movement (republicanism) of which women increasingly were seen as emblematic. Irish political women were not attacked primarily or solely as a means of discrediting any specifically women's issues for which they were agitating, but as part of a broader effort to feminize, and thus disgrace, Irish republicanism. Pro-Treatyites characterized the arguments voiced by female Irish politicians as revolutionary detritus, useful as attention-getters and emotion-generators during the revolution, but less useful and even dangerous during the more sober subsequent period of state-building. Gendered language was used to denigrate both female politicians and republicans, as Free Staters attempted to create a new state free from the influence of both. As a result, the debates over the Anglo-Irish Treaty, which saw a significant shift in the reception accorded to female politicians and their arguments, marked a key point in the political marginalization of Irish women, and was therefore an important turning point in modern Irish history.

Peter Hart has called revolutionary republicanism 'the most female-dependent major movement in modern Irish history'.[2] During the revolution, women spoke at political meetings; raised money for active, wounded and imprisoned IRA men; contributed to the political work of Sinn Féin; carried messages, nursed, sewed clothes and provided safe houses for the IRA. Mary and Muriel MacSwiney undertook a speaking tour in the United States, with Mary staying nearly a year and crisscrossing the country. Six women reached the pinnacle of formal political activity, elected as Sinn Féin candidates for the Second Dáil. Four of these women were related to martyred Irish revolutionaries: Mary MacSwiney's brother Terence had undergone a lengthy and fatal hunger strike in late 1920; Kate O'Callaghan's husband Michael, a former lord mayor of Limerick, had been murdered in his house by Black and Tans; Margaret Pearse's two sons Patrick and William were executed in the wake of the Easter Rising, as was Kathleen Clarke's husband, Thomas. The other two female TDs, Countess Constance Markievicz and Dr Ada English, had not suffered such losses but often identified themselves publicly with these women who had.

Female activists during the revolution pushed for greater equality for women and desired to expand the limited suffrage granted to women in 1918. The 1918 Cumann na mBan constitution pledged the organization 'to follow the policy of the Republican Proclamation [of 1916] by seeing that women take up their proper position in the life of the nation'.[3] Sinn Féin also accepted women as equal members, and its constitution promised 'that the equality of men and women in this organization be emphasized in all speeches and leaflets'.[4] Margaret Ward has argued that active Irish women generally subordinated their feminism to nationalism during the revolution, and while there is an element of truth in this assertion, it does not mean that women subordinated their political agency during the revolution. They certainly disagreed, among themselves and with male revolutionaries, about the relative primacy of nationalism versus feminism, but these women were the makers of their own political destinies during the revolution in ways that have not been sufficiently emphasized by historians. Other than in the sphere of military action, where women's involvement was generally quite circumscribed, there is little evidence that female activists were controlled by male politicians.

While not following direct orders from men, female politicians were limited by the political discourse of the time, itself primarily a male creation. They could, like Hanna Sheehy-Skeffington, blaze their own trails and introduce advanced feminist positions into Irish political discourse, but the more tempting path was to emphasize familiar and time-worn Irish themes. As a result, female politicians frequently invoked women's roles as culture-bearers, instilling nationalist values in succeeding generations. They referenced the archetypal mother – often Hibernia, Erin or the Virgin Mary – accepting the sacrifice of her sons. And they often embodied the Victorian stereotype of a mourning woman, with the practice of keening giving this image a particularly Irish flavour. In fact, the dominance of the discourse of sacrifice during the revolutionary period – obviously a key trope during any violent revolution, but particularly powerful given Ireland's long history of failed revolts – meant that women had to access this language in order to be taken seriously as politicians. Men could sacrifice or risk their lives through military activity. Women, on the other hand, had to use a feminized discourse of sacrifice in order to attain maximum viability. This meant that female relatives of deceased patriots were in a particularly fruitful political place, as they had a greater ability than other women to access this potent language.

Lacking the overt ability to sacrifice their lives in the military – while the Irish Citizen Army welcomed female soldiers, the IRA did not – women had to establish their right to use the language of sacrifice. They did this by highlighting different types of particularly female sacrifice. The first was economic, as they called attention to the financial straits of women whose male breadwinners were dead, imprisoned or on the run.[5] They sought a more directly gendered angle in describing a second type of suffering: the physical harm done or threatened to women by Crown forces. The *Irish Bulletin* constantly chronicled attacks on women and often used vaguely sexualized language in describing women in various stages of indecency or undress during police raids. These articles also frequently mentioned that these raids reduced women to hysterics. Kate O'Callaghan wrote a pamphlet describing in close detail the violation of her home and the murder of her husband: 'I shall never forget the agony I suffered as I lay there screaming and helpless while I watched them [the Black and Tans] running down the grass in the shaft of light from the hall door. I crawled back to my husband and fell across his body, all my being crying out to God to spare him to me. I had never seen anybody die.'[6]

Although O'Callaghan was a witness to her husband's death, and MacSwiney was frequently at the bedside of her dying brother during his hunger strike, these political women also emphasized that they were not merely witnesses to these male sacrifices, but were more intimately connected with or implicated in them. They asserted that the sacrifice was shared: the male aspect was the death, and the female aspect was allowing the death, blessing it and carrying the burden thereafter. This strategy gave women a potent foothold, albeit a highly gendered one, into the discourse of sacrifice. Margaret Pearse made this claim in a letter to the government arguing for a larger pension, noting: 'I gave, willingly, my only two boys in prime of manhood.'[7] An earlier letter from Mrs Pearse asserted: 'I have only done as every Irish mother would do, willingly as I did, give their beloved ones for Ireland and for freedom.'[8] Others perceived the women in this sacrificial light as well. An introduction given for one of Muriel MacSwiney's 1920 appearances in America emphasized that 'Mrs MacSwiney's heroism in permitting her husband to make the supreme sacrifice for Ireland had given her a high place among the world's heroines.'[9]

This assertion that female relatives had a decisive role in a male sacrifice led to a belief that the sacrifice was shared, and the line between sacrificial victim and witness blurred even further. Grace Gifford, penniless and in need of money after her husband Joseph Plunkett's execution, claimed: 'I think my having to go into the workhouse on the anniversary of my husband's sacrifice and my own will hardly fail to shock.'[10] A letter to Muriel MacSwiney in 1920 stated: 'Ireland I am sure will ever be grateful for the sacrifice you have made.'[11] This access to the sacrificial act allowed female politicians to strengthen their connections to the deceased and also to access the powerful language of sacrifice, a common weapon in the Sinn Féin arsenal. This strategy also allowed women to talk credibly about the suffering brought on by war, a key topic in revolutionary Ireland. Mary Mac-Swiney told the Dáil:

> You men that talk need not talk to us about war ... It is the women who suffer the most of the hardships that war brings. You can go out in the excitement of the fight and it brings its own honour and its own glory. We have to sit at home and work in more humble ways. We have to endure the agony, the sunshines, the torture of misery and the privations which war brings, the horror of nightly visitations to our houses and their consequences. It is easier for you than it is for us.[12]

In a revolutionary movement suffused with martial language and soldier-politicians, women had to talk about sacrifice and war in order to have political credibility. Their co-option and feminization of the language of sacrifice allowed them to do this. This wartime suffering and sacrifice became key components of women's political identities. This rhetoric tapped into the archetype of the suffering mother in Irish culture, particularly the image of the Virgin Mary. A priest made this claim explicitly to Margaret Pearse: 'Mary gave her Son freely for the Redemption of the human race though it cost her the bitterest sorrow. You gave your sons to save Ireland's soul; and as the sacrifice has been both acceptable and efficacious, Mary ... will obtain from her Divine Son grace to sweeten the bitter memories of Easter 1916.'[13] Mrs Pearse defined herself frequently as a mother – specifically, the 'dearly loved mother of two of the noblest and bravest sons of Ireland' – and could not have failed to realize the obvious connection to the Virgin Mary in Ireland's Catholic culture. An Irish-American supporter told her: 'You have always been to me the embodiment of the courageous Irish motherhood which has brought Ireland to its advanced political position.' Another correspondent called her the 'Mother of Patrick', capitalizing the title in the same way as the Virgin's name.[14] Mrs Pearse was also asked for relics of her dead relatives, furthering the connection with the cult of the saints and the Virgin.[15]

These women did not sacrifice their lives, or risk their lives in military engagements, but they too sacrificed by offering up their male relatives to Ireland, and then handling the consequences of that sacrifice after the men had died. Their sacrifice was represented as both active and shared, and it gave those women who had lost relatives political identities, and allowed them to function as a bridge between public and private suffering and commemoration. They grieved privately, but also brought their grief into the public arena in order to serve as an example for others and, crucially, to spur further sacrifices for the cause. This suffering became a critical component of the debates over the Anglo-Irish Treaty.

Once the Treaty was brought to the Dáil on 14 December 1921, the six female TDs each made powerful speeches against the Treaty, and those who could drew on their own history of suffering in order to augment their political legitimacy. This discourse was not their only contribution to the debate – Markievicz talked extensively of her desire for a Connolly-inspired workers' republic, for example – but it was one of the most powerful and frequently noted. All six women wore mourning dress to the Dáil meetings, as the two female TDs who had not lost relatives associated themselves with the others through this very public gesture. This image of the suffering and grieving relative seemed to offer women unimpeachable legitimacy, and drew on themes that had been accepted by male revolutionaries during the war. It also connected women to the language of sacrifice that had dominated revolutionary-era rhetoric. These women had, quite reasonably, staked their political legitimacy in large part on the continued viability of their martyred relatives. Given the obsession with these sacrifices during the war, this seemed like a logical strategy. However, as part of the pro-Treatyites' attempt to promote the compromise Treaty, they moved away from the 'emotional' language of the revolution toward a more self-consciously sober and restrained discourse of state-building and pragmatism. This paradigm shift threatened women's political identity insofar as it was connected to the martyrs, and allowed Free Staters to denigrate both women and republicans for relying overmuch on this emotional language.

All six women in the Dáil voted against the Treaty, and their emphasis on their surrogacy for their male relatives was one of the more distinguishing features of women's anti-Treaty rhetoric. Several female TDs, for example, frequently claimed to be in the Dáil because of the dead. While a memo noted that MacSwiney was sent on her

American publicity tour because of her 'brilliancy and her oratorical ability', she herself admitted: 'I have reached many people who have never before heard a word on the Irish Question. That I reached them was mainly due to Terry's death and the interest it excited.'[16] In the Dáil, MacSwiney said: 'I consider the fact that what I went through for seventy-four days at Brixton gives me a right to speak for the honour of my nation now.'[17] Brixton Prison was where Terence MacSwiney had carried out his fatal seventy-four-day hunger strike. Kate O'Callaghan referred to the 'people of Limerick who elected me deputy of this Dáil two months after my husband's murder, and because of that murder'. She also said: 'Lest anybody should afterwards question my right to stand here and criticise and condemn this Treaty, I want it to be understood here and now that I have the clearest right in the world. I paid a big price for that Treaty and for my right to stand here.'[18] The price, of course, was the murder of her husband. Even before the Treaty, Margaret Pearse had said: 'she had been elected here on account of her beloved boys. She was very happy she had been elected, though she was almost an ornament here, so that the name of a Pearse would be in the first Irish parliament.'[19]

In addition to gaining the right to speak from the dead, the women claimed to speak for the dead. They often directly quoted the words of their deceased relations and attempted to use their privileged connections with the martyrs in order to fix the meaning of those words. Since the legacies of the revolution and its participants were very much contested during the Treaty debates, this was a very controversial claim. Those female TDs who had lost men claimed that their men did not die for a compromise Free State but for an unfettered Republic, and would have opposed the Treaty had they lived. The dead were thus marshalled against the Treaty, in part to counter the majority of the living who seemed to favour it. Mary MacSwiney punctuated her private session speech with repeated assertions that 'I stand here in the name of the dead', and called on the TDs to 'vote in the name of the dead to unite against this Treaty'.[20] She also said: 'I claim that the daily torture of seventy-four days of unspeakable suffering gives me a claim to speak for [Terence] and myself.'[21] The question was, therefore, how to most effectively monopolize the words and the names of the dead. One way was to claim gnostic knowledge, relaying conversations held with their relatives in private moments. Both Kathleen Clarke and Mary MacSwiney told the Dáil that Tom Clarke and Terence MacSwiney emphasized in their dying moments that all talk of compromise with the British should cease. Margaret Pearse made a similar claim with regards to a final letter that Patrick attempted to smuggle out of Kilmainham Gaol.[22]

Several of the women also explicitly rejected any attempt by pro-Treatyites to interpret the legacies of their relatives. Kathleen Clarke challenged: 'Is there anyone here who would tell me that Tom Clarke lifted his hand for that thing [the Treaty]? Is there anyone here who would tell me that any of the young men who fought and fell in 1916 would have lifted their hands for it?'[23] Kate O'Callaghan said: 'I challenge any Deputy in this Dáil to deny my husband's devotion to the Republic, a devotion he sealed with his blood. I would ask the gentlemen who say he was never a Republican ... to leave my husband's name out of the matter.'[24] And Margaret Pearse told the Dáil: 'If I signed that Treaty or accepted it I assure you I would not have any night's rest, for I would be haunted by the ghosts of my sons.'[25] During her public speech, she echoed this theme: 'It has been said here on several occasions that Pádraig Pearse would have accepted this Treaty. I deny it. As his mother I deny it, and on his account I will not accept it. Neither would his brother Willie accept it, because his brother was part and parcel of him.'[26]

Any attempt by others to interpret the legacy of these men differently was declared to be off-limits by these women, who claimed special knowledge based on years of access to the private men, as well as privileged conversations held near the end of the martyrs' lives. Many of these men had complex legacies: after all, Pearse and Clarke had surrendered in 1916 rather than fighting on against insurmountable odds, and Terence MacSwiney's Cork Brigade remained famously inactive in 1916. These complexities were put aside as the men were unambiguously placed in the republican camp. Treatyites were denied the right to alternate interpretations: as Kate O'Callaghan said, they were to leave her husband's name out of the matter. Mary MacSwiney, although conceding that she did 'not speak of my right any more than I do of others to allude to those who have gone', then requested 'those here tonight who are putting expediency before principle to kindly leave the names of the dead out of their speeches'.[27] Annie MacSwiney, another of Terence's sisters, demanded that his former friend Richard Mulcahy return his mementoes of Terence, as Mulcahy's Treatyite stance gave him no further right to such remembrances.[28] The ties of blood and marriage trumped those of friendship and comradeship. The women fashioned themselves as the only acceptable surrogates for their dead men, and then tried to use these powers to sway the Dáil against the Treaty.

This was all filtered through the different discourse with which the women spoke. Male revolutionaries tended to talk of their dead comrades as soldiers or statesmen. Women did this too, but also emphasized the familial relationships they had with their dead men, something that generally could not be claimed by others in the Dáil. Wearing black to the debates highlighted this familial style, as this was not a form of mourning associated with soldiers. The frequent discussion of private conversations also contributed to this different tone, emphasizing that some key knowledge of these men could not be gleaned solely from public actions and pronouncements. The women also equated their undoubted private suffering with some form of national suffering, including the wider suffering of other women who had lost relatives and the long-term suffering of Ireland as a whole. Kate O'Callaghan's Dáil speech against the Treaty masterfully wove together personal and national suffering, and demonstrated the potency of this discourse. She asked: 'Now what have all these hundreds of years of struggle been for? What has it been about? What has been the agony and the sorrow for? Why was my husband murdered? Why am I a widow? Was it that I should come here and give my vote for a Treaty that puts Ireland within the British Empire?'[29] This connection between women and a very particular kind of suffering and mourning was also used as the foundation of the oft-repeated claim that the women of Ireland would oppose the Treaty. Mrs Pearse said: 'I have been through Ireland for the past few years and I know the hearts and sorrows of the wives of Ireland. I have studied them; no one studied them more, and let no one here say that these women from their hearts could say they accept that Treaty.' She finished her speech by striking a note of defiance against those who charged that women were misusing the dead:

> One Deputy mentioned here about rattling the bones of the dead. I only wish we could recall them. Remember, the day will come ... when those bones shall be lifted as if they were the bones of saints. We won't let them rattle. No, but we will hold what they upheld, and no matter what anyone says I feel that I and others here have a right to speak in the name of their dead.[30]

Here Mrs Pearse linked women specifically to suffering by equating women to their 'hearts and sorrows', and she then cited that characterization in concluding that Irish women would reject the Treaty. MacSwiney admitted that some Irish people would turn away from the Republic and accept the Treaty, but 'not the best, not those who have suffered; not those who have faith in the justice of their cause, and regard for the honour of their dead'.[31] MacSwiney assumed that suffering conditioned people to take the republican side, and both she and Mrs Pearse assumed a proprietary role over the dead, referring to them as 'their' dead. Certainly, not all women's rhetoric in the Dáil was couched in this way, but enough of it was to be remarked upon frequently by male politicians. A republican pamphlet demanded that Free State soldiers 'Ask yourselves on which side is the mother of the Pearses, the widows of Tom Clarke, The O'Rahilly, Éamon Ceannt, Joseph Plunkett, James Connolly; on which side are the relatives of Ashe, MacSwiney, Kevin Barry, Dick McKee? … Is there a name of Easter Week, or since, that does not accuse you?'[32]

This rhetorical strategy continued during the Civil War, and proved difficult for Free Staters to counter. Attacking mourning women, or claiming that they misunderstood their relatives, was politically problematic and risked the appearance of heartlessness. Rather than contest these issues directly, the Treatyites decided instead to denigrate the entire discourse with which women spoke, and in so doing delegitimize republicanism as a whole. The Treatyites attacked women's use of the dead in particular, and claimed that the use of this tactic by the women demonstrated general weaknesses of republicanism. In their quest to define a politics that excluded and delegitimized republicans, pro-Treatyites defined a politics that excluded and delegitimized women. They feminized republicanism and used familiar stereotypes of women – in fact, the same stereotypes traditionally used by the colonizing English against the colonized Irish – to undermine support for republicanism.[33]

They did this in a number of ways. First, some Free Staters said it was improper to mention the dead at all in this political context. Fionán Lynch told the Dáil: 'We have had a great deal of emotion and a great deal of emotional speeches about the dead. I say for myself that the bones of the dead have been rattled indecently in the face of this assembly.'[34] Michael Collins admonished those who invoked the dead: 'we [pro-Treatyites] have refrained from reading letters from the relatives of the dead. We have too much respect for the dead.'[35] Collins also said: 'There is no man here who has more regard for the dead men than I have. I don't think it is fair to be quoting them against us. I think the decision ought to be a clear decision on the documents as they are before us, on the Treaty as it is before us … Don't let us put the responsibility, the individual responsibility, upon anybody else.'[36]

Collins charged that the invocation of the dead minimized the responsibility of the living. As he told the Dáil: 'Deputies have spoken about whether dead men would approve of it [the Treaty], and they have spoken of whether children yet unborn would approve of it, but few of them have spoken as to whether the living approve of it.'[37]

In addition to arguing that the dead had no place in a political debate, pro-Treatyites also took issue with attempts to ascertain what deceased individuals would have thought of the Treaty had they lived. Gearoid O'Sullivan said: 'I speak of Dick McKee and Peadar Clancy. Very few had the courage to see the tricolour draped on their coffins and screw the lids on their coffins. I have been thinking ever since I saw this treaty of many conversations I had on these two men and I certainly would not say that either of them would vote against this Treaty.'[38] Piaras Béaslaí said: 'We have no right to say how any man who is dead would have voted', and Éamon Duggan asserted his own interpretive right: 'I say that I shall interpret for myself what their [the martyrs'] views were and would be if they were here today, and that no other man or woman has the right to interpret them for me.'[39] Fionán Lynch refused to be limited by the putative views of his dead colleagues: 'Now I am alive, and I took my chance of being killed as well as any white man in this assembly, and I challenge any man to deny that. Now I am here to interpret myself, and I stand for this Treaty.'[40] Lynch specifically referred to men in this passage, implying that women were not able to risk their lives for the nation. He later denied to women the right to interpret the dead: 'if I were dead, and if I were to be interpreted, I should ask to be interpreted by the men who soldiered with me and by the men who worked with me in the National movement'.[41] This argument deliberately privileged the views of (masculine) fellow soldiers over female relatives. Finally, pro-Treatyites characterized this women's discourse as both personal and emotional, and thus out of place in what purported to be a rational discussion of Ireland's future. Batt O'Connor, a friend of Michael Collins, said in a letter:

> There is not much real division noticeable at all among the people, but the women are 'holy terrors'. They are mudslinging and name calling and spiting and froughting [sic] to the mouth like angry cats, and always casting up about their relatives that died for Ireland. I think the Irish people will not be in a hurry again to elect women to represent them.[42]

Seán Milroy admitted to the Dáil:

> It is time we realised where we are drifting to. I heard today passionate speeches. I heard today speeches that did not make people smile. I heard from Mrs O'Callaghan today one of the most pathetic stories I ever listened to. It is not a thing to smile at, but a thing that cut to the heart of anyone listening to it.

Milroy then contrasted the women's approach with his own: 'I am not going to appeal to anything but your real and clear conception of what Ireland's national interests are.'[43]

Treatyites also charged that many of these women became excessively emotional because of their suffering. Desmond FitzGerald said that Mary MacSwiney 'was a fanatic and not quite normal after Brixton'.[44] Alec MacCabe, in the most sustained attack on the women in the Dáil, echoed FitzGerald, saying: 'it may be that Miss MacSwiney's mind and outlook are distorted by the terrible experiences she has passed through. If so, there is some excuse for ...' He was unable to finish his sentence, as he was immediately interrupted by an angry MacSwiney, who assured MacCabe that she was 'quite sane on the point' and ordered him to 'leave out my experiences'.[45] On the other hand, Richard Mulcahy decided that women took up opposition to the Treaty because they had not suffered enough, and did not run any risks to their lives during the war. Critiquing a hostile letter from Annie MacSwiney, Mulcahy observed: 'it [the letter] can be regarded as epitomizing the quintessence of the feeling of the non-fighters, non-responsibles'.[6] This charge that women adopted extreme positions because they did not have to fear for their lives – either from the British during the Anglo-Irish war or the Free Staters later – was repeated frequently during the Civil War. Factors that were used to bolster women's credibility during the Anglo-Irish war, particularly the suffering that they went through, were now being used to undermine their arguments and question their sanity.

The women's discourse was also criticized for being excessively personal. MacCabe, again, launched the most direct attack of this kind:

> Now, nobody objects to people voting against the Treaty because they have a personal grievance against England, but I do suggest that it is unfair asking other people to vote for their grievance, for this is what it really amounts to. Is it not enough to have eight, nine or ten votes as the case may be, but not sufficient anyhow to

defeat the Treaty, cast on this personal issue? Where does the country come in? I would remind all those Teachtaí who have such grievances that they were not sent here to avenge the wrongs committed in the war ... I would, therefore, appeal to them to rise above their personal prejudices and think of themselves, not as the sisters or wives or mothers or brothers of dead patriots, but as representatives of the people, with the fate of a country in their hands.

MacCabe made another dig at the references to the dead, dryly noting: 'the earth belongs to those who are on it, and not to those who are under it, and to the living and not the dead we owe our votes'. He then attacked MacSwiney again, asking:

Is there one woman in this assembly who could rise to the great opportunity, one woman who would sink her feelings, sink her cravings for vengeance, sink her principles even, and, sacrificing her personality as others sacrificed their lives, vote for the good of her country. Such an act of self-elimination would, in my opinion, appeal to the whole world as an act worthy of a countrywoman of Terence MacSwiney.[47]

Mocking the women's attempt to sacrifice themselves – they could only sacrifice their personalities – MacCabe implied that the only way for Mary to replicate Terence's sacrifice was to abandon her interpretation of his principles, a 'self-elimination'. This denigration of the personal language put women's particular arguments outside the bounds of politics and reason. Pro-Treaty TD Professor Whelehan also contrasted personal appeals with reason and rationality: 'I submit that the appeals against this Treaty have been appeals to the heart and not to the reason or to the judgment. I submit that, and often I found that my heart was touched by several personal appeals here, and that I had to urge my judgment to do what was correct.'[48] The women's personal appeals, therefore, were to be overcome by reason, a faculty that the women presumably did not use in voicing those appeals.

The charge that women were emotional, personal and irrational was extended to all of republicanism, as the relatively high profiles that female politicians held in the republican movement made the delegitimation of women a crucial component of the undermining of republicanism as a whole. This path was more tempting during the Civil War, when women assumed even greater visibility within the republican movement, itself often mockingly referred to as the 'Women and Childers Party'. Political women were assumed to be unbalanced, and gendered language was used to castigate both women and republicans and to remove their arguments from the parameters of rational debate. Kevin O'Higgins told the Dáil at the height of the Civil War that 'this country is not a stage or a platform whereon certain neurotic women and a certain megalomaniac kind of men may cut their capers.'[49] O'Higgins also said that the Treaty was passed 'despite the most frantic appeals to passion and emotion', and that republican leaders '[got] a lot of silly, neurotic women to back them ... and a lot of silly neurotic young boys to do likewise'.[50] Ernest Blythe characterized opposition to the Treaty as 'to a very large extent indeed irrational', and W.T. Cosgrave described republicans as 'people whose mental balance is bad'.[51] The lines between republicanism and femininity were often blurred, as the Free State/republican difference was illustrated by Free Staters using language derived from the more recognizable male/female difference. Alec MacCabe demonstrated this by decrying the 'wild women and the effeminate men' in the republican movement.[52] Women themselves, as well as possessing stereotypical 'feminine' qualities, were assumed to embody the distinguishing characteristics of republicanism, and then were savagely attacked as contrasting unfavourably with the rational, forward-looking and sober Free Staters. Even when not specifically discussing women, gendered terms like 'hysterical' or 'neurotic' were used to characterize republicanism.

Nowhere was this more evident than in the debates over Mary MacSwiney's Civil War hunger strikes. The Free State government decided that female politicians bore significant responsibility for the continuation of the Civil War, and therefore had to be arrested and incarcerated. In discussing a later arrest of Mary MacSwiney, Cosgrave said:

> It must be admitted that until steps were taken to arrest certain active women, considerable damage and considerable loss of life were occasioned in the city and in other parts of the country. Since they have been arrested, these activities have to a very large extent ceased. We know, on the information at our disposal, that if it were not for the active co-operation of women, this particular onslaught on people's rights, liberties and property would not have continued to anything like the same length of time.[53]

Blythe echoed Cosgrave in this: 'We know that a terrible amount of destruction of life and property would not have occurred if it had not been for the active participation of large numbers of women in the struggle. It is as necessary for us, for the protection of the community, to hold women prisoners as it is to hold men prisoners.'[54]

Mary MacSwiney was arrested in November 1922, and again in April 1923. Each time, she went on hunger strike. Unlike her brother, though, Mary was not treated as a hero by many elements of the former revolutionary community. Terence's hunger strike was the centrepiece of Sinn Féin propaganda in late 1920, while Treatyites condemned Mary's as a selfish and irrational act. The change in the manner that the two hunger strikes were discussed highlights not only the obvious gender differences between the strikers, but also the very different political circumstances in which the strikes took place.

From the beginning, Mary MacSwiney was determined to recreate her brother's great sacrifice. She referred to Mountjoy, the prison in which she was held, as a 'second Brixton', and told the archbishop of Dublin: 'I have begun a hunger strike and with God's help will carry it through as bravely as my sainted brother did, and for exactly the same cause, and with equal justification.'[55] Republican propaganda echoed this claim, making a great deal out of Mary's connection to Terence. Often, she was just referred to in speeches, official letters and broadsheets as a 'sister of Terence MacSwiney', with her familial relationship forming the essence of her public identity.[56] De Valera told Mary that her cause was the same as Terence's, and said that Mary and her sister Annie (who was on hunger strike outside the prison as well) were 'both acting as voluntary soldiers offering your lives as a sacrifice in a worthy cause'.[57] A copy of *Poblacht na hÉireann*, a republican broadsheet, said Mary 'is being allowed to die, as her brother died in Brixton Prison two years ago, in the same protest and for the same faith'.[58]

Outside observers frequently made the same obvious connection between Terence and Mary. Archbishop Byrne of Dublin urged Cosgrave not to allow MacSwiney to die, as 'she is the sister of Terence MacSwiney and if she dies, the same way, cannot fail to share some of his "martyr's apotheosis"'. J.P. Dowdall of Cork wrote to the government and said: 'the association of hunger-striking and death in consequence of same as in the case of Terence MacSwiney is too closely reminiscent of the struggle with England and all that it implied in the recent past'. George Lyons, a Sinn Féiner and Treatyite, warned Cosgrave: 'she is the sister of the one who owes his place in our history because of a hunger strike. She owes her place in Irish politics solely to that fame of her brother. She owes it to that fame of her brother's to go on hunger strike and according to her mentality she has no alternative.' One Dublin woman told Cosgrave:

> She [Mary] is Terence MacSwiney's sister and ... the Irish state cannot see her kill herself, thus making two tragedies in that family. This may seem to you a reason of mere sentiment, but sentiment plays a powerful part in human affairs ... If she and those women who abet her proclaim their triumph over your Government [at being released] woman's triumph is but a frail thing after all.[59]

Republican propaganda presented Mary as replicating Terence's decline and death. Unable to sacrifice her life during the War of Independence, this was a way for Mary to inhabit her brother's sacrifice and finally demonstrate that she too could suffer in exactly the same way. It was the apex of the female politicians' frequent emphasis on suffering and familial relations. An issue of the republican paper *Straight Talk* highlighted the key issue: 'It falls to the lot of Miss MacSwiney to take up the work of her brother Terence ... Will the Provisional Government bring about the repetition of the greatest episode of all Irish history in the person of Terence's sister?'[60] Free Staters, however, responded quite differently to the strike than Sinn Féiners had to Terence's strike. The stark difference reflects the very real changes in the rules of political discourse and the acceptance of female politicians that had transpired since the signing of the Treaty and the sundering of the revolutionary movement.

Government supporters now gendered the whole notion of a hunger strike. Kevin O'Higgins derogatorily referred to the 'women's weapon of the hunger-strike', and George Lyons implied that MacSwiney went on hunger strike because 'she is a woman ... and according to feminine psychology, being unfitted to inflict hurt upon a man, she inflicts it upon herself'.[61] In discussing later hunger strikes, Deputy William Magennis (albeit arguing for the strikers' release) noted that a hunger strike was 'not, when seriously regarded, the performance of a rational being'.[62] The hunger strike was thus both irrational and a reflection of women's physical impotence. No such language would have been deployed against Terence MacSwiney in 1920.

Cosgrave, in responding to members of the church hierarchy's concern for Mary's life, emphasized the negative role women played in Civil War politics. He told Archbishop Byrne: 'Your Grace may not be wholly cognizant of the prominent and destructive part played by women in the present deplorable revolt against the definitely expressed will of the vast majority of the Irish people, and against those sacred principles upon which civilisation and even Christianity itself is founded.' He also told Cardinal Logue: 'the release of a leader so prominent and so fanatical as Miss MacSwiney ... would tend but to encourage in their mad courses the young people of both sexes whom she has goaded into revolt against both ecclesiastical and constitutional authority'. Cosgrave concluded: 'The Government can but hope that Miss MacSwiney may yet come to an appreciation of the fundamental differences between her protest and that of her gallant brother.'[63] This was another point that the Free Staters hammered home, as they denied any similarities to Terence's sacrifice. Patrick Hogan, the outspoken minister for agriculture, said: 'there is no analogy good, bad, or indifferent. None whatsoever.'[64] Richard Mulcahy told the imprisoned MacSwiney that he interpreted her brother's principles quite differently than she did, and later referred to Mary's 'caricature of her brother's sacrifice'.[65]

Ernest Blythe, with characteristic bluntness, told the Dáil: 'In most cases, the matter [a hunger strike] is simply a bluff. Of course, it might end fatally. Some prisoners, women of a particular age, who might not be so reasonable as they would be in normal circumstances, might perhaps go further.'[66] This comment, made near the end of MacSwiney's second hunger strike in May 1923, invoked menopause as the catalyst, a charge that would be replicated more explicitly in the medical reports about MacSwiney made by prison doctors. The first medical officer who examined her observed:

> She has been complaining of headaches, diffuse pains, flushes, etc. for the past three months and has been undergoing treatment, I believe. In my opinion, these symptoms, taken in conjunction with her age and three recent missed periods, point definitely to the onset of menopause. This will have a very important bearing on the duration of her hunger-strike – the climacteric being so commonly a period of great mental and physical instability in so many women. In recent time she must have had severe emotional disturbances. These have certainly affected her mental outlook. I feel it essential to put on record that this present additional strain of facing a long hunger-strike, combined with her past experience in this same trouble and her present disturbed mental equilibrium from the climacteric may conceivably culminat[e] in unhinging her mind.

The director of medical services passed on these concerns in a report to the Provisional Government: 'another complication following in this case is the unstable highly strung mentality of the prisoner, which renders a mental collapse as likely as a physical one'.[67] This framed in medical terms the diagnosis of republicanism that Free Staters had made since the Treaty debates. The 'past experience' of suffering and sacrifice, paired with the revolution itself – 'a period of great physical and mental instability' – caused republicans to clutch at the fantasy of the Republic. The peculiar mental makeup of republicans, linked expressly to femininity, had rendered them unable to pass from the emotional wave of revolution to the sober tranquillity of state-building. Unhinged by the sufferings of heroes, they had no idea what to do in a post-heroic age. Such a diagnosis negated the high ideals for which Mary MacSwiney claimed to be striking and exploded the link with her fallen brother. Rhetorically, it was a powerful strategy and epitomizes the feminization of republicanism that came to dominate Cumann na nGaedheal thinking.

The Treaty and Civil War marked a change in Irish political discourse and a change in the location of much of that discourse, as the focus shifted from Westminster to Leinster House. This proved to be a turning point for Irish political women, as the conditions that favoured their growing involvement during the revolution suddenly evaporated, and the political ground shifted under their feet. The political culture suddenly became more hostile to women, in part because of a need to debunk the powerful arguments made by republican women, and in part because of the Free State government's difficulties in connecting itself to the Irish revolutionary tradition. Several prominent political women had staked a portion of their political legitimacy on their connection with hallowed martyrs, only to see those connections denigrated as emotional, sentimental and personal during the Treaty debates and Civil War. This is not to say that the female politicians were responsible for their own marginalization, but merely to point out that the means by which they gained influence proved to be a key reason for their subsequent loss of influence. Female politicians, as is often the case in a fundamentally patriarchal society, were seen as a vulnerable point in the republican coalition, and were attacked as such. These attacks blurred the lines between women and republicans, and attempted to cast both out of the infant Free State. The promise of female political activity during the revolution had to wait several decades to be even partially fulfilled, and thus the Treaty marked a turning point in Irish history for female politicians.

CHAPTER FOUR

The Problem of Equality: Women's Activist Campaigns in Ireland, 1920–40

MARIA LUDDY

The turn of the twentieth century was a very vibrant period in Irish political history which saw increasing numbers of women taking to public life – as political activists, as elected members of boards of guardians or in local government. They were teachers in universities, nurses and doctors in hospitals. Women combined cultural and political nationalism in the establishment of new societies, such as Inghinidhe na hÉireann, the first radical nationalist organization formed by women, for women. The organization was home to a generation of women activists including Maud Gonne, Helena Molony and Kathleen Lynn, all formidable public figures for much of the first half of the twentieth century.[1] The establishment of the Ulster Women's Council in 1911 to oppose home rule saw the politicization of thousands of Irish women, primarily in the north of Ireland. By 1913 the council claimed to have a membership in the region of 200,000 and remained an active force throughout the century.[2] New suffrage societies, including the Irish Women's Franchise League (1908), utilized more public and what some considered 'aggressive' means to win the vote for women. In 1918 the British parliament gave women over 30, meeting certain qualifications, the right to vote. Whether or not it had any real impact on improving women's lot in society, the vote had symbolic value, allowing women some level of electoral equality with men. The ideal of equality with men had been a constant refrain in feminist activism in Ireland from the early nineteenth century. However, that equality was often limited by notions of class and working-class women had little to gain from that campaign.[3]

The establishment of the Irish Women Workers' Union (IWWU) in 1911 by Delia and Jim Larkin saw the beginnings of a vibrant force within trade unionism. It was the first general union for women in Ireland, and was inaugurated after a successful pay strike by 3,000 women at Jacob's biscuit factory in August 1911. The union suffered a number of upheavals and internal disputes in its first few years. Delia Larkin resigned as secretary in July 1915 and her place was taken by Helena Molony. From a working-class background, Molony combined her nationalist and trade union activities throughout her career. She was secretary to Inghinidhe na hÉireann and edited their journal *Bean na hÉireann*.[4] Molony worked closely with and was greatly influenced by James Connolly and, as a member of his Citizen Army, took part in the Easter Rising. By 1918 Louie Bennett and Helen Chenevix had become the honorary secretaries of the union. From its inception the IWWU initiated the clearest alliance of working- and middle-class women in Ireland. Individually its members played a role in the cause of Irish nationalism, and collectively through union activity shaped Irish women's working lives.[5] In 1918 Louie Bennett observed that the most notable development of the women's movement in Ireland was the growth in trade unionism among women workers.[6] The expansion of women's trade unionism was believed to be 'the best possible contribution to the whole cause of feminism. There can be no real freedom or independence for women until they are economically free.'[7] The growing numbers involved in the trade union movement allowed women to express their needs as workers, and also in many cases to successfully challenge their exploitation. The union and its leadership were to play a significant role in fighting for women's economic equality in Ireland.

Women played an active role in the fight for Irish independence through their involvement in the Easter Rising of 1916, the War of Independence 1919–21 and the Civil War 1922–3. Equal citizenship had been guaranteed to Irish men and women under the Proclamation of 1916. Active lobbying, particularly by women, saw all Irish citizens over the age of 21 enfranchised under the Irish Free State Constitution enacted in June 1922. The early twentieth century was an exciting period for women's activism on political and economic issues. Ideas of equality and equal citizenship became central in many women's minds to understanding their significance and place in an independent Irish state. How equality was understood, or expected to work in practice, was not always clearly articulated, and as a concept equality was often framed or understood in gendered and class terms. Through an examination of activist campaigns, however, we can come to a clearer understanding of what was meant or implied by the term.

Social issues that involved family life, reproduction and economic equality provoked campaigns by women throughout the century, particularly after the establishment of the Irish Free State. For instance, the Irish Housewives Association (IHA), formed in 1942, sought originally to demand fair prices and fair distribution of goods during the period of the Emergency and it proved to be an effective pressure group throughout the second half of the twentieth century.[8] The IHA was later instrumental in encouraging the government to establish a Commission on the Status of Women in March 1970.[9] In the same year the establishment of the Irish Women's Liberation Movement brought a new generation of women to embrace political and social activism. One of the major issues pursued by the movement was contraception, a campaign which brought it infamy and publicity, particularly when on 22 May 1971 a group of women made a trip to Belfast to purchase contraceptives which they openly and blatantly brought back to Dublin.[10] It was not until 1979 that anti-contraception laws were removed from the statute books. The Commission on the Status of Women published its final report in December 1972 outlining forty-nine areas of discrimination against women in Ireland.[11] One of the consequences of the report was the formation of a Council for the Status of Women, which was to monitor the implementation of the commission's recommendations and also be alert to other areas where women might face discrimination. The Council for the Status of Women through vigorous campaigning has been influential in shaping government policy and action in areas relating to, among other issues, equality legislation and domestic abuse.[12]

The nature and extent of women's activism in the struggle for independence would suggest that Irish women were well placed to benefit from the roles they had played in that struggle. However, women did not retain a high profile in the political affairs of the country and from the foundation of the Free State women's political, economic and social rights were gradually eroded. The implementation of restrictive legislation in the economic and political spheres found echoes in the social sphere. For instance, divorce, previously available through Act of Parliament, was banned in 1925; the 1927 Juries Act made it very difficult for women to sit on juries. The 1929 Censorship of Publications Bill prohibited the advertisement of contraceptives, while the 1935 Criminal Law Amendment Act prohibited the sale of contraceptives. Other legislation, to be discussed below, also had repercussions on how women could live their lives in Ireland.

Given the many political, social, cultural and economic changes that occurred in Ireland in the twentieth century and their relevance to women it is difficult to mark out any single event or campaign that can encapsulate a momentous change in Irish women's lived experiences. It was always going to be difficult to dislodge generally held views that women's lives must remain centred around the home and the family. From the foundation of the Free State there is no doubt but that both the state and the church emphatically presented women's place as being in the home and the ideal role of the Irish woman was as mother. Whatever equality might mean, it was always circumscribed by this belief in the domestic nature of women.

Equality in the labour market was always contentious. Concern about women's paid labour in the nineteenth century was often less about her right to work than the conditions under which she worked. Thus legislation tended to focus on 'protection', limiting, for instance, women's working hours and attempting to improve actual working conditions. Economic independence for women rarely surfaced as a sustained campaigning issue for Irish nineteenth-century feminists.[13] For suffragists, the acquisition of the vote was considered a superior aim to that of ensuring economic independence for women. The right to work, however, did remain a central point of importance to women trade unionists and to women political activists from the foundation of the Free State. Attempts to restrict women's access to employment were strongly resisted by women activists. Important campaigns were instigated around the Civil Service Amendment Bill (1925), the Marriage Bar, the Conditions of Employment Bill (1935) and the campaign against the draft Constitution of 1937. In this article I want to explore these campaigns and to place them in what I consider to be a fundamental discursive argument utilized by activists that had its origin and power in the 1916 Proclamation. Much of women's political activism in the 1920s and 1930s was informed by their understanding of both the 1916 Proclamation and certain articles in the 1922 Constitution. From the 1916 Proclamation the phrase 'The Republic guarantees religious and civil liberty, equal rights and equal opportunities to all its citizens ...' was the standard against which government policy, particularly where it affected women, was measured. Article 3 of the 1922 Constitution, which guaranteed equality to all Irish citizens, strengthened the position outlined in the Proclamation.[14]

The ideals of equality implied by both these documents held a vital place in the vocabulary of women's political activism in the 1920s and 1930s.[15] Invoking both the 1916 Proclamation and the relevant sections of the 1922 Constitution, women campaigned against government attempts to limit their rights as citizens and specifically their rights as workers. Within the context of the theme of this book I would argue that these phrases, particularly that from the Proclamation, offered a fundamental and irrevocable foundation for campaigns of equality fought in the 1920s and 1930s. The language of equality expressed in the Proclamation, sanctified by the deaths of the Rising's leaders and the campaign for independence, and consolidated in the 1922 Constitution, offered women activists an essential understanding of their status in Irish society. While it was a status consistently under attack, these phrases remained an enduring legacy for activist women. The discursive importance of the 1916 Proclamation and the 1922 Constitution to the campaigns undertaken by women activists in the 1920s and 1930s mark, arguably, the most significant turning points for Irish women in the twentieth century.

The campaigns to be discussed below all related directly to issues of equality, citizenship and rights, the right to work being a fundamental right of any citizen.[16] The essential and continuous link among these campaigns was the constant reference to the fundamental right to equality promised women in the 1916 Proclamation and reinforced in the 1922 Constitution. This proclamation was the benchmark by which women's groups measured the performance of various governments with regard to the rights of women as workers and citizens. It was a standard that was rarely met by any government in the period.

THE CIVIL SERVICE AMENDMENT ACT

In 1924 the government passed a Civil Service Regulation Act that opened all competitive examinations to all citizens of Ireland or those born in Ireland.[17] However, in the autumn of the same year it was announced that an examination for junior administrative positions would be restricted to men only.[18] The Irish Women Citizens and Local Government Association (IWCLGA) took advice on the matter and threatened legal action if the government attempted to exclude on the basis of sex.[19] The attorney general, in his advice to the Executive Council on the matter argued that, according to the Civil Service Regulation Act, the Civil Service Commission had no power to make regulations excluding women from this examination. Indeed, he noted that such examinations were open to all citizens of the Free State who 'pay the fees and possess the qualifications as to age, health, and character prescribed by the regulations'.[20] The government then, in 1925, introduced a bill, the Civil Service Amendment Bill, which the minister for finance noted was 'to deal with the difficulties which arose when it was discovered that under existing legislation the Civil Service Commission had not the power to confine examinations to members of one particular sex'.[21] The minister argued that 'in certain situations in the Civil Service you must discriminate with regard to sex'.[22] He noted that there was also the possibility of confining examinations to women for posts such as typists and telephonists. Women were more suitable for typing work and those grades, he believed, were best confined to women.[23] It was also argued that women should not be in positions where they would be 'controlling men of mature years'.[24] The bill met with considerable opposition within the Dáil. Quoting Article 3 of the 1922 Constitution, Deputy Cooper argued that every citizen was entitled to equal opportunities. He observed one of the great changes to have occurred in society was the fact that 'women left home to take up a career and, in consequence, you now have women in almost every sphere of life except the Church, and the Army'.[25] It was, he noted, 'the most revolutionary thing that has happened in our time'. Cooper warned that the bill 'was a step in the wrong direction' and saw it as a 'retrograde step'.[26] Cooper further argued that the bill would introduce the 'principle of sex-disqualification, which does not at present exist in our legislation'.[27] Deputy Alton stated that the bill 'is tending to put back the clock and to drive women down into the lower civil service posts and to confine the higher administrative and executive posts to men only'.[28]

A number of the male TDs were concerned with the powers the bill seemed to give to the Civil Service Commission, and to future ministers in limiting progress through the ranks of the civil service.[29] Deputy Hewat, who also opposed the bill, argued that 'we must recognize that women occupy a position of equality today with men that never would have been contemplated years ago'.[30] But there was an inherent contradiction in the evocation of equality. Women, most deputies agreed, were not suited to all posts in the civil service, and they believed the legislation was unnecessary to limit their work in the service. Most men and women, it was believed, already understood and accepted an ideology of work that would inhibit women applying for 'male posts'. According to this belief the legislation introduced by the government was unnecessary and the real issue was about excessive ministerial power.

Professor William Magennis, TD, provided a severe criticism of the bill and saw it as a 'bill for sex disqualification'.[31] It was evident to him that the bill was a means to prevent women from entering into the higher grades of the civil service. It was, he said a 'denial of democracy' to inhibit or prohibit educated women from progressing through the civil service. 'We were,' he argued, 'the first in the world to introduce equality between man and woman, to recognize a common citizenship irrespective of sex, and now we are proceeding to do away with that. Why? ... what has occurred in recent history that would justify us doing away with that equality?'[32] He saw the bill as 'reactionary and against the spirit in which the Constitution was enacted'.[33] And yet Magennis, like many individuals, could also argue that 'no woman will apply for appointment to a position where the fact of being a woman is an obvious and natural disqualification'.[34] Equality, as it was understood in a 'common-sense' way, was in itself inherently restrictive.

Ironically, it was Margaret Collins O'Driscoll, one of the few women in the Dáil, who supported the bill. Collins O'Driscoll, who 'had been canvassed by very influential members of my sex' to oppose the bill, could not, she stated, 'see that it infringes our rights under the Constitution in any respect. I am not enamoured of this bill ... I must admit it limits to a certain extent the appointments for which women are eligible.' But, she argued, 'the more I study the bill the more I see that I would be injuring my sex by voting against it'. Accepting the arguments that had been put forward by the minister for finance in proposing the bill, she believed that women would only be excluded from a small number of posts in the service.[35] It was always possible, she noted, that more women deputies would be returned to the Dáil in the next election and they could then amend the legislation.[36] Collins O'Driscoll was, with other deputies, perpetuating gendered claims to appropriate occupations for women and reaffirming an ideal that women should not have to work or were temporary workers until they married.

When the bill was introduced in the Senate on 17 December 1925 it was noted to be an 'objectionable' measure.[37] Senator Eileen Costello quoted Article 3 of the Constitution before stating that 'the bringing in of this Bill by the Government is unjust ... morally wrong, and ... monstrously unfair'.[38] Costello could see no reason why such a bill had been brought forward. 'Does it mean,' she asked,

> that there has been such a rush of women for the various posts that the Government finds it necessary to bring in this Bill? I have not heard anything about such a rush. I believe that the Ministers maintain that for some posts women are unsuitable. I rather think the word that should be used is 'unwanted'. They are synonymous terms in the mind of the Minister.[39]

Jennie Wyse Power, who had been an activist since the days of the Ladies' Land League and was a former president of Sinn Féin, also objected to the bill and bemoaned its introduction by men 'who were associated in the fight [for independence] with women who played their part at a time when sex and money were not considerations'.[40] Wyse Power also argued that 'no consultation of any kind' had taken place with any representative women on the subject before the bill was introduced.[41] Ignoring women's views on policy and legal proposals was to remain a point of contention for women's groups throughout the period.

The argument over the bill was also carried on outside the houses of the oireachtas. In a letter to the *Irish Independent*, Mary Hayden and Ethel McNaghten of the Irish Women Citizens and Local Government Association informed readers that they had taken advice on the bill and that if it were passed it would be unconstitutional.[42] In another letter to the press the IWCLGA 'bitterly resented' the bill, seeing it as an attempt 'to legalise the exclusion of women, however competent or suitable, on the grounds of sex alone, from the executive and administrative posts of the Civil Service'.[43] The association argued:

> On the one hand, the advantage which the Government hopes to secure by the Bill is but a slight temporary facility in administration, whilst, on the other, the heavy price which women are called upon to pay for the temporary facility is the total loss to generations of women of careers which it has been proved they are perfectly competent to fill.[44]

While the IWCLGA acknowledged that equality had been granted under the 1922 Constitution, women could not be complacent about that equality. It was a responsibility of all women to help to 'build up the State'. If they neglected this duty they could find themselves in a state 'where customs and practices they would regret and dislike' would be implemented.[45] Agnes O'Farrelly declared that the bill was 'insidious and far reaching and hit at the new status of women as citizens. It was a blow they did not expect from the youthful Government of the Free State.'[46]

The bill was passed in the Dáil but defeated in the Senate.[47] Its defeat in the Senate owed much to the arguments made by the women senators, and by feminists outside the oireachtas, who reaffirmed the rights of women under the promise of equality proposed in the 1916 Proclamation.

The concept of 'equal pay' was never taken seriously by government in this period. The minister for finance observed that the notion of equal pay within the civil service was unfeasible. 'An ideal such as "equal pay",' he argued, 'could not be realized in the Saorstát at present. The budget must be balanced and any reasonable means that would assist to that end would have to be used.' At the same time the minister noted women to be unreliable workers. For instance, he argued that 'most women will retire, generally after six years, when they have become entitled to a marriage gratuity and leave the service to marry. There must then be added the fact, ascertained beyond question by official records, that the sick leave of women in the Service is more than one half again as that of men.'[48] The belief that women workers were expendable was made clear in another government memorandum on the discharge of temporary staff in December 1925. It was noted that the order of discharge for temporary staff was prioritized as follows: '(a) Persons not wholly dependent on their earnings (in particular married women); (b) Unmarried men and women; (c) Other officers selected so far as possible in such order as to inflict a minimum of hardship on those dependent on their earnings.'[49]

Likewise, when the government mooted the establishment of a Committee of Unemployment in 1927, the trade unionist Louie Bennett suggested that the interests of unemployed women might be best served by the presence of a woman on the committee. The government decided that 'the committee should not be chosen with a view to giving representation to different sections of the unemployed but to individuals who had knowledge of labour and the "general conditions of the country"'.[50] In response Bennett was to write to the minister for industry and commerce noting that:

My Committee are extremely indignant at the implication contained in your letter that no woman can be found in Ireland who
has as intimate a knowledge of general conditions in the country
as the men now selected for the Unemployment Committee. My
Committee assert that such a point of view certainly betrays a
strangely inadequate knowledge on the part of the Government
on the intellectual resources of this country.[51]

The attempt to limit, through legislation, women's opportunities
in the workplace was rationalized from the nineteenth century as
necessary to protect the inferior status and capacity of the woman
worker. P.S. O'Hegarty, secretary, Department of Posts and Telegraphs,
responded to the Commission of Inquiry into the Civil Service that
'our experience is that as a unit the woman Civil Servant is not as good
as the man ... segregation in the past has the advantage of
enabling women to be promoted to posts which they could not have
been promoted to if they had to compete with male officers of a
similar grade.'[52]

THE MARRIAGE BAR

During the debates on the Civil Service Amendment Bill the minister
for industry and commerce commented that 'there is great wastage in
the female staff through marriage'.[53] In the first years of the Free State
there was evident and growing government concern with the employment of married women. In Ireland, as in many other countries
throughout the nineteenth and into the twentieth century, many
women expected to spend time looking after siblings and parents, but
they also expected to have access in time to their own home and family.
Working-class women certainly also expected to earn wages before
marriage, an expectation that extended to the middle classes by the
end of the nineteenth century. Many women supported themselves and
their families through their efforts, but it was generally accepted that
ideally all women should marry, have children and centre their life
within the domestic sphere. Of course, there was a discrepancy
between the widely held ideological belief that women's place was in
the home and the fact that many women either wanted or needed to
engage in waged employment. In 1926, for example, there were
1,127,077 females over the age of 12 in the state. Of that number
about 31 per cent (343,894) were in employment. The majority of

women workers were to be found in agriculture, about 35 per cent (121,894), and domestic service, about 32 per cent (109,461).[54] In 1926, 37 per cent of the female population over the age of 15 years were married, and a further 12 per cent were widowed. The majority of women aged 15 and over, about 43 per cent of the female population, were unmarried.[55] Despite the numbers of single women in the country, women's citizenship rights became bound up with their family commitments. Their right to work was gradually eroded in an attempt to consign them to the domestic sphere.

From April 1924 women who held permanent posts in the civil service were obliged to resign on marriage.[56] Mary Kettle, who had consistently fought for the rights of women in the early twentieth century, was to note with regard to this marriage bar that 'women from their entry until they reach the ages of 45 or 50 are looked on as if they were loitering with intent to commit a felony – the felony in this case being matrimony'.[57] Employment following marriage was not supported by government, or indeed by the general public. In the early 1930s a high level of unemployment among male national school teachers led the government to consider introducing a marriage ban for women teachers. In January 1932 the general secretary of the Irish National Teachers' Organisation (INTO), the trade union for primary school teachers, received a letter from the Department of Education revealing that it was proposing to introduce such a marriage ban. The union responded that, among other issues, such a ban would be unconstitutional. The union also argued that imposing such a ban would discourage women from marrying and that there was no general support for such a regulation.[58] The government attempted to justify the ban by alleging that married female teachers could not give their full attention to both school and home and something would suffer in consequence. It also argued that considerable jealousy was aroused in the community where a good income was available to married couples who might both be teachers, or where teachers were married to substantial farmers. It was stated that savings would be made on salaries that could be put to training more teachers. It was also noted that 'the absence of a female teacher for two months surrounding childbirth is a considerable upset'.[59] All female teachers who became primary teachers after 1 October 1934 had to retire on marriage.[60] This marriage bar was not revoked until July 1958.

Both the civil service marriage ban and the ban on female teachers were directed at middle-class women. Marriage was believed to provide financial security to women and children and as such the state of marriage itself negated or reduced women's claim to remunerative employment. Much of the lobbying and campaigning around the marriage ban for teachers was conducted by the INTO and there was little engagement with the issue by feminists.[61] However, the government's attempts to control the employment of working-class women proved a more flammable proposition. It was clear from the implementation of the marriage ban that marriage could, and indeed did, define and restrict women's right to work. The government was now proposing to limit the right to work of single women. For feminists, equality and citizenship rights were considered to be under severe threat.

CONDITIONS OF EMPLOYMENT BILL

By the end of the nineteenth century gender determined access to employment, and gender ideology shaped the rights men and women had at work. The male breadwinner was privileged as a worker, while women's employment was viewed as a temporary measure until security was achieved through marriage. Women did not have equal economic citizenship with men. They did not have equal access with men to the full range of employment opportunities. Women were discouraged from competing with or, worse, displacing men from employment. By the 1930s economic difficulties saw many countries introduce legislation to restrict women's working opportunities. It was widely believed, as one commentator noted, that 'the moral effect of unemployment on men is worse than on women, especially where they are married and have a family'.[62] In 1933 Seán Lemass, the minister for industry and commerce, noted that:

> If employment is to be balanced in the Saorstát, certain avenues must be reserved for men. In other countries, employment is given to men in heavy industries, heavy engineering, manufacture of machinery ... In the Saorstát heavy industries are not at present carried on to an appreciable extent ... the Minister is convinced of the necessity for statutory prohibition, for without it, women may rapidly be recruited for most classes of industry that are likely to be developed here.[63]

To combat the possibility of such a development the Conditions of Employment Bill was introduced into the Dáil on 11 April 1935, and was to be part of a series of legislation intended to address all occupations and to allow:

> Where undesirable exploitation of labour occurs, machinery for the regulation of working conditions, which will prevent abuses, and which will enable the State to exercise a general supervision over these conditions of employment.[64]

During the debate on the bill the minister spoke of the 'invasion of industry by women'.[65] The real fear expressed, however, was that if certain industries were to develop in Ireland women might find employment more easily than men. Therefore the government wanted the power to 'ensure that men will continue to be employed'.[66] Lemass stated in the Dáil that the aim of the bill was 'to arrest any tendency which may develop in future to substitute female for male labour in consequence of alterations in the mechanical methods of production in industry'.[67] Section 12 of the bill gave the government power to restrict or prohibit the employment of women in industry.

Deputy McGilligan opposed the bill, stating that it was 'reactionary in its tendencies' and 'undesirable' in providing too much power to the minister.[68] Although he accepted that some occupations were 'undesirable for women', he opposed this bill because it seemed to want to 'oust women from employment – to let men in because women are women and men are men'.[69]

There was little support for the women's case in the Dáil from Labour TDs. Deputy Norton argued that 'man is the natural breadwinner of the family, on him devolves the responsibility, in most cases, of providing for his wife and family'. Women, he stated, were difficult to unionize and he saw them as 'more birds-of-passage' in industry. Women found industrial employment 'because they are cheap, because they can be adapted to new mechanical processes and because they are, from the employer's point of view, very docile and, from the trade union point of view, extremely difficult to organise'. Section 12 of the bill, he declared, would not be used to 'exclude women from industry, or from employment for which they are peculiarly suited'.[70] The support provided by the Labour Party for the bill facilitated its passage in the Dáil.

Senator Jennie Wyse Power found the bill 'regrettable'. She recalled that after the Rising a number of women who had lost their jobs assured her that 'when our own men are in power, we shall have equal rights'.[71] She also noted the position of the Labour Party on the bill and commented that there was no 'standing shoulder to shoulder'.[72] Senator Kathleen Clarke, while accepting the principle that women workers might need some level of protection, was opposed to the section regarding women. She considered it

> ... from the point of principle alone, a principle on which the Party to which the Minister belongs are in agreement – the principle of equal rights and equal opportunities for all the citizens of this State.

She wondered what James Connolly would have made of Labour's stand on a bill she believed was 'the thin end of the wedge against women'.[73] Clarke noted that 'the 1916 Proclamation gave to every citizen equal rights and equal opportunities'. If the government was to legislate to curtail how one section of the community might earn a living, then, she asked, where were the 'equal opportunities provided for in that proclamation?'[74] There was little or no support for the deletion of Section 12 of the bill from male trade unionists, who believed it was men who had a right to work, not women. Women's employment had, for these trade unionists, a social and economic cost that should not be borne. One commentator, claiming to express the views of the general population, observed that women's employment in industry was 'contrary to nature, it splits up the Christian family and ... it delays and discourages marriage'.[75] Women's right to work was limited because of their gender; the government and male trade unionists sought to 'protect' working women, but protection saw limitations and restrictions placed on women's ability to work. Guarantees of equality framed in the 1916 Proclamation and the 1922 Constitution would not be upheld when men's occupations were endangered.

The Irish Women Workers' Union engaged in an intense campaign against Section 12 of the bill. It argued that 'legislation which deprives one section of the community of their free rights as workers is a form of tyranny which no self-respecting citizen can tolerate, and is a step backwards to serfdom'.[76] They saw this type of legislation as an 'encroachment on the rights of women workers and on their personal liberty'.[78] In a memo to de Valera, who was head of government, Louie Bennett stated that after 1916 women 'anticipated that the establishment of an Irish government would mean for them the establishment of equal rights with men'. 'In certain matters,' she noted, such as the citizenship laws, their [women's] hopes have been justified, but more recent legislation shows a violent movement in the opposite direction, depriving women of fundamental liberties, and suggesting that the government is permitting itself to be influenced by the incentive which is overthrowing the democratic freedom and establishing bureaucratic dictatorships in certain European countries.[78]

Bennett stated that, with this bill, 'women in industry would no longer be free citizens with full control over their lives and work'.[79] It was, Bennett noted, 'a strange proposal from a government which declared adherence to the Republican programme of 1916 and to James Connolly's principles of equal rights for all'.[80] At the Irish Trade Union Congress in August 1935 Louie Bennett introduced a motion that 'Congress reaffirms its allegiance to the fundamental principle of equal rights and equal democratic opportunities for all citizens and equal pay for equal work'.[81] However, little support for the motion was forthcoming, with one delegate declaring, 'woman is the queen of our hearts and of our homes, and for God's sake let us try to keep her there'. Helena Molony noted that it was 'terrible to find such reactionary opinion expressed ... by responsible leaders of Labour in support of a capitalist Minister in setting up a barrier against one set of citizens'.[82]

The Conditions of Employment Act came into force on 29 May 1936 and while no minister ever invoked the powers provided to him under Section 16 of the act, it sent a clear message to Irish women workers.[83] The legislative initiatives undertaken to limit women's employment opportunities in the 1920s and 1930s made women activists wary of trusting governments and politicians to enforce the spirit of the 1916 Proclamation and the 1922 Constitution with regards to equality. This distrust was fully evident in the campaign against the draft Constitution of 1937.

THE CAMPAIGN AGAINST THE DRAFT CONSTITUTION

It was not only Irish society that saw women, whether married or single, primarily in terms of their reproductive capacities and responsibilities to home and children. Most of western society had difficulty seeing women as equal citizens. While many women welcomed the 1937 Constitution's attempts to reinforce the status of women as wives and mothers, they were not willing to support this move when it appeared simultaneously to undermine their rights as workers. The campaign conducted against the draft Constitution saw the evocation of the language of equality and citizenship form the basis of much of the objections raised towards the draft.

On 24 May 1934 Éamon de Valera, president of the Executive Council, established a committee of four civil servants to examine the Irish Free State Constitution of 1922. A draft of the proposed new Constitution was published on 1 May 1937.

John A. Costello, Fine Gael Dáil deputy and ex-attorney general, was one of the first to draw attention to the position of women under the draft Constitution. In a long article in the *Irish Independent* on 6 May, which contained two paragraphs on women, he wrote, 'We read the somewhat grandiose statement that all citizens shall be held equal before the law, but we then discover that the substance of that declaration is taken away by the provision that the State may, if it likes, in its legislation declare them to be unequal.' He argued that in introducing legislation the state, because it could take 'due regard to differences of capacity, physical and moral, and of social function', was allowing itself immense powers. That provision, he argued, read in conjunction with the constitutional declaration of 'the inadequate strength of women' and the omission of the significant words 'without distinction of sex' contained in Articles 3 and 14 of the existing Constitution, 'must,' he noted, 'appear curious in view of the substantially equal rights of voting and otherwise at present accorded to women'. Costello claimed that, under the draft Constitution, women did not have, 'as a constitutional right', any claim to the exercise of the franchise on equal terms with men. As it stood, the draft offered its framer as a 'whole burnt offering to feminists and feminist associations'.[84]

The journalist Gertrude Gaffney responded to the draft Constitution in her regular column in the *Irish Independent*.[85] She objected to several assumptions made within the draft and called on women to mobilize themselves into action. The 'death knell of the working woman is sounded in this new constitution', she wrote. 'Mr de Valera has always been a reactionary where women are concerned. He dislikes and distrusts us as a sex and his aim ever since he came into office has been to put us into what he considers is our place and keep us there.' Under the proposed Constitution, Gaffney argued, 'we are to be no longer citizens entitled to enjoy equal rights under a democratic Constitution, but laws are to be enacted which will take into consideration our "differences of capacity, physical and moral, and of social function"'. Gaffney observed de Valera's skill in reaffirming the principles of 1916 but commented that the inclusion of conditional clauses would result in 'exterminating us [as workers] by degrees'. Were de Valera to descend to reality, she observed, he would see that 'ninety per cent of women who work for a living in this country do so because they must'. The argument revolved around commonly held beliefs that to remove women from the workforce would immediately lead to a reduction in male unemployment. Gaffney believed that de Valera, conscious of the 'nightmare of unemployment', was using the cue of economic depression as a means to further restrict women's rights as workers. It was, for Gaffney and many other women activists, a complete rejection of the principles of the 1916 Proclamation.

Within a few days both the Joint Committee of Women's Societies and Social Workers and the Women Graduates' Association (WGA) took up Costello's and Gaffney's points. At a meeting of the WGA it was noted that 'the omission of the principle of equal rights and opportunities enunciated in the Proclamation of 1916 and confirmed in Article 3 of the Constitution of Saorstát Éireann was deplored as "sinister and retrogressive"'.[86] It was clear to the WGA that Articles 40, 41 and 45 opened the possibility of reactionary legislation being enacted against women. It was decided to appoint an emergency committee to publicize the issues relating to women arising from the draft Constitution, to work with other groups to delete the 'offending' articles and to restore Article 3 of the Free State Constitution.

Mary Kettle, chairwoman of the Joint Committee, called upon women to examine carefully the so-called 'protection' clauses of the new Constitution. She maintained that, if these articles became law, no working woman, whether she worked in trade, factory or profession, would have any security whatever. Since the establishment of the state, she added, women had become accustomed to regard Article 3 of the 1922 Constitution as the charter of their liberties. If de Valera disliked the phraseology of that article so much he could always fall back on the 'classic simplicity' of the Proclamation of the Republic, which stated: 'The Republic guarantees religious and civil liberty, equal rights and equal opportunities to all its citizens.' Such a statement, Kettle concluded, was unequivocal and would satisfy all women.[87]

In the Dáil debate on the draft Constitution, Deputy Rowlette noted that 'there has not been for many years such a condition of alarm among the women, as to their rights as citizens of the country, as has been aroused by certain clauses in the constitution'.[88] Deputy O'Sullivan declared that women were much more afraid of economic discrimination than political discrimination. He also noted that 'these women are not all of the class who hold advanced views. Many of them are moderate, conservative women, who hold views which are by no means advanced.'[89] These women, he said, feared 'for their political position' but they were much more afraid of what may happen in practice as to the taking away of opportunities to work.[90] Mrs Helena Concannon noted the concerns raised by the Joint Committee and the Women Graduates' Association and asked de Valera to satisfy himself that any future interpretation of the disputed articles could not lessen the status of women. It was clear to her at least that 'the framers of the constitution had no intention in their minds to interfere in the slightest way with the rights of women and I am glad to have that assurance'.[91]

Louie Bennett wrote to de Valera as president of the Executive Council stating the views of the Irish Women Workers' Union to the draft Constitution.[92] She noted that their objection to certain clauses in the Constitution was 'inspired by a real anxiety to safeguard the position of women irrespective of class or party prejudices'. 'Most of us,' she continued, 'would wish to subscribe without cavil to the proposed constitution, but for many of us it contains points of serious danger', not for what it actually expressed but for the ambiguity of the clauses and the danger of multiple interpretations. The IWWU believed that Article 40.1 'tends to place women in a different category of citizenship from men and in a different position from men' with regard to the law. Given the evidence of fascist governments, Bennett argued, this clause gave power to the government to initiate legislation that would be detrimental to women's equality. The 'most indefensible' clause, however, was Section 4.2 of Article 45. It took from women the right to choose their own avocation in life. The letter argued that this clause would give the state power to decide what avocations were suited to a citizen's sex and strength. 'It would be hardly possible,' the letter continued, 'to make a more deadly encroachment upon the liberty of the individual than to deprive him or her of this right.' The same clause, it argued, opened the door to 'fascist legislation of a very objectionable type'.[93]

Opposition to the draft Constitution by republican women was motivated by what they saw as a betrayal of the principles of the 1916

Proclamation. A statement from Cumann na mBan observed that 'this constitution does not satisfy the aspirations of the Irish people. If the Proclamation of Easter Week meant anything, it meant the end of capitalism and the introduction of equal rights and opportunities for all. Our charter of freedom was laid down in the proclamation of Easter week. Only the establishment of a republic in accordance with that proclamation will satisfy our aspirations.'[94]

The referendum on the Constitution was held on 1 July 1937, and was accepted by 685,105 votes to 526,945, a majority for 158,160. Whether the Constitution had any real practical impact on women's lives is open to debate. What is significant for the purposes of this article is the constant evocation of both the 1916 Proclamation and the 1922 Constitution and the language of equality which was an essential element of both documents. While the various campaigns engaged in by women activists in the 1920s and 1930s were about practical issues that would affect women's rights as workers and citizens, they were also about the importance of the concept of equality as expressed in the Proclamation and the 1922 Constitution. The simple promise of equality found in these documents held more resonance for women activists than any of the rhetoric of the suffrage campaign, which did not argue for the equality of all women. The Proclamation and the 1922 Constitution gave women activists the power to protest against the discursive construction prevalent in Irish society that all women, whatever their marital status, and whether they were mothers or not, were enmeshed in traditional families. Although by 1922 Irish women had the vote on the same terms as Irish men, it was to the language of the 1916 Proclamation and the 1922 Constitution that they turned when their rights and duties as citizens came under fire. We have, as yet, little sense of how women related to the formal political parties that existed in Ireland after independence, and we have little sense of how they voted, or if gender played any significant role in voting patterns. Women's organizations such as the Irish Women Citizens and Local Government Association, the Joint Committee of Women's Societies and Social Workers (1935), the Irish Women Workers' Union, the Women Graduates' Association and even some campaigning groups of republican women provided women with a political space in which to continue to campaign for the influence of women in the social, political, economic and cultural spheres of Irish life. There was, at times, a considerable challenge to the gender order of society and common cause made among different women's organizations.

Until the 1940s much of that uniting force was shaped by an under-standing of the equality promised in 1916, and given legislative power in the 1922 Constitution.

CHAPTER FIVE

Nuanced Neutrality and Irish Identity: An Idiosyncratic Legacy

THOMAS E. HACHEY

The concept of 'neutrality' has been an integral part of Ireland's political, even social, vocabulary for well over a half century. It also has been the subject of a large body of literature that grew exponentially during that same period of time, much of it representing quality scholarship from the pens of specialists extending from the disciplines of history and politics to literature and sociology. Yet, despite such collective and careful scrutiny, neutrality has had, and continues to have, an unresolved aspect about it that can elude any shared sense of that concept in Ireland. That circumstance appears to be all the more remarkable when one considers how, with the Irish language in decline and the influence of the Roman Catholic Church in eclipse, neutrality has evolved as a discernable, even emblematic, feature of Irish identity. It is, therefore, worth revisiting the etiology of that development, particularly the way in which the meaning of neutrality has been embraced and understood by the Irish populace, as well as by successive Dublin governments. Therefore, it becomes necessary to ask: what distinction is there between perception and practice in Ireland's time-honoured commitment to a policy of neutrality, and what will the impact of international developments of the twenty-first century have upon its character or sustainability?

Ronan Fanning traces Ireland's propensity toward neutrality back to the isolationism reflected in both the home rule and separatist traditions. He also recalls, for example, how Sir Roger Casement published a proposal in 1913 advocating the neutralization of an independent Ireland, and how James Connolly, in 1914, assumed the presidency of an organization known as the Irish Neutrality League. But Fanning, and others, would agree that it is misleading to attach the label of neutrality to this period of intense nationalist passion.[1] Indeed, prior to the First World War, Irish nationalists were motivated by anti-British sentiment and very few of them would have had any commitment to a specific concept of neutrality.[2] And, correspondingly, there is scant reference to that term to be found in either regional or national newspapers before or during the First World War, suggesting, as it does, that the subject had not become a part of any contemporary discourse.[3]

During the immediate post-war years, Irish political leaders most likely would have favoured a policy of military neutrality for their country, but few of them would have made it their first priority. It was, for example, during a 1920 fundraising tour of America that Éamon de Valera affirmed that Ireland would not participate in any future wars on behalf of the empire, while also assuring London that such abstention by an independent Ireland would never imperil British security. It was in the hope of demonstrating the sincerity of that pledge that he proposed making Ireland's relationship to Britain analogous to the one that obtained between Cuba and the United States.[4] Quite apart from the negative reaction that that remark provoked among militant Irish nationalists who recoiled at the thought of any subordinate status, it also revealed how de Valera, at least at that time, was unconcerned about setting the foundation for any future policy of Irish neutrality.

During the contentious 1921 Anglo-Irish Treaty negotiations, Michael Collins exhibited a similar disposition. His objective was, at minimum, the creation of a virtually autonomous dominion with primary allegiance to an Irish Constitution, not to the king. That priority took precedence over the nationalist concern about how Britain's continued occupation of three naval ports in the proposed Free State might compromise Irish sovereignty. When Colonial Secretary Winston Churchill arranged to have Admiral David Beatty explain to Collins how critical were the so-called 'treaty ports' to British security, Collins is said to have replied, 'Of course you must have the ports. They are necessary for your life.'[5] Arthur Griffith concurred. These men were pragmatists, and their assent did not suggest any indifference toward the possible adoption of some future policy of neutrality for Ireland. Collins would later tell those who condemned the Treaty that it would provide 'the freedom to achieve freedom', while Griffith felt especially optimistic, despite knowing that the presence of British forces in those Irish ports might very well result in Ireland being drawn into a war. Griffith was also prepared to wait on events and is said to have privately envisioned future situations in which neutrality could and would be preserved at the discretion of an Irish government.[6]

However, it was not neutrality but rather 'collective security' that dominated political discussion in the aftermath of the First World War, particularly among the smaller European countries. Within a year of the untimely deaths of Griffith and Collins in 1922, the newly established Free State government passed the League of Nations (Guarantee) Act in both houses of the oireachtas. It acknowledged that the Executive Council of Dáil Éireann would be authorized to impose economic or military sanctions in conjunction with the League.[7] Moreover, in October of 1923, Eoin MacNeill assured the Imperial Conference in London that if any challenge to the League's principles were to arise, he was entirely confident the Dublin government could be depended upon to do its duty.[8] Despite the fact that debates in the Dáil did occasionally reveal some ambivalence about the Free State's foreign policy, it would be erroneous to assume that neutrality was given much attention by the Irish people or politicians in the early 1920s.[9]

William Cosgrave's Cumann na nGaedheal government worked as co-operatively as it could with its British counterpart throughout that decade, while simultaneously remaining supportive of the League of Nations and collective security. However, a sea change occurred in Irish politics in August 1927 when Éamon de Valera led his Fianna Fáil followers into the Dáil and, in the general election the following month, his party assumed the leading oppositional role in the Irish parliament. The first flashpoint occurred only a few weeks later when the minister for defence proposed a plan to strengthen Ireland's security with reforms intended for the armed forces. De Valera objected vociferously. He declared that neutrality was the proper policy for the Irish Free State and warned against any collaborative military relationship with Britain, save in the instance of an invasion of the British Isles by some external power.[10] The debate that followed is not memorable so much for its impact on security reform, which was nil, but rather for the fact that it represented one of the earliest calls in the Dáil for Ireland to embrace a policy of military neutrality.

Patrick Keatinge has shown how Ireland's early endorsement of the concept of collective security might have tempered any national conversation about neutrality. Implicit in the League's proposition was a commitment by member nations to assist the victim of aggression. And although the principal focus was on economic sanctions, the participating countries were fully expected to permit the transporting of troops across their territories which was, of course, a notable departure from one of the primary expectations of classical neutrality.[11]

Irish foreign policy during the 1920s, quite apart from the League, was also largely determined by the way in which the Free State's role at the Imperial Conferences contributed substantially to the redefinition of dominion status within the British Commonwealth. Hence, as Michael Kennedy has reasoned, the ten years between 1922 and 1932, when Dublin's participation in international affairs was largely relegated to issues relating to the League, or to Commonwealth affairs, might very well be seen as 'a more suitable precursor of contemporary Irish foreign policy than the experiment of "mutual, non-participatory Ireland" from the mid 1930s until 1948'.[12]

Fianna Fáil came to power in the general election of 1932, and it is noteworthy how very little mention was made by the competing parties about the subject of neutrality in the campaign speeches and proclamations. The League of Nations was a prominent topic in most of the commentary relating to foreign affairs, but much of the discourse among politicians and the general populace focused largely on domestic economic conditions. De Valera represented himself as being philosophically committed to the proclaimed ideals of the League of Nations, but as a pragmatic realist he recognized the limitations of collective security in the geopolitical circumstances of that decade. As Martha Kavanagh has noted, he may even have contemplated preparing the Free State for a retreat from the Geneva Accord as early as 1932, and he doubtless recognized its probable demise following the League's capitulation to the 1935 Italian invasion of Abyssinia. Speaking before the League's assembly in Geneva on 3 July of that year, de Valera signalled his defection from the policy of collective security by urging small countries 'to look to strengthen their own defences'.[13] Ironically, that was advice de Valera would later be criticized for failing to act upon in Ireland.

There is little evidence in the press, the Dáil debates, or in the published documents on Irish foreign policy to support those who continue to perceive any general disposition toward, or possibly some formulation of, an Irish policy of military neutrality prior to 1936.[14] It is true that de Valera did make statements, beginning as early as 1935, that pointed in the general direction of neutrality, but there is also some evidence that he was quite prepared to enter a defensive military alliance with Great Britain if a resolution could have been reached on the partition issue.[15]

Partition was in fact an unacceptable bifurcation of what de Valera perceived as the *de jure*, even if not the *de facto*, national territory on the island of Ireland. But, like neutrality, it was not his primary objective. Sovereignty was his first priority and he succeeded in attaining much of that goal with the adoption of the 1937 Irish Constitution in which he played a major role in both its creation and ratification.[16] The Irish state, renamed Éire, became a republic in everything but name, now only 'associated' with other Commonwealth dominions, and retaining linkage to the British Crown for limited external purposes only.[17] De Valera would subsequently fully achieve his goal of virtual sovereignty for the twenty-six-county Irish state with the Anglo-Irish agreements of April 1938 which transferred the harbour defences at Berehaven, Cobh and Lough Swilly to the Irish government.

Although the 1937 Constitution did claim jurisdiction over all thirty-two of Ireland's counties, it realistically acknowledged the existence of Britain's bona fide authority in the six counties of Northern Ireland. Article 3 specifically states 'that a united Ireland shall be brought about only by peaceful means with the consent of a majority of the people, democratically expressed, in both jurisdictions in the island'.[18] De Valera kept the contentious issue of partition subordinate to his unrelenting pursuit of complete sovereignty.

Neutrality, of course, was never an end in itself, but rather a means to an end. As Ronan Fanning has argued, neither de Valera nor any of his revolutionary colleagues were ever ideologically committed to any theory or doctrine of neutrality. For them, neutrality was the ultimate manifestation of sovereign independence.[19] Whether or not that conviction was widely shared, neutrality was nonetheless catapulted into the national conversation by the growing awareness among people that war was an imminent possibility in the Europe of the late 1930s. It marked a significant change from the Ireland of earlier years when the term had very limited currency, with little sense of passion or resolution. Clair Wills' splendid book, *That Neutral Ireland*, is one of the more recent and inclusive accounts of how Irish domestic opinion gravitated toward favouring a policy of military neutrality in the years immediately preceding the Second World War. Among the general populace, she affirms, there was near complete consensus in support for a policy that was seen as a 'practical stance dictated by military and political necessities, not an ideological declaration, or the expression of a moral choice'.[20]

On 3 September 1939 Britain and France declared war on Germany after the Reich had refused to halt its invasion of Poland, and de Valera responded with a prompt declaration of neutrality. Both de Valera and his political opponents agreed on the necessity of neutrality for essentially the same three reasons: avoiding involvement in a European war, the very real prospect of a civil war over Irish Republican Army action involving Northern Ireland, and the opportunity to showcase the Dublin government's indisputable sovereignty.[21] But in the span of only a few short months a new spin was given to the neutrality stance that would continue to resonate periodically, in one form or another, down to the present day. Joseph Walshe, the enigmatic and highly secretive secretary to the Department of External Affairs, sent an 11 July 1940 confidential memorandum to de Valera, who held the portfolios for both the office of taoiseach and foreign minister. The memorandum is indicative of the extent to which the Dublin government was prepared to portray Ireland's abstention as a manifestation of Irish national identity, even at this early date. Walshe wrote:

> Neutrality was not entered upon for the purpose of being used as a bargaining factor. It represented, and does represent, the fundamental attitude of the entire people. It is just as much a part of the national position as the desire to remain Irish, and we can no more abandon it than we can everything that constitutes our national distinctiveness.[22]

It seems likely, however, that de Valera, at least at this point in time, was more immediately concerned with how he might obtain Britain's and Germany's assent to Ireland's proclaimed neutrality. Such compliance was fundamentally more essential to the success of his policy than was any definitional sense of national identity. And that instinctive pragmatism was in evidence when he sought to explain to Dr Eduard Hempel, the German minister to Ireland, how the magnitude of Ireland's trade with, and geographical proximity to, Great Britain required Dublin to show a certain degree of consideration for the United Kingdom, despite Dublin's profound desire to pursue a policy of neutrality.[23]

Acrimonious exchanges between London and Dublin still did occur as each side occasionally distorted genuine issues for propaganda purposes. Partition, for example, was no doubt a genuine concern to the Irish government but de Valera also manipulated it for his own purposes in seeking to make neutrality respectable. Throughout the war, he repeatedly complained that it was the English who occupied Ireland, and not the Ulster unionists. It was a clever stratagem, particularly when directed toward the significant number of Irish-Americans who, after Pearl Harbor, were unreservedly committed to the United States joining the Allies in the war, and who were prone to make Éire feel uncomfortable about neutrality unless distracted by other issues.[24] In truth, however, de Valera would not have abandoned neutrality, with or without partition, given that Ireland's entering the war would have exposed the country to aerial bombardment, and to IRA insurgency.[25]

Prime Minister Winston Churchill was equally disingenuous in accusing neutral Ireland with harbouring German spies and promoting espionage via wireless radio at the German legation in Dublin. In so doing, Churchill lent additional credibility to occasional hyperbolic accounts of enemy intrigue in Ireland that were being sent to Washington at the time by David Gray, the American minister in Dublin.[26] The British, it should be noted, had successfully broken the German cipher (codenamed Pandora), making it possible for them to read even the most sensitive diplomatic communications between the Berlin government and its Dublin legation.[27] Churchill nevertheless continued to fulminate about the peril of German spies operating in Ireland.

Later in the war, British complaints would diminish notably, especially criticisms pertaining to Éire's refusal to allow the Royal Navy access to strategic ports, as well as its refusal to enter the conflict in support of the Allies. The reasons were twofold: one is that experience in the early and critical years of the war had shown that the Irish ports were not as vital as some British officials had previously supposed and, secondly, Britain simply did not have the capability of defending Éire if that country were to have been drawn into the hostilities. That assessment was candidly admitted by

Dominions Secretary Clement Attlee in a March 1943 memorandum
to Foreign Secretary Anthony Eden. In it Attlee warned against
the danger of pressuring de Valera into allowing a British military presence in Éire for fear that de Valera should suddenly agree. Attlee concluded:

> It would be tantamount to bringing Éire into the war, and we
> should have to supply her not only protection (anti-aircraft
> equipment, etc.) [but] also with civilian supplies. I thought it
> doubtful that one could spare enough of this at the present time
> and that the strategic facilities would probably be dearly bought
> at such a price.[28]

And the wisdom of that calculation had been dramatically illustrated
in 1940 when the German Luftwaffe reduced a large part of the English city of Coventry to ashes, despite the numerous anti-aircraft guns
and fighter planes dispatched to defend it.[29]

Eunan O'Halpin's insightful and comprehensive study, *Spying on
Ireland: British Intelligence and Irish Neutrality During the Second
World War*, convincingly illustrates this point: rather than posing
a threat to the British war effort, neutrality offered the Allied side
significant advantages.[30] That reality, however, was insufficiently
appreciated in both Washington and London. One need not revisit
the now familiar details of the infamous 'American Note', other than
consider the impact it had upon both Irish official and public attitudes
toward neutrality. While the United States was understandably
apprehensive about the presence of Japanese and German legations in
Dublin while D-Day invasion plans were directed from the British
Isles, the State Department's request to expel all Axis diplomats from
Ireland had the implied tone of an ultimatum. And the fact that it was
delivered by David Gray, the keenly disliked American minister, only
added to de Valera's profound irritation. He rejected the proposal
without hesitation and angrily reminded Washington of the extraordinary measures Ireland had taken to prevent Axis espionage.[31] The
taoiseach's public support for the policy of neutrality was demon-
strably strengthened by Washington's insensitivity, evidenced by the
electoral gains won by the Fianna Fáil party in the general election
that year.[32]

And Churchill's own missteps and heavy-handed treatment of de
Valera also contributed to the Irish leader's near unanimous support
for neutrality among the different political parties in the Dáil, as well

as within the Irish populace at large. Churchill never forgave Ireland for what he thought to be her illegal and unpardonable determination to remain neutral.[33] One historian has even suggested that Churchill perceived Ireland in much the same way as he did Iraq, Persia, Egypt and Afghanistan, as scarcely a sovereign state in any sense, but rather a former colony or protectorate churlishly opposed to making common cause.[34] The British prime minister did indeed dispute Ireland's claim to be a sovereign state, but Ireland's geographical proximity to Britain also very probably heavily influenced Churchill's attitude toward that country.[35]

De Valera, of course, exhibited a capacity for controversy injurious to his own policy when he insisted upon calling upon the German minister in Dublin to express formal condolence following the death of Adolf Hitler. To his mind he was strictly observing the conventional protocols of neutrality since he had paid a similar visit to the American legation in Dublin a few months earlier after Franklin Roosevelt had died. Such a gesture, he assured the Irish minister in Washington, was a compulsory courtesy and did not signify either approval or disapproval of the state in question, or its leader.[36]

As it happened, de Valera's visit took place just as the full horrors of Nazi extermination camps were being widely reported in the international media. To a significant number of Irish people, to say nothing of the outrage among some British and American citizens, it appeared that the taoiseach had sacrificed ideals for symbols.[37] An even stranger turn of events followed when the British prime minister unintentionally helped restore the Irish leader's popularity, at least in Ireland. Churchill turned to the airwaves to broadcast an intemperate diatribe in which he provocatively declared how the London government had shown great forbearance in leaving 'the Dublin government to frolic with the Germans'. De Valera waited four days before delivering his own radio reply, and the moderate, statesmanlike tone of his address gave the Irish taoiseach a psychological and moral advantage. With the Nazi example so close at hand, de Valera took full advantage of the British prime minister's excessive language, declaring, 'Mr Churchill makes it clear that in certain circumstances he would have violated our neutrality and that he would justify his actions by Britain's necessity ... and when this necessity became sufficiently great, other people's rights were not to count.'[38]

Despite the deprivations endured by a large part of the Irish population during the war, significant enough, even if not at all comparable to that suffered by many civilians in the European theatre, neutrality itself remained exceedingly popular with the large majority of Irish citizens at the end of that horrendous and costly conflict. In the Dáil, there was near unanimity endorsing the Irish government's policy, and the deputy leader of Fine Gael, James Dillon, was expelled from the party for his public repudiation of neutrality. Elizabeth Bowen, a novelist and British intelligence gatherer, later observed that neutrality had been almost universally embraced in Ireland as a positive value that engendered a sense of self respect. And Sir John Maffey, Britain's diplomatic representative in Dublin, was firmly convinced that neutrality transcended all political parties and personalities, declaring, 'the creed of Ireland today is neutrality; no government could exist that departed from that principle'.[39]

Hence, while the concept of, and support for, neutrality scarcely extended even to the elites in Ireland prior to the mid or late 1930s, there is no doubt regarding its strong support among the Irish population from 1939 to 1945.[40] What divides many historians, of course, whether traditionalists or revisionists, is the retrospective assessment today of that wartime neutrality. Trevor Salmon, for example, argues that Ireland's objective was simply to stay out of the war, 'not necessarily following an impartial policy, or a policy conditioned upon insistence on and respect for neutral rights and duties, or a policy limited by well-known rules and obligations. Rather, it was a policy based on bending with the wind through discrimination and compromise.'[41] Unlike Switzerland, Ireland never took seriously the need to defend neutrality by creating a credible military force. Irish leaders sought instead to avoid all circumstances likely to draw the country into war. Salmon insists that this was not neutrality but non-belligerency, and he provides numerous examples of how and why Ireland's professed policy of neutrality during the Second World War failed to meet the criterion normally associated with neutrality and nonalignment.[42]

Garret FitzGerald fully concurs with Salmon, finding de Valera's military defence status to have been woefully inadequate during the Second World War. 'Non-belligerent', he insisted, best characterized Ireland's posture, and FitzGerald further contends that the scale of assistance given by Ireland to Britain was wholly incompatible with the concept of neutrality under international law. To underscore that argument, he cites a British cabinet memorandum of February 1945 which detailed ten specific ways in which the Dublin government provided significant wartime support for the United Kingdom.[43]

Brian Girvin takes a different revisionist approach, arguing that Ireland's failure to enter the war in 1943, when it would have cost the country nothing compared with what it could have gained, illustrates how little neutrality had to do with national interest, versus how much with political ideology. He is particularly critical of what he perceives to be de Valera's myopic isolationism that led to Ireland's post-war economic stagnation. Girvin accuses the taoiseach of pursuing a policy of non-alignment that went so far as to portray the Axis and the Allies as moral equivalents.[44]

The debate, of course, continues and a book published as recently as 2009, entitled *Behind the Green Curtain: Ireland's Phoney Neutrality During World War II*, purports to show how both Britain and the United States distorted Ireland's role in the conflict for their own political purposes. The author, T. Ryle Dwyer, maintains that Ireland was never neutral during the war and relates how de Valera secretly assured the British that he was prepared to extend all possible assistance, short of involving Ireland in the hostilities.[45]

As previously noted, however, de Valera's adherence to what he chose to call neutrality was broadly popular among the people of Ireland, irrespective of political party. There also exist numerous interpretations of why this was so, and Ernie O'Malley, an eminent revolutionary leader of a previous generation, published an especially interesting one in 1946. O'Malley recalled how, since the Civil War, there had been a good deal of apathy and scepticism among the younger generation in Ireland. They criticized some of their elders for nostalgic accounts of the real or imagined deeds in a past life, despite their later penchant to substitute political or economic gain for integrity and idealism. He wrote:

> Neutrality helped to change this cynical pessimism, and out of neutrality grew a new loyalty to a country that needed service. Younger sons of Imperialists served in the ranks of the Volunteer Defence Force with the sons of separatists. Men who had fought against each other in the bitter civil war met again as comrades, or served on committees and, as war savaged Europe, memories of our own struggle were softened and made gentle. The healing of the aching sores resulting from the civil war were for some the most important result of neutrality.[46]

Neutrality may very well have had a bonding influence among Irish people of different backgrounds and political persuasions, but it nonetheless was not a readily identifiable nor commonly understood concept among that same populace. In the absence of the kind of meticulously calculated social science analyses of public opinion available today, it is difficult to ascertain what the term 'neutrality' implied for Irish citizens in the immediate post-war era. Certainly, there was a reflexive sense of gratitude for a policy that had largely spared Éire's population the horrors of aerial bombardment, as much of Europe and the counties of Northern Ireland had experienced. And, to a certain extent, it helped foster among many people, as Eunan O'Halpin reminds us, 'enduring illusions about the moral basis of staying out of other people's wars'.[47] For these and other reasons it remained popular in public opinion, even if it also continued to elude any definitional consensus of precisely what 'neutrality' was intended to mean.

In fairness, there may have been a similar degree of ambiguity among members of the Irish government concerning the implications of Ireland's professed policy of neutrality in the post-war years. There is no evidence that there ever existed a shared sense of some ideological, or doctrinal, commitment to anything approaching an international standard of classical neutrality. There was, however, a high degree of unanimity favouring a pragmatic, if not opportunistic, implementation of that policy.[48]

Ireland's economy remained stagnant in the aftermath of the Second World War, and Fianna Fáil was defeated in the 1948 election by a coalition of Fine Gael and smaller political parties. The new government, under John Costello, exhibited the same obsession with sovereignty, vis-à-vis Britain, as had its predecessor. After repealing the External Relations Act and declaring the formal establishment of the Irish Republic, the Fine Gael coalition prepared to address the only remaining issue of consequence in Anglo-Irish relations: partition.[49] An early opportunity presented itself in January 1949 when the United States invited Ireland to join the North Atlantic Treaty Organization (NATO), created as a counterweight to the Soviet Union. Costello's government expressed an open willingness to join, as long as it could enter the alliance as a united Ireland. Washington promptly declined that proposal, but it served to confirm how the Irish would have traded neutrality for an end to partition.[50] De Valera publicly admitted that, had he been in power, he too would have

urged NATO membership for Ireland in return for national reunifi-
cation.[51] Neither the coalition government headed by Fine Gael
nor the Fianna Fáil leading opposition party appeared particularly
concerned with how Ireland's entry into a military alliance would
effectively negate the nation's ostensible policy of neutrality.

De Valera's party returned to power between 1951 and 1954, during which time any national discussion, in and out of government,
on the subject of neutrality usually focused on popular anti-militarism
sentiment rather than on the state's role in ensuring national security.
Indeed, the Irish government exhibited no enthusiasm for international
affairs, budgeting less than a fifth of the money for defence than the
Irish general staff thought was needed in order to maintain a credible
neutrality.[52]

The second coalition government, again under the leadership of
John Costello, held office between 1954 and 1957. Neutrality was
not frequently referenced in Dáil debates or in the media, with one
notable exception: the 1955 admission of Ireland into the United
Nations. Although a few members in the Department of External
Affairs did express some apprehension over the implications contained in the United Nations commitment to collective security, that
concern quickly dissipated after the Korean conflict made it clear that
participation in collective actions was voluntary, not compulsory.[53]
Otherwise, neutrality was seldom mentioned in any official or public discourse. During Costello's second brief tenure as taoiseach, the
Irish government committed itself to three principles: fidelity to the
UN charter; avoiding assimilation by ideological rivals; and preserv-
ing 'Christian civilization' by resisting the spread of communism. If
there existed any doubt as to where the loyalty of this self-professed
neutral lay, the Costello government also affirmed: 'We belong to the
great community of states, made up of the United States of America,
Canada, and Western Europe.'[54]

With the 1957 Fianna Fáil electoral victory, de Valera appointed
Frank Aiken minister for external affairs, with full responsibility over
Ireland's delegation to the United Nations. Aiken had been a former
chief of staff of the Irish Republican Army and was a fervent anti-
colonialist. He quickly became de Valera's point man in resuscitating
neutrality for a taoiseach who viewed the policy as a desirable
anchor in the increasingly turbulent realm of international affairs.
Aiken believed that such a posture afforded Ireland a rare opportunity to act as a bridge between conflicting groups in the UN.

Although the Dublin government continued to be generally aligned with the West, it voted with emerging 'third world' nations on numerous occasions. Ireland also sent troops to participate in UN peacekeeping operations, and nine Irish soldiers were killed during a 1960 mission in the Congo. Public reaction was supportive, however, reflecting a sense of national pride, with the high cost in human life seen 'as an affirmation of Ireland's willingness as a neutral state to risk the lives of its soldiers in defence of peace rather than in prosecution of war'.[55]

In June 1959, Éamon de Valera stepped down as taoiseach and was elected to the largely ceremonial office of president of the Republic of Ireland. His departure from political office did not result in the abandonment of the Dublin government's policy of neutrality, but it did represent a final nail in the coffin of a doctrine of strategic security that had been largely crafted and perpetrated by him since its formal inception in September 1939. The succession of Seán Lemass as taoiseach very arguably can be viewed as precipitating the most significant review and repositioning of Irish neutrality since the advent of the de Valera era twenty-seven years earlier. Lemass was first and foremost an Atlanticist, interested in bringing foreign investments into Ireland and improving economic relations with Britain and America. Ireland's activist and independent role at the UN was soon modified as Fianna Fáil's new leader reined in the Irish delegation. During the decade that followed, or essentially between 1961 and 1972, Irish policymakers redefined the interest of such core values as sovereignty and neutrality at a time when Irish public attention was often distracted by the meetings being held between the leaders of Northern Ireland and the Republic, or the 1966 festivities commemorating the fiftieth anniversary of the Easter Rising, or the eruption of violence in Northern Ireland.[56]

Isolationist and somewhat xenophobic, post-war Ireland rejected NATO when it perceived no national gain from membership, but embraced the UN because it provided an opportunity for the Dublin government to assert its sovereign independence from Britain while serving humanitarian world causes. Ireland was initially cautious about the European Economic Community (EEC), however, despite its appeal in Western Europe. Paula Wylie explains how there was little intuitive understanding in Ireland of the original motivation for the greater integration among continental European nations after the war. It was the fear of conflict resulting from Cold War tensions that first inspired the 1948 Congress of Europe, and then the 1949 Council of Europe. Wylie argues that Ireland did not feel similarly threatened and therefore felt less inhibited. She also insists that Europeans were mistaken in suspecting that Irish disinterest was attributable to the belief that non-association gave Dublin greater leverage in sustaining independence from Britain.[57] Seán Lemass, whose priorities differed from those of de Valera, revealed a keen interest in seeking entry into the EEC after it was discovered in 1961 that Britain was about to apply for membership. In the Dáil debates that followed, the Irish government argued the economic advantages that entry into the EEC would yield, while the opposition warned that the country's inclusion could compromise its policy of neutrality. Lemass, however, displayed little concern about what the consequences might be for the ever persistent, but never statutorily established, policy of Irish neutrality.[58] At the urging of the taoiseach, the Dáil agreed to apply for membership a few months later.

Lemass perhaps may have perceived Ireland's frequently proclaimed neutrality as an irrelevant domestic issue over which there was merely some divided opinion, but the EEC Council of Ministers did not take such an indulgent view. The EEC had first begun as an economic community but there was a clear expectation among its members that it would progressively evolve into a political and defensive union. Every member of the EEC was also a member of NATO and, predictably, the United States was decidedly cool to the prospect of having a self-described neutral joining this pro-Western group of nations. It was, therefore, with the intent of reassuring both the Americans and the EEC Council of Ministers that the Fianna Fáil minister for lands, Michael Moran, attempted to distance the Irish government from the policy of neutrality when he publicly declared 'a policy of neutrality here in the present world division between communism and freedom was never laid down by us or indeed envisioned by our people. Neutrality in this context is not a policy to which we would ever want to appear committed.'[59] On 5 September 1962, seven months following the Moran statement, Lemass gave the following response in answer to a European journalist's question about Ireland's neutrality appearing to be incompatible with NATO. Lemass affirmed: 'We do not wish, in the conflict between free democracies and the communist empires, to be thought of as neutral. We are not neutral and do not wish to be regarded as such, even though we have not got specific commitments of a military kind

under any international agreement.'[60] The taoiseach's careful quali-
fication reflected the fact that there did exist opposition to NATO in
various elements within Irish society and no purpose would have
been served by provoking those people while the Dublin government
was seeking to undertake a reappraisal of neutrality, in tandem with
the realities and responsibilities of EEC membership.[61]

Whether or not the Council of Ministers, or the United States
Department of State, were in any way moved by Seán Lemass's willingness to jettison Irish neutrality in exchange for EEC membership,
it mattered very little once Charles de Gaulle intervened. The French
president vetoed Britain's application, and Ireland was given a painful
reminder of her economic dependence on Britain when told to put its
own application on hold. As the president of the EEC Commission
publicly remarked, 'Britain can possibly come in without Ireland but
Ireland cannot come in without Britain.'[62] Both countries, of course,
waited until 1973 before gaining admission to the European Economic Community.

In the interim, both Seán Lemass and his successor, Jack Lynch,
occasionally glossed over the implications for neutrality contained in
the language of the Treaties of Rome and Paris as they repeatedly
insisted that those documents did not entail any military or defence
commitments for member states of the EEC. On other occasions,
however, they made statements that underscored what some
commentators in Ireland increasingly spoke of as the government's
policy of ad hoc neutrality. Seán Lemass, for example, openly
conceded as early as 1962 that 'a military commitment will be an
inevitable consequence of our joining the Common Market and ultimately we would be prepared to yield even the technical label of our
neutrality'.[63] And Dr Patrick Hillery, the minister for external affairs
in 1970, spoke for the Lynch government in declaring that 'while
Ireland remained neutral during the Second World War we have
never adopted a permanent policy of neutrality in the doctrinaire or
ideological sense'.[64] When Ireland did take its place as a member of
the EEC 'neither the Irish public nor its leadership believed that
political co-operation with the EEC threatened neutrality'.[65] Indeed,
in a 1972 national referendum, fully 83 per cent of the electorate
voted in favour of Ireland's entry into that body. The public's affinity
for neutrality may have been sufficiently anaesthetized by the
reassuring ambiguity in which the Irish government appeared to
promise compliance with EEC objectives without making unequivocal

commitments of any kind.[66] But the fact remains, as J.J. Lee has observed, that few countries have made so heavy an emotional investment in the analysis of neutrality as have Irish politicians, who have ensured 'that it remains a subject that has not been conclusively defined'.[67]

Although neutrality was a prominent subject in both the Dáil debates and in the popular press prior to the 1972 referendum that overwhelmingly endorsed Ireland's entry into the EEC, it was a secondary issue compared to the attention given to the economic benefits that Ireland would receive from membership. For much of the decade that followed, only scant attention was given to the topic of neutrality, despite the international tensions reverberating from the revolution in Iran and Soviet intervention in Afghanistan, all of which prompted a global reassessment of security arrangements.[68]

British Prime Minister Margaret Thatcher met with her Irish counterpart, Charles Haughey, in December 1980, ostensibly for the purpose of discussing a resolution of the Northern Ireland conflict. Newspapers, however, leaked the story that the two leaders had agreed to an Anglo-Irish military alliance. Thatcher quickly distanced herself from that report while Haughey, who was attacked on the issue by neutrality advocates in the Dáil, refused to confirm the story on the grounds of confidentiality. Moreover, he did nothing to allay their concerns by further remarking that Irish neutrality would be at an end once the European Community (EC) achieved full political union.[69]

During this 11 March Dáil discussion, Haughey chided Fine Gael leader Garret FitzGerald by quoting his statement that appeared in *The Irish Times* of 8 February 1980, in which he declared, 'There really isn't any such thing as neutrality today: we are part of Western Europe and our interests coincide with theirs.'[70] FitzGerald replied by asserting that Fine Gael favoured military neutrality through non-participation in existing defence alliances of the West 'because we believe this policy accords with the current sentiments of our people, and secondly, because … Ireland can play a more useful role in promoting world peace outside these organizations than it would be likely [sic] we could do within them'.[71] That rejoinder came close to revealing how FitzGerald favoured ad hoc neutrality only because he could not disavow a practice that enjoyed such strong support within his own party.[72]

Both Fianna Fáil and Fine Gael went to great pains to underscore

how each was solemnly committed to what one might generously de-
scribe as a carefully contrived, abstract concept of neutrality. It was
very much the same delicate dance in which both parties engaged for
much of the next two decades. Deputy Brian Lenihan, the minister
for foreign affairs, offered his own explanation of the 11 March
debate, illustrating that Ireland could be ideologically partisan while
remaining militarily neutral. After remarking that the country's entry
into the EEC had not entailed any defence obligations, he declared,
'We are neutral in a military sense, but we are not neutral in a political
sense. That is the net position.'[73] That may indeed have represented
a meaningful distinction to the Dublin government, but it did not
alter how Ireland was perceived by others within the international
community. Among the so-called non-aligned nations, for example,
Ireland's profession of neutrality was given little credence. In a 1979
survey of the Organization of African Unity and Arab League members,
not a single one identified Ireland as neutral or non-aligned, as some
33 per cent did in the instance of Austria.[74]

In the 1980s, the European Union's (EU's) increased interest
in security issues all but ensured that neutrality would maintain a
visible political profile in Ireland. The respective attitudes of the Irish
parties and electorate also become more complicated as the Labour
Party and other neutrality proponents revised their definition of the
policy, with demands for what they called 'active' and 'positive' neutrality that generally translated into opposing any security or defence
co-operation with foreign military alliances.[75] That may partly
explain the reversal in Charles Haughey's position when the Falk-
lands War erupted in the spring of 1982. Initially, the Irish government condemned the Argentinean invasion and supported Britain by
participating in the EEC embargo against all imports from Argentina.
Once British troops entered into combat, however, and especially
after the sinking of an Argentine ship, the *General Belgrano*,
the Dublin government agreed with those who were claiming that
Ireland's traditional neutral stance no longer could be sustained once
military action superseded economic sanctions.[76]

Throughout much of the 1980s – from December 1982 to March
1987 – Garret FitzGerald headed a Fine Gael–Labour coalition
government that sought to promote Irish integration within the
European Economic Community. Specifically, he attempted to maintain what had been the objective of the preceding Fianna Fáil government: eventual Irish participation in the Community's defence

while also ensuring that the decisions of the EEC did not prejudice Ireland's existing position as a non-member of a military alliance. Fianna Fáil, however, not only opposed such efforts but also declined to embrace its own pre-1982 unambiguous rejection of neutrality upon returning to power in 1988. It was a strategy motivated by calculating and cynical party politics, by no means then unique to Fianna Fáil. The electorate had no agreed concept about what was intended by the use of the term 'neutrality', and politicians from virtually all political parties sought approval by affirming their commitment to what was clearly popular, even if undefined.[77] Given the scope of such propagandizing and posturing, it is little wonder that a 1985 public opinion poll revealed a notable gap in the public's comprehension of the issue – 20 per cent of respondents, when asked 'What does "Irish neutrality" mean to you?', gave answers that showed that their understanding of the policy was either vague or non-existent.[78]

Ireland's membership in the more aggressively integrated European Union of the 1990s witnessed a dramatic expansion of the Irish economy. This was also a time when some in Ireland began to wonder if the cornucopian Celtic Tiger came at too great a price, namely the nation's distinctive form of neutrality. But the public discourse on the topic of neutrality had less to do with European, or global, developments than with such abstract principles 'as sovereignty, independence, and anti-militarism, together with a historical reflex to keep a distance from large neighbours'.[79]

By the end of the 1990s, every notable European neutral except Switzerland had joined the European Union. As Austria, Finland and Sweden entered the EU, Ireland, a veteran member of two decades, now appeared ready to participate in European security arrangements, including its 1999 inclusion in NATO's Partnership for Peace. Remarkably, both Fianna Fáil and Fine Gael supported joining the Partnership, reasoning that Irish involvement in NATO peacekeeping did not violate the principle of neutrality.[80]

There was vocal dissent in Ireland against such initiatives, of course, and one of the more active groups was the Peace and Neutrality Alliance (PANA), established in Dublin in December 1996. Its objectives included a policy for the disarmament and demilitarization of the EU; refusing to allow Ireland to co-operate with any nation maintaining nuclear weapons; restricting Irish troops to service abroad only as peacekeepers under the auspices of the UN;

and the pursuit of a positive and independent foreign policy that eschewed any and all military alliances.[81]

In June 1997, the coalition government of Fine Gael, Labour and Democratic Left was displaced by a new Fianna Fáil–Progressive Democrat coalition under Bertie Ahern as taoiseach and Mary Harney as tánaiste. The Irish economy soared in 1997 when Ireland's Gross National Product (GNP) increased by almost 9 per cent. Moreover, government projections anticipated continued economic growth and improvement in living standards over the next five years. Although the poorest section of the population did not share in that unprecedented surge in prosperity, general satisfaction with the fiscal health of the country very probably made new departures in the international arena more palatable, even if they contained implications for the holy grail of neutrality. In December 1996, the United Nations Security Council authorized the creation of a force for an eighteen-month period to help pacify the conflict in Bosnia. The force comprised some 30,000 troops from thirty-six countries under NATO command, but in support of the UN mandate. In May 1997, the Dáil approved participation of forty-nine Irish troops for the peacekeeping mission. Moreover, an Irish officer was assigned to NATO headquarters in Belgium as a liaison officer. Labour deputy and leader Dick Spring defended such Irish involvement and argued that it was consistent with the country's foreign policy traditions and objectives.[82] One indication that there still existed significant differences of opinion about the proper course of Irish foreign policy among the Irish political leadership is the fact that Dessie O'Malley, whose Progressive Democrats party was the supporting coalition member in Bertie Ahern's government, publicly denounced Ireland's participation in the Bosnian crisis.

On 11 September 2001 Al Qaeda operatives hijacked commercial airliners and crashed them into the World Trade Center in New York and the Pentagon in Washington, D.C., which led to an American retaliatory strike against the terrorist sanctuaries in Afghanistan. When the US invaded Iraq in 2003, Irish citizens began protesting against the use of Shannon airport to refuel US military aircraft and the controversial rendition flights for captured combatants.

Moreover, in a December 2001 public address, Irish Minister for Foreign Affairs Brian Cowen had sought to assure his countrymen that their overall concern about an increasingly centralized EU was misplaced. He told his audience that while joining the European Union had perhaps resulted in some loss of sovereignty for the state, no differently than for other European Union members, the benefits that accrued for the nation's welfare far eclipsed that loss. Cowen noted how Ireland's sovereignty was perhaps least trammelled upon during the immediate post-war years of the 1950s, but who, he asked, would want to return to those grey, isolated days? He went on, however, to declare that EU membership did not entail any mutual defence commitment, nor did it affect Ireland's position as a non-member of a military alliance.[83]

Reassurances of this kind were not enough to mollify public wariness over the Irish government's growing involvement in European security arrangements. Ireland was already committed to providing resources for the European Security and Defence Policy (ESDP), whose tasks encompassed humanitarian, rescue and peace-keeping responsibilities. Irish involvement with that agency, however, was subject only to the decision of the Dublin government, rather than to any directive from the EU. Yet despite such provisions precluding any encroachment of Irish sovereignty, there was little appetite among the electorate for participation in a common defence scheme.[84]

There emerged indisputable evidence during the first decade of the new millennium that majority opinion in Ireland did not share the government's enthusiasm for increased integration with the European Union. The debate over the Nice Treaty in 2001, both in the Dáil and in the media, revealed genuine anxiety regarding how that document would impact upon Irish neutrality. But those same accounts reveal how another principal objection to the Nice Treaty was concern that it could marginalize the rights of smaller nations. Ireland is the only member of the European Union that requires ratification of such treaties via referendums, and most of the leaders in the major parties were stunned when voters rejected the treaty in June 2001. After predictable recriminations in which the legislative members blamed one another for the defeat of a treaty that would have included admitting Eastern European applicants to the EU, a second referendum was scheduled for 2002. The vote this time did endorse the Nice Treaty, but only after a restriction was inserted into the Constitution prohibiting Irish participation in an EU common defence arrangement. It should be noted that this new constitutional provision, reluctantly agreed to by the Fianna Fáil–Progressive Democrats government, made no specific reference to neutrality. Moreover, it allowed the government to assent to the establishment of a common EC defence, provided that Ireland could retain the option to abstain from participation.[85]

Despite the evident opposition to any further Irish participation in European Union security planning, Bertie Ahern proceeded to explore an EU invitation to consider supporting the European Union's emergency defence arrangements. Ireland's Minister for Defence Willie O'Dea attempted to quell resistance to that prospect when he announced on 10 February 2006 that Irish involvement in such a capacity would only occur with strict adherence to the 'triple lock' mechanism. That term referred to the Irish government's repeated pledge to never commit Ireland to any military undertaking without triple approval; the Irish government, the Dáil and the United Nations would all need to grant consent before Ireland would assume any external military undertaking.[86] That pledge did help diminish some opposition to exploring the feasibility of Irish involvement, but other critics expressed concern that a Dáil recess was but one example of how the 'triple lock' might prove difficult to implement in any time-sensitive circumstance.

The first and second referendums on the Nice Treaty, together with accompanying and often contentious debates, took place at a time when the Irish economy was generally thriving. By 2007, however, property sales were in a tailspin, manufacturing jobs were being lost due to Ireland's diminished competitiveness and the banks were in crisis. The country went from possessing the fastest-growing economy among 'first world' nations to having the worst recession among that same cohort. It was also the time in which Ireland would hold a referendum on the Lisbon Treaty that proposed expanding the EU membership from fifteen to twenty-seven. Once more, critics in Ireland urged the electorate to reject the government's appeal for ratification, arguing that the influx of so many new members into the EU would disadvantage Ireland's standing in that body during a particularly precarious time for the Irish economy. And, remarkably, the political leadership was again caught by surprise when the referendum failed to win approval. Neutrality was not the chief concern of opponents to ratification, but the government took no chances and sought to disabuse voters of the notion that the Lisbon Treaty would, as Sinn Féin and other leftist parties claimed, dilute the country's policy of neutrality. In successfully winning ratification by a second referendum in October 2009, the government received assistance from a number of celebrities including Ireland's Nobel Laureate poet Séamus Heaney. He dismissed the notion that the country's sovereignty would be negated by absorption into a European super-state and warned his countrymen of the consequences to the nation's culture if the Lisbon Treaty was rejected a second time.[87]

As Ireland entered the second decade of the twenty-first century, the often ambiguous or contradictory positions toward neutrality of the major political parties became more consistently transparent. Irish views have been Europeanized, especially with reference to EU security and defence co-operation, but the debates among them remain firmly rooted in domestic politics. The Fianna Fáil party is reluctant to move toward a common EU defence and still regards neutrality as its badge of independence and link to what it perceives to be Ireland's proud tradition. And while the Fianna Fáil party has been increasingly receptive to greater co-operation with the EU on matters involving common defence, it insists that the government and the Dáil must retain control over military decisions, such as the deployment of troops.[88]

Fine Gael is the more pro-European of the two main political parties and had long ago advocated exploration of the EEC member-ship, even before Seán Lemass announced the decision to apply. Fine Gael has also exhibited greater interest in and support for the process and goals of European integration beyond the benefits of member-ship. The party lacks, of course, the historical connection with the policy of neutrality specifically articulated by de Valera, and its receptivity to defence integration is consistent with Fine Gael's less nationalist attitude toward issues that touch on neutrality and sover-eignty. It has, for example, advocated the removal of the 'triple lock' so as to enable rapid deployment of troops in EU crisis management operations.[89] But Fine Gael has not been in a position to form a majority government, which has led to agreements with potential partners that either diluted or compromised the party's intended approach to international relations. For example, the junior party in Fine Gael-led governments since Ireland's admission into the EEC has invariably been the Labour Party. And Labour, of course, has held opposite views to Fine Gael on neutrality, and been wary of any security co-operation with the EU.[90]

Whether it was Fianna Fáil, Fine Gael, Labour, the Progressive Democrats, Sinn Féin or others, party politics was but one of three domestic factors that have contributed to Ireland's persistent attach-ment to the policy of neutrality: the other two were public opinion and the role of interest groups.[91] Neal Jesse, utilizing detailed public opinion surveys on neutrality not available for earlier time periods, reveals how the public's interpretation of neutrality could appear inconsistent. A 1992 poll, for example, cited 46 per cent of respondents affirming that neutrality meant either 'no involvement in wars', or 'no military alliances'.[92] But a 1996 poll reported that 57 per cent of the respondents believed that 'Ireland should come to the aid of another [EU] Member State if attacked'.[93] And, lastly, interest groups like the Irish Sovereignty Movement and the Peace and Neutrality Alliance have helped to solidify, in the minds of the people, what Patrick Keatinge has described as the 'traditional symbol and national myth' of Irish neutrality.[94]

Technological, geopolitical, economic and other realities of the twenty-first century have profoundly altered the dynamics that shape the international landscape. Those pervasive changes will almost certainly have a direct impact upon the Irish understanding of, and support for, the policy of neutrality in the foreseeable future. What remains to be seen is whether or not both the Irish government and the electorate it serves will have a shared perception of what precisely is intended by this somewhat iconic, even if vaguely embraced, feature of Ireland's national identity.

National borders and sovereign jurisdictions are being made increasingly vulnerable not only to such traditional challenges as illegal immigration and asylum seekers but also to internet security, private military contractors, and international criminal and non-state terrorist organizations. Indeed, the standardization of international commercial law and business practices have, as Michael O'Sullivan explains, contributed to a globalization phenomenon that has rendered traditional attitudes toward neutrality somewhat moot. Already the long-established Irish opposition to military alliances has been incrementally qualified to embrace both security-based EU co-operative undertakings and an exponential expansion in the Europeanization of law enforcement. Particularly significant is the fact that neither has been viewed as compromising neutrality by an ever more flexible Irish government, and a supportive population.[95]

In summary, therefore, there is little agreement over whether or not Irish neutrality was seriously explored in the first decades of the twentieth century. Political elites, rather than public interest groups, engaged in what limited dialogue there was on the topic prior to the Second World War. Ireland profited from the fact that she had no traditional enemies, apart from Britain, and was so geographically isolated from the rest of Europe that none of the great powers perceived any advantage in compelling that nation to join one alliance or another. And Ireland's determination to escape British dominance and procure sovereign independence became an objective that eclipsed neutrality as a priority. It was Ireland's admission to the European Union (initially the EEC), more than any other development, that enabled the Dublin government to achieve the status of a nation totally independent of Great Britain.[96] The Belfast Agreement of 1998 greatly reduced the proximate danger of violence from Northern Ireland and heralded the opening of a new era in Anglo-Irish relations.

Ronan Fanning has aptly described the way in which neutrality has been one of the more notable characteristics of Irish security policy in the successive stages of dependence, independence and interdependence. He observes that when Ireland was dependent upon Britain, neutrality was the policy to which it aspired; upon gaining independence, it became the policy which it practised; and when Ireland and Britain became interdependent in the post-Second World War era, neutrality continued to be the policy to which Ireland remained unalterably committed.[97] But Professor Fanning's thoughtful analysis predated Dublin's eventual decision to join the Partnership for Peace, a determination that has been subsequently followed by an ever more active involvement in European military and security arrangements.

It would be incorrect, or at least premature, to speak now of the 'demise' of Irish neutrality, but the transformative changes noted above will inevitably require a re-conceptualization of this long-revered national posture with which many in Ireland remain emotionally, if not philosophically, committed. What appears as the one certainty in Ireland's near-term future is the continued strengthening of the nation's relationship with other members of the European Union. EU membership was seen to be an invaluable asset by the country at large during the affluent decade of the Celtic Tiger, and shortly thereafter it became Ireland's best hope in averting economic collapse during the wake of massive bank failures following the world economic recession, beginning approximately in 2008.

Despite its prominence in both Irish public and legislative discourse up to the present day, and its frequent reference during recent debates over the ratification of the Lisbon Treaty, the term 'neutrality' in Ireland often connotes something more comparable to a cultural temperament than it does a national policy. The Irish may often differ when attempting to define the nature of that doctrine, but most will insist that they know how it should be appropriately exercised. That ethereal approach is reasonably consistent with the expressed perspective of United States Supreme Court Justice Potter Stewart who, in 1964, famously attempted to explain what is obscene by saying, 'I shall not today attempt further to define the kinds of material I understand to be embraced ... but I know it when I see it.' Frequently revered and occasionally reviled, neutrality is an Irish mindset that is likely to endure long after the term has lost all resonance within the world at large.

CHAPTER SIX

Modernity, the Past and Politics in Post-War Ireland

ENDA DELANEY

Towards the end of the 1950s Ireland changed from a traditional, rural, homogenous society to the present urbanized-
industrialized society. The malaise of modern Irish society has
been created by the non-replacement of traditional values by
a system aimed at greater efficiency, self-reliance and discipline. At best we have evolved a fragmented or polarized value
system with pressure groups pursuing sectional interests often
at the expense of the common good.[1]

In what was a futuristic assessment of independent Ireland's prospects
by the new millennium published in 1982, the director of An Foras
Forbartha (National Institute for Physical Planning and Construction
Research), Liam Downey, underscored the rapid pace of change that
occurred in independent Ireland in the second half of the twentieth
century. Established in 1964, An Foras Forbartha was a state agency
that conducted research on the urban built environment.[2] Like many
other contemporary observers, Downey cited the rapid pace of
urbanization in the 1960s and 1970s as a sign of Ireland's emergent
'modernity'. In the course of this *fin-de-siècle* rumination Downey also
identified the consequences of these changes, in what he described as
the contemporary 'malaise of modern Irish society'. Individualist self-
interest was seen as the defining feature of this 'new' Ireland, replacing
a communitarian ethos that had emphasized the 'common good' and
the primacy of the interests of the wider community over individual or
sectional concerns. This assertion may be questioned, as sectional
interests such as farming organizations, professional groups and the
labour movement had long sought to influence public policy since the

foundation of independent Ireland, albeit discreetly – and perhaps more perniciously – behind closed doors.[3] Nevertheless, Downey was correct in identifying the rapid pace of economic, social and cultural change that had reshaped Ireland since the 1960s, and historians would agree that in the last forty years of the twentieth century a far-reaching transformation took place.[4] These developments profoundly altered the nature of Irish society, and his comments reflect the widely accepted view that independent Ireland had wholeheartedly and un-reservedly embraced this 'new' modernity, with far-reaching conse-quences for both Irish values and social cohesion. Given the extent and nature of the changes that occurred in the 1960s, should this decade, like the more recent era of the Celtic Tiger, constitute a watershed in late modern Irish history, marking out both sharp discontinuities with the past and Ireland's embrace of modernity?[5]

Historians, cultural theorists and social scientists – with their different techniques, perspectives and methodologies – have great difficulty in even agreeing what constitutes modernity in the first place.[6] Modernity has attracted particular attention from historically informed social and cultural theorists including towering figures such as Perry Anderson, Marshall Berman, Anthony Giddens, Jürgen Haber-mas and Zygmunt Baumann as well as Charles Taylor and a whole host of other scholars in sociology, literature, political science, philosophy and cultural studies.[7] Anderson perceptively describes it as 'neither economic process nor cultural vision but the historical experience me-diating the one to another'.[8] In this discussion, modernity is used as a qualitative category in the sense of its being a lived experience rather that a period in history or a descriptor of the development of societies. Indeed, a defining and problematic element is that there was a shared consciousness of this modernity.

Even with this conceptual permissiveness and obvious interpreta-tive difficulties, some points of agreement do, however, emerge. First and foremost, modernity is a long-term, diffuse process rather than a strictly delineated chronological period, and is not bound by any par-ticular opening and end dates.[9] Secondly, Western modernity, once viewed by historians and social scientists as the benchmark against which to measure the 'progress' of other 'developing' societies, is a Eurocentric starting point at which to begin: the shortcomings and inherent assumptions of such an approach have been exposed with devastating effect by scholars concerned with non-Western countries, most persuasively in the pioneering work of Dipesh Chakrabarty.[10]

Lastly, established pre-modern social practices and cultural frameworks did not simply disappear overnight with the sudden onset of post-Enlightenment 'modernity'.

Moreover, it was the uneasy relationship between traditional conceptions of society and those ostensibly 'modern' values which is particularly relevant to twentieth-century Ireland.[11] At particular points, conflict arose between different visions of Irish modernity such as the role of religion in the 'new' Ireland, the effects of constant interactions with other 'modern' societies (in particular the Anglo-American world), and, not least, the impact of advanced capitalism and economic development on an economy that was based primarily on agricultural production until the late 1950s. Lacking the drama of political events in twentieth-century Irish history such as the 1916 Rising, the end of British rule in 1921 or de Valera's accession to power in March 1932, the process by which independent Ireland became self-consciously 'modern' in the 1960s is just as significant, yet historians have had relatively little to say about this topic. The Irish historiographical revolution of the mid-twentieth century in particular was centred on the primacy of the archive and close readings of documentary material, and few historians have ventured into the field of conceptually driven accounts of the Irish past. In fact, the most engaging and original discussions that seek to interrogate the extent, nature and consequences of Irish modernity have come from literature critics, cultural theorists and folklore specialists.[12]

I

Instinctively, historians think in chronological periods as they seek to impose some form of structure on the inherent diversity of the past, and in this respect the historiography of late modern Ireland is no different. Equally, historians identify patterns, and the 'social shape' of the past tends to work in cycles: up-down, decline-progress-decline, zigzag, and so on.[13] For twentieth-century Ireland, the narrative might be sketched out in the following broad brush terms: a dramatic era of war and revolution from the turn of the century until 1923, thereafter followed by a period of consolidation and nation-building in the 1920s and 1930s, leading to independent Ireland's ultimate isolation during the Second World War. An even gloomier period from the late 1940s until the end of the 1950s is often described in terms such as 'morass' or 'stagnation'.[14] But the general climate changed in the 1960s, rather euphemistically captured in the description as being the 'best of decades'.[15] Another period of economic stagnation, marked by widespread unemployment and emigration, followed in the 1980s and early 1990s. Last but certainly not least we have the emergence of the Celtic Tiger from the mid-1990s until the first decade of the twentieth-first century. For wider consumption, such periods are often labelled or branded by association with particular leading politicians, such as the age of de Valera, the Lemass era, or the Haughey years, reflecting the preoccupation of many Irish historians with key personalities as the drivers of political change.[16]

Such periods of historical time often take on readily identifiable features and tropes. For instance, the age of de Valera was characterized by a rather austere and dogmatic Gaelic Catholic nationalism. Yet the narrative of the first inter-party government underlines the optimism fuelled by Clann na Poblachta's radicalism and the end of Fianna Fáil's dominance, an optimism that unravelled very quickly in the face of internal divisions, conflict with the hierarchy of the Roman Catholic Church, and the medical profession during the Mother and Child Scheme in 1951. For the Lemass era, the phrases that most often spring to mind are pragmatism, 'modern' and outward looking, after decades of introspection and isolation following independence. In the writings of some historians, Lemass sometimes takes on a near-heroic personage: J.J. Lee adopts an almost hagiographical approach in his upbeat assessment, published in the late 1970s, of his tenure as taoiseach between 1959 and 1966. Not alone did he drive on industrialization, but Lemass initiated the process of challenging traditional, pessimistic views about Ireland's ability to be a successful country:

> Despite all the encouragements and setbacks, and there would be many, despite the clinging survivals of earlier mentalities, Lemass succeeded in establishing a bridgehead in which the productive forces in Irish society could take root, and gradually – however gradually – push back the parasitic forces.[17]

Attributing change to the dynamism of political leaders is standard practice for historians, though such an approach tends to underestimate deeper and less obvious social, economic and cultural forces.

The discontinuities when decisive changes actually occurred are often described as turning-points, milestones or watersheds. The following turning-points are most commonly used in standard historical narratives of twentieth-century Ireland: the 1916 Rising, the formation of Dáil Éireann in 1919, and the signing of the Anglo-Irish

Treaty and subsequent establishment of the Irish Free State in 1921–2. The year 1932, de Valera's ascent to power, is often described as a key milestone, in that the transfer of democratic power occurred smoothly, as is the publication of *Economic Development* in 1958 which represented a rejection of Ireland's traditional inward-looking economic policy. Finally, the entry of independent Ireland into the European Economic Community in 1973 marked a significant shift in political orientation, away from the tortuously complex British–Irish relationship and toward a broader set of European relationships. Such dates on the 'timeline' of twentieth-century Irish history often mark the opening and closing dates for many synthetic accounts. For instance, Roy Foster declares that the terminal date of his coverage of 1972 in his monumental survey of Irish history was appropriate because it 'may be taken as the year when many old moulds were broken with apparent decisiveness', and he is referring to the removal of the 'special position' of the Roman Catholic Church from the Irish Constitution of 1937 by a constitutional referendum, the suspension of the Stormont administration in Northern Ireland and the eventual entry of independent Ireland into the EEC.[18] J.J. Lee chooses the Anglo-Irish Agreement of 1985 as the last act of his invigorating interpretative account of twentieth-century Ireland, seeing it as a decisive shift in British–Irish relations, although with the ever helpful benefit of hindsight, the Hillsborough Agreement was less significant than it might have seemed at this time. More recent accounts have opted for the Belfast Agreement of 1998 as the final act in the long history of modern Ireland.[19]

One of the central arguments to be advanced is that while this approach – concentrating on particular people, watersheds, events or milestones – is instructive for political and constitutional historians, it obscures the complex and overlapping patterns of social and cultural change. Even though the 1960s are seen as the high-point of the modernization of Ireland, elements of continuity with the past co-existed within this strange kind of modernity, and the emergence of the 'new' Ireland was not simply a product of this decade but of a much longer historical pedigree. In fact, as Roy Foster noted in 1988, 'a good deal of what characterized the country in the mid-twentieth century was obdurately pre-modern'.[20]

II

The view that independent Ireland only fully engaged with modernity in the 1960s is a gross over-simplification. This view is most fully expressed by Fergal Tobin in his feel-good book *The Best of Decades: Ireland in the 1960s,* first published in 1984, and over twenty years later still the standard account of Ireland during that decade. Whereas for British society the 'age of affluence' was in the 1950s, this same characterization can be applied to independent Ireland in the following decade. According to Tobin, the 1960s were a crucial watershed in the transformation of late modern Ireland:

> History does not fall neatly into decades, nor do historical transformations occur clearly and completely. But no one in Ireland in 1970, looking back on the decade that had just ended, could doubt that the country had seen unprecedented changes. The isolation and introspections of generations did not finally disappear – in some degree they never can – but the blinds were let up, the windows were thrown open, the doors were unlocked; and good, bad or indifferent, the modern world came in among us at last.[21]

The 1940s and 1950s were associated with stagnation and isolation, and then seemingly out of nowhere in the 1960s sprang a cultural revolution that fundamentally reshaped Irish society. This outlook is a linear and dichotomous model of social and cultural change that lacks complexity, nuance and conceptual rigour.

Ireland's proximity to one of the world's most advanced economies ensured that modernity was never far away from the minds of the postwar generation. A number of authors, including the historians Mary E. Daly and Brian Girvin and the sociologist Damian Hannan have charted the profound and far-reaching changes that occurred in rural and small-town Ireland between independence and the 1960s.[22] A significant factor in why one out of every three people born in 1946 had left Ireland by the late 1960s was that the visions of modernity that provided the cultural frameworks for understanding one's position in the world sat uneasily with the harsh and often glum realities of rural and small-town life.[23] As Damian Hannan perceptively argued in the early 1970s when discussing the huge exodus from post-war Ireland, 'this widespread existence of British points of reference for judging the adequacy of conditions at home is probably one of the most influential local consequences of our recent emigration history'.[24] Newspapers and radio offered glimpses of a different way of life based on material well-being, a consumer-based social scene organized around popular activities such as dancing and going to the cinema, and, most importantly, a vision of a future that centred on the fulfilment of individual aspirations. In other words, what have come to be seen as central features of the 'modern way of life' were just across the water, and thousands of emigrants had direct experiences with these ways of life through travel to Britain.

British newspapers were read widely in Ireland, especially the more popular variants. A conservative Catholic cleric, the Rev. Robert Devane SJ, estimated that nearly 400,000 British Sunday newspapers were imported every week and even proposed in 1950 that the government should impose a special tariff on cheap imported newspapers and magazines to protect 'innocent' Irish minds.[25] Together with the alleged pernicious influence of newspapers, those living on the eastern coast of Ireland and close to the border with Northern Ireland could listen to the even more insidious British wireless service. Detailed research on listening habits undertaken by Radio Éireann in the early 1950s indicated that BBC Radio Light and Radio Luxembourg, both designed to appeal to a younger audience, were very popular across all social groups.[26]

One of the most ubiquitous expressions of modernity was the cinema. Irish audiences invariably watched American, or to a lesser extent, British films as an indigenous industry had not developed to any degree.[27] By the mid-1930s it was reckoned that four-fifths of the films shown in Irish cinemas came from Hollywood.[28] For some conservative critics, the cinema was the 'celluloid menace', a powerful source that 'confirmed the unthinking in their lack of thinking, and has filled their lives with a colourful and varied vacuity'.[29] A night out at the 'pictures' was by a long stretch the most popular form of leisure activity in Ireland by the mid-twentieth century: one estimate produced in 1954 suggested that roughly one in three people frequented the 'palace of dreams' at least once each week.[30] Knowledge of the wider world was viewed through this Technicolor lens, leading to some unfavourable comparisons between life in rural Ireland and the cinematic representations of modernity contained in Hollywood's portrayal of material success, city life and private morality. As the film historian Kevin Rockett has argued, Irish cinema-goers were confronted with 'a radically contrasting world and lifestyle which necessarily challenged traditional Irish notions of morality and order and highlighted their own material lack, both personally and as a nation'.[31] Even if the notoriously strict censorship policy operated by the state removed licentious or sexually suggestive scenes from Hollywood films, the more basic message that people elsewhere had better lives still undermined traditional Irish nationalist values.[32] This sense of a disjuncture between life in Ireland and Hollywood representations was identified by an educationalist writing in 1944:

> It is interesting to consider the average farm labourer, walking five or six miles … to go to the pictures, and then that way home again in our Irish rain. What has he seen that has the slightest relation to life as he knows it? He has seen night-club queens covered by a few spangles, Chicago gangsters talking a peculiar argot, society playboys babbling airily of Reno divorce. He has seen crooning cowboys, coal-black mammies, typists clad in Schiaparelli models living in luxurious flats, and millionaires living in Babylonian palaces. He is going home to fall into his bed in the loft, to rise the next morning and feed the pigs. What does he make of it all?[33]

Young Irish people were avid cinemagoers. While it is somewhat facile to overstate the effect of the powerful images of 'modern life' contained in American and British films on the mentalities of a complete generation, films offered a tantalizing taste of the alternative lifestyles available in the prosperous industrial economies. In 1948, a civil servant and member of the Commission on Emigration reflected on the effects of these perceptions:

> It may be that, in years gone by, such persons have been content to live virtually on a subsistence basis, but the cinema, radio, newspapers and friends are now luring them into the attitude that they should not be satisfied with [this] but should leave home and get wages to enable them to raise their standards, get married and have homes of their own. Who can blame them?[34]

Contemporaries often alleged that females were especially influenced by such glamorous portrayals of American life, although this tells us more about the gendered nature of discourse and the lack of understanding of the rising aspirations of young women rather than any innate differences.[35]

And even the depth of the reaction to the alleged bastion of antimodernism, the Catholic Church in independent Ireland, may offer hard evidence of the inroads that modernity was making into Irish consciousness well before the widespread and well-documented changes that occurred in the 1960s. Louise Fuller's impressive work on Irish Catholic culture since 1950 shows how many of the changes that occurred in Irish society in the 1960s and 1970s were related to processes that were well underway beforehand.[36] Censorship and other forms of cultural protectionism which either clerics or lay Catholics advocated could be read not simply as signs of Ireland's backwardness, but rather the real and genuine challenge that modernity posed to the traditional values promulgated by both church and state. And not all was as it might seem about the moral and social authority of the Catholic Church, and perhaps more imaginative strategies of historical research are required to test this truism. The views of disaffected intellectuals such as the group of writers associated with *The Bell* in the late 1940s and early 1950s are often seen as a marker of discontent with the authoritarian censorship practised by the Irish state, which was in part a reflection of the omnipotent power of the Catholic Church.[37] But this was a very small and rarefied section of Irish society with cosmopolitan reference points and frequent international inter-actions. For instance, when a future archbishop of Westminster, Fr John Heenan, visited Dublin during the war in 1941, he wrote a series of articles for the *Catholic Herald* which inter alia suggested that many young people he had talked to in the city were anti-clerical, and that the level of religious instruction was far below the standard required and that when they went abroad they would not be 'in a position to de-fend and sustain the faith'.[38] Archbishop McQuaid wrote to William Godfrey in November 1941, who was then the apostolic delegate to Britain, to complain about the article which he thought was 'a scan-dalously offensive calumny' against Catholic Dublin.[39] Godfrey diplo-matically refused to do anything and politely suggested to McQuaid that he should raise the matter with the papal nuncio in Ireland.[40]

Throughout the post-war period large numbers of Irish people had varying degrees of engagement with modernity, in the sense of expe-riencing aspects of life or value-systems that were widely acknow-ledged to be new and very different. The massive exodus to Britain from the Second World War onwards together with the cultural encounters provoked by cinema, radio and later television helped to foster an ethos which ascribed primacy to individual well-being and achievement and created the sense of living through a period on which 'traditional' values, attitudes and social norms were changing.

III

If we accept that a distinguishing feature of this modernity is a shared sense of living through something new and something quite different, what role is there for the past, or history? The success of the golden jubilee celebrations of the Easter Rising in April 1966 indicated that recent history had not been consigned to complete oblivion.[41] On the other hand, as the distinguished French historian Pierre Nora has observed, when historical events are commemorated, it is usually a sure sign that they have passed from living memory only to be codified as sites of memory.[42] However, with the emerging civil rights campaign in Northern Ireland together with the sectarian murders by the newly formed Ulster Volunteer Force (UVF) of three people in May and June 1966, contested versions of the past would soon again take centre stage in the simmering conflict.

Seán Lemass was, as John Horgan describes him, 'an enigmatic patriot', a politician whose historical vision was far less developed than de Valera. Lemass, however, was no flag-waver and even during the golden jubilee commemoration of the Easter Rising he took a back-seat, leaving the 'chief' de Valera to take centre stage, which was important as he was running for re-election against Tom O'Higgins. His foreword to the official record of commemoration was somewhat muted, and Lemass preferred to concentrate on thanking all those involved and a brief mention at the end of the 'stirring events of Easter 1916'.[43] Lemass laconically observed that the golden jubilee celebrations marked 'the end of a chapter: as one of the generation, this marked the end of the road for me'.[44]

Shortly after coming to office in 1959, Lemass outlined his understanding of patriotism:

> Personally, I believe that national progress of any kind depends largely upon an upsurge of patriotism – a revival of patriotism, if you will directed towards constructive purposes. Patriotism, as I understand it, is a combination of love of country, pride in its history, traditions and cultures, and a determination to add to its prestige and achievements.[45]

Lemass was not the only public figure who conceived patriotism in pragmatic terms. In the late 1950s the bishop of Clonfert, Dr William Philbin, then regarded as one of the few Catholic bishops whose 'speeches and articles on social questions attracted interest because of their originality of theme', published a pamphlet in which he articulated an alternative version of patriotism.[46] Moving beyond the usual exhortations to love one's country, Philbin argued for what be best described as a civic form of patriotism, based less on visceral and sentimental elements and more concerned with improving communal well-being and fostering economic progress.[47] And, as Philbin argued in an article published in 1957 in the influential journal *Studies*, pragmatic rather than rhetorical yardsticks were more relevant:

> Our greatest neglect of all – the capital sin of our young Irish state – is our failure to provide for our young people an acceptable alternative to emigration. Our version of history has tended to make us think of freedom as an end in itself and of independent government – like marriage in a fairy story – as the solution of all ills.[48]

While perhaps not too much should be made of the views of a select number of élite figures, it does seem that by the late 1950s there was a sense that this 'new' Irish nationalism was not based on appeals to the cherished fallen heroes of the Irish pantheon but on practical improvements in the everyday lives of citizens of the Irish state. In this respect, the emphasis on pragmatic or 'civic' citizenship mirrored similar discussions that were taking place in Britain at this time, prompted by the prominent sociologist T.H. Marshall, who argued in 1950 for 'social' citizenship, centred on the achievement of economic security through the provision of welfare.[49]

Lemass was a master of what might be described as the rhetoric of progress and often associated national pride as being intimately linked to economic development. Throughout his term as taoiseach, the political vocabulary shifted from the historical wrongs of British–Irish relations over the previous eight centuries, or what he pithily referred to as the Irish disposition 'to be sorry for ourselves', to a self-consciously 'modern' outlook. As Tom Garvin has argued, Fianna Fáil's ideology was based on the difficult balancing act of espousing traditional values that reflected the outlook of its support base with a commitment to economic modernization.[50] While enthusiastically endorsing the agenda of modernization, Lemass was also well aware of the potential side-effects of promoting this image of 'new' Ireland on the traditional Fianna Fáil support base within the rural working-class population.[51]

It is perhaps also worth noting that this understanding of patriotism was reflected by some of the views expressed by the Irish living overseas, who to a large degree had rejected patriotism based on simple nostalgia a long time ago. This was the 'disenchanted generation' that had seen the illusory nature of the so-called gains from independence. Like Lemass they measured the achievement of independence in concrete rather than abstract terms. As Mary E. Daly has documented, Irish officials in New York in the mid-1950s observed that generational frictions existed between the recent arrivals and the more established American Irish, often due to sentimental attitudes toward the old country, which compared starkly to the realities of life in post-war Ireland.[52] The new generation of arrivals after the Second World War were 'rather less zealous and less interested in the Anti-Partition movement than one might expect or even hope', and in the view of the Irish Consul-General in New York, Paul Keating, this was a cause of conflict with the established American Irish.[53]

> One reason for this I think is that the attitude of people who grew up in an independent Ireland is different to that of people who knew Ireland before 1922, or perhaps only by hearsay. I think a great deal of the sentimentalism and romanticism of so many Irish-Americans grates on the younger people coming to this country. I think they are also at times irritated by the assumption which prevails in some quarters that they know nothing and I certainly know some who resent very much being told that it was the Irish-Americans who won the war for independence in Ireland. On this account there is a clash.[54]

Similarly, the patriotism of the Irish in Britain was limited to participation in 'national activities' and a conspicuous lack of interest in sustained political involvement to place partition on the wider British political agenda. After years of trying to engender interest in Irish politics, another unnamed activist remarked rather unkindly in the late 1960s that 'all they're good for now is cursing the English on Saturday night with their free National Health teeth'.[55] Life in England had apparently taken its toll on the national fervour of the displaced migrants. Bitterness toward the Irish body politic was frequently expressed by migrants, and it was widely perceived that it was the inadequate policies of successive governments that had forced thousands to leave in the first place.[56] As Kevin O'Connor noted, Irish nationalism had served the post-war generation badly: 'Tri-colour flag waving and lip-service to the sacred cows of the Republic, after all, had not provided them with the means to earn a living there, and many of the young immigrants were impatient with such rhetoric.'[57]

Disillusionment and disenchantment with the founding tenets of Irish nationalism was evidence of intergenerational conflict during the 1950s and 1960s. For the generation who had participated in the Irish revolution, the past was central to their self-image and understanding of the present. By the early 1960s, however, such viewpoints were looking increasingly anachronistic, given that independence had been secured nearly a half-century ago.

The rapid pace of change in the 1960s naturally created uncertainties and fuelled anxieties about the adverse effects of modernity in all its various guises. Urbanization, the emphasis on individual self-fulfilment, and the consequent decline in social solidarity were the subjects of public debate. But the topic that attracted the most publicity was the intrusion of the 'modern' world on 'traditional' Irish lifestyles through the medium of television. The negative impact of television was the subject of much debate well before the establishment of the Irish national service on 31 December 1961.[58] Even at its inception, in the much-quoted televised address on the inauguration of Radio Telefís Éireann, President Éamon de Valera expressed the view that the power of the new medium was a double-edged sword:

> I must admit that sometimes when I think of T.V. and radio and their immense power, I feel somewhat afraid ... Never before was there in the hands of man an instrument so powerful to influence the thoughts and actions of the multitude.[59]

And he continued that while television 'can build up the character of the whole people', it could also 'lead, through demoralization, to decadence and dissolution'.[60]

IV

Other sources of conflict were emerging outside of Ireland that had an Irish dimension. Generational tensions were evident from the mid-1960s, most notably in the campaign for equal rights for women and the moves towards the liberalization of Irish sexual mores.[61] These well-known debates are often framed in the context of the declining moral and social authority of Irish Catholicism in the face of international and domestic challenges, but they may also be viewed as elements of a much longer 'fear of the modern', to use Tom Garvin's phrase, a long-standing feature of Irish nationalism since the late nineteenth century.[62] For instance, life in large anonymous cities was seen as dangerous and with many negative effects both for the individual and the wider nation. De Valera remarked in a Dáil speech in 1938 that 'country life is better for our people and a nation is a better and a strong nation if it is based on country life rather than on city life and city conditions'.[63] For a generation who viewed the simple rural existence as the most desirable lifestyle, the steady decline in the rural population was a lamentable consequence of modernity. One of the recurring themes in the debate about the effects of emigration on post-war Irish society was the perception that life in British and American cities was anathema to the Irish 'character'.[64]

But the 'new' modern Ireland that began to take shape in the 1960s was not without its social problems, which were discussed more openly and frequently than ever before, and on the basis of empirical research rather than impressionistic opinions. One journalist, Michael Viney of *The Irish Times*, set about investigating aspects of the 'hidden Irelands', and catalogued a whole range of social problems from alcoholism to poverty and mental illness. As Diarmaid Ferriter has remarked, Viney became 'almost a one-man department of sociology as he explored Ireland's dark corners'.[65] These were not new problems, of course, though the discussion of these sensitive issues was rarely conducted in the public sphere. Other journalists such as John Healy also explored pressing social issues such as the terminal decline of rural communities in the west of Ireland, a topic that was aired with increasing frequency in the 1960s as rural depopulation was seen as draining away the lifeblood of whole communities. Healy's touching elegy to his home-town, Charlestown, County Mayo, first published in *The Irish Times* as a series of articles in 1967, appeared under the title *Death of an Irish Town* and was a stark reminder that large-scale migration to cities and large towns had profound consequences for those who were left behind in this declining rural population.[66]

While Viney and Healy were journalists who based their findings on first-hand observation, academic research expanded enormously in the 1950s and 1960s with the emergence of professional social science in both Irish universities and other independent bodies such as the Economic and Social Research Institute, founded in 1960.[67] From the late 1950s onwards, a large number of sociological investigations into aspects of life in rural Ireland were completed by individuals and groups sponsored by government departments, semi-state organizations and other public bodies.[68] For instance, the sociologist John Jackson completed a detailed analysis of the effect of emigration on the town of Skibbereen in West Cork in the early 1960s, research that was funded by the Irish National Productivity Committee, a national body in which employers and trade unions were involved.[69] Another landmark in the development of professional social science in Ireland was the publication of the Limerick Rural Survey in 1964, sponsored by the rural development organization Muintir na Tíre and described by J.H. Whyte as the 'first sociological study of an Irish rural area since the work of the Harvard anthropologists Arensberg and Kimball in the 1930s'.[70] This was completed under the direction of Dr Jeremiah Newman, then professor of sociology at Maynooth College and later the bishop of Limerick. Throughout the 1960s and 1970s a large number of sociological studies appeared with clear implications for public policy on the future of rural Ireland, the effects of urbanization and even the very fabric of Irish society itself.

The communication of scholarly research to inform public debate was not, however, confined to social scientists. The Thomas Davis Lectures broadcast on Radio Éireann from 1953 sought to communicate 'the best in contemporary Irish scholarship presented in a form which would hold the interest of the intelligent non-specialist listener'.[71] The series was the brainchild of Professor T.W. Moody of Trinity College Dublin, joint founding editor of *Irish Historical Studies*, a key figure in the professionalization of Irish history and a member of the Irish Broadcasting Council.[72] Throughout the 1950s and 1960s the broadcast lectures, many of which were subsequently published in cheap attractive paperbacks, explored issues relating to the Irish past, some of which were deeply sensitive and inherently controversial such as the Irish revolution and the 1916 Rising. According to the series editor, Rev. F.X. Martin of University College Dublin, Radio Éireann was at first reluctant to accept the proposal for a series on 1916 since 'the rising, hitherto treated as a sacrosanct national epic, was now to be examined in a detached spirit by a group of Irish and British historians'.[73] The dangers of exploring near-contemporary topics were neatly illustrated by the fate of a self-consciously iconoclastic article on 1916 by a mild-mannered Jesuit priest, Fr Francis Shaw: the journal *Studies* held over publication from 1966 until it eventually appeared in 1972 after the death of its author.[74]

V

Traditional interpretations of the post-war history of independent Ireland need to be revisited, as we seek to reconstruct the cultural, social and intellectual frameworks through which people understood the changing everyday world around them. A major shortcoming with the existing historiography is that the 'high' political narrative has been superimposed on the history of the complete society. Historians have made extensive use of official government records, yet for the most part, such documentation only offers an insight into the views of the politician or the bureaucrat. In political terms, independent Ireland in 1945 was isolated, protectionist and insulated from the wider European and Anglo-American world. But this does not necessarily mean that modernity in the sense of being a lived experience developed when Ireland suddenly became 'modern' in the 1960s. In this respect, the changes that were introduced such as the liberalization of the economy (in particular the attraction of overseas investment), the challenges to existing cultural orthodoxies through the media, especially television, and the attempts to introduce measures to reduce social inequality by allowing greater access to the secondary and university system may be paradoxically seen as merely the political establishment following on what were widely perceived by the state's citizenry to be the basic features of a developed, equitable and 'modern' society. This raises tantalizing questions about how subaltern groups drove on social and cultural change in post-war Ireland, often credited as being the unique 'achievement' of the tiny university-educated liberal middle-class élite.

The role of the professional expert as purveyor of knowledge and 'driving forward a vision of the future' was a distinctive feature of late modernity in the western world.[75] As a number of scholars examining post-war British society have argued, over time this extended beyond the realm of simply seeking to influence public policy:

> By the 1950s the authority of experts had become central not only to economic management and social policy, but also to the areas of cultural taste, the urban and rural environments, consumer behaviour and the psychological well-being of communities.[76]

The archaeology of knowledge, to employ a Foucaultian term, and the role of intellectuals of differing backgrounds in shaping both the terms and content of public debate in post-war Ireland is yet to be systematically explored by historians. Lee's sustained analysis of the place of ideas in public debate in twentieth-century Ireland – or perhaps more accurately the absence of sustained intellectual engagement between policy-makers and intellectuals – is a characteristically thoughtful starting point for such an investigation.[77] Other work also indicates the potential for an approach that combines the history of ideas with social and cultural history to reconstruct how values, concepts and mores were formulated, articulated and received.[78] At the heart of such an analysis should be the relationship between social power, authority and knowledge: in other words, who were the 'brokers' of this 'new' modernity and where did the sources of social power and lines of authority rest in post-war Ireland? [79]

'Ireland is an Unusual Place': President Kennedy's 1963 Visit and the Complexity of Recognition

MIKE CRONIN*

State visits by US presidents to Ireland have become commonplace events in recent years, with three of the last four residents of the Oval Office landing at Dublin or Shannon airport for brief trips (George W. Bush, 2004; Bill Clinton, 1995 and 2000; Ronald Reagan, 1984). Prior to the arrival of Reagan, the only other official presidential visitors to those shores had been Richard Nixon in 1970 and John F. Kennedy, the thirty-fifth president of the United States of America, in 1963.[1]

Importantly, the Irish saw Kennedy as more than a visiting dignitary. He was the great-grandson of Patrick Kennedy, born 1823, native of County Wexford and an emigrant to the United States. President Kennedy epitomized the success of the Irish–American project. In him was embodied a narrative that had begun with pre-Famine emigration from Ireland, and ended with his successful return as the most powerful man in the world. Kennedy's visit was also different in that it had no clear political purpose. Whereas Bush (US–European relations), Clinton (Northern Ireland peace process)[2] and Reagan (Cold War politics) had clear foreign policy initiatives to pursue when visiting Ireland, Kennedy's trip has always been posted as a self-indulgent act, a trip driven by personal rather than political motivations. As one writer has recently concluded, Kennedy's 'movements aroused great public interest, and the visit seemed to symbolize the boom atmosphere of the early 1960s'.[3]

As this article will explain, the historical understanding of Kennedy's visit has been one that has centred on a widespread popular memory of the event, the impact of contemporary television coverage, and the added poignancy given to the president's time in Ireland because of his assassination five months later. Given that the visit of Kennedy is so well remembered, indeed is seen as an iconic moment during the Irish process of its emergence from relative isolation in the late 1950s and early 1960s, it is surprising that the event has never been fully interrogated by historians. Dermot Keogh has pointed to the significance of the Kennedy visit, arguing that while it was 'magical for Ireland', the spectacle personified the Ireland of Fianna Fáil Taoiseach Seán Lemass.[4] During his visit Kennedy identified with his Irish audience and 'elevated the role of Ireland in world history'. His youth, wealth and belief in free enterprise and social reform made into flesh the image of what Fianna Fáil wanted to be. As Keogh concluded, 'after the visit, it was possible to believe that the Lemass tide would raise all boats'.[5]

Does then Kennedy's four-day visit say more about Ireland in the early 1960s than it does about a presidential self-indulgence? Or do we need to search for deeper meanings that can be attached to the visit? Put simply, what was the purpose of Kennedy's time in Ireland, how was it projected and managed by the Irish government, and why has it not been better analyzed? To understand the nature of the visit it is perhaps best to examine one reading of the event which challenges the modernizing context advanced by Keogh. Fergal Tobin, rather than seeing Kennedy's time in Ireland as one that spoke to the modernism of the economic reforms of Lemass, argued that 'Kennedy spoke to an Ireland that was passing away.' As such his visit and in particular his speeches, echoing as they did tales of emigration and exile, spoke to a nation that was an 'inert, defeated country which never ceased to contemplate its own miseries and kept warm its old resentments'. On this reading, Kennedy thus offered a bridge between the new industrialized and European nation dreamt of by Lemass and the insular certainties of de Valera's Ireland. The changes instigated by Lemass had shifted the traditions of national identity that had underpinned Ireland for decades, but which, for many in the country, failed to offer an 'alternative definition of nationality as comprehensive and as comforting as that which John Kennedy recalled in the last days of June 1963'.[6] The difficulties of giving Kennedy's visit clear and consensual meaning lies in the complexity of recognition: were the Irish seeing the youthful, wealthy and powerful visitor as a product of what they might aspire to as Ireland developed and modernized in the 1960s? Or did he symbolize the happy ending to a long and painful history of poverty and emigration? For the Irish, Kennedy's presence offered them a mirror to see both a reflection of what they had been and what they might become. The complexity was which reflection they would most recognize and relate to.

THE PURPOSES OF STATE VISITS

Before moving on to the specifics of Kennedy's 1963 visit, and its localized meanings, it is important to understand what the perceived function of state visits actually is. In the most recent literature, the purpose of such a visit has been defined as when 'one nation's leader has the opportunity to reach the public of another nation's, through ceremonial events, improvisational moments and press coverage of the visit [and] to influence and improve public perceptions of a country's national image'.[7] The literature that relates to state visits in other countries is contemporary in focus, and while there has been work on nineteenth- and early twentieth-century royal visits to Ireland, certainly no work has been carried out on the impact of twentieth-century state visits.[8] It has been argued, by Manheim for example, that the state visit has been transformed in recent decades away from a 'government to government' or 'diplomat to diplomat' interaction, to include more recently 'government to people' or public diplomacy initiatives.[9] Public diplomacy is a process whereby governments seek to communicate with foreign publics as a method of heightening an understanding of its aims and policies. Although there were official engagements during Kennedy's visit, it is remembered for and was focused on his interaction with the large crowds of Irish people that he met. While much of the work enabling communication between foreign governments and the people of another nation has been undertaken by cultural organizations (e.g. the British Council), at public events (e.g. World's Fairs, Olympic Games) and through the media and tourist industries, the state visit can deliver, in a short period of time and through a high media profile, 'political advocacy and cultural communication advocacy'.[10]

For any state visit it is important that the visiting dignitary is allowed to promote their own country and its role as a partner to the host nation, and be exposed to a showcase image of the nation that they are visiting. In a mutually advantageous process, both visitor and host allow positive images of themselves to be projected by the media and consumed by the populations of both nations.[11] Major public events such as state visits are said to 'evoke socio-psychological processes of group identification'.[12] But what is actually represented by the national dignitary in state visits, and how does their presence create such group identification?

Heads of state, such as the president of the United States, are endowed with representative status by virtue of their position. In the case of the United States (and in this context the Republic of Ireland), presidents derive their status as a product of the Constitution and their electoral mandate to hold the most senior office. As a result the nation is effectively embodied by the president, and s/he becomes the principal representative of the nation. In order for the United States to be officially represented at any major event or gathering, the president (or an appointed officer, ambassador or secretary of state) must be in attendance. Some office holders, by virtue of their skills and popular appeal, the feelings of consensus that they produce, or their role as figurehead in a time of national crisis, will produce heightened feelings of representativeness and identification, and thus enhanced group identification with their own nation and that which they visit compared to other previous/future office holders. This is especially important in the context of Kennedy. In 1963, even before the heightening of his reputation and the mythologizing of him that followed his assassination, he was immensely popular. He was youthful and glamorous, used the mass media to promote himself as a populist president, had successfully led America through the Cuban missile crisis, and at the Berlin Wall shortly before his arrival in Ireland had added a personal and popular dimension to the Cold War struggle by identifying himself with the people of West Berlin.[13]

The role of Kennedy while in Ireland was as president of the United States, making an official visit to the Republic at the invitation of President de Valera: this meeting of the relevant heads of states symbolized and embodied the relationship between the two nations. While the visit is often remembered for its friendliness and Kennedy's interactions with the crowd, it has to be remembered that all Kennedy's activities and speeches during his visit were carefully choreographed. State visits and official speeches have specific functions and are restricted by protocol and the function, of both visitor and host, as the representative of their nation.[14] The role of Kennedy, Lemass and de Valera is therefore restrictive: all their interaction, especially that which was public during visits, at functions and in giving speeches, was controlled. All acted in a manner becoming of their office, promoted their own national interest and perspective, yet remained alert to the central function of the visit, which was the cultivation of a mutual atmosphere of recognition and representation. Whether at state events or civic visits, when receiving honorary degrees or in public speeches mediated by newspaper, radio and television, Kennedy as visitor spoke to the citizens of the Irish Republic as a whole, and as president of the United States delivered a series of messages which all Americans tacitly endorsed.

PLANNING THE VISIT

The initial process of inviting Kennedy to Ireland began in the spring of 1962. On 14 March 1962, Robert Briscoe, the lord mayor of Dublin, had met Kennedy in Washington. On leaving, Briscoe asked the president when he intended to visit Ireland. It was reported that Kennedy was enthusiastic and was keen to travel to Ireland, but that he needed some special occasion as a justification for absenting himself from day-to-day business in the United States. Kennedy also made it clear that he did not simply want a restful visit, but that he wanted 'all the works' on his arrival in Dublin.[15] The Irish embassy was keen to facilitate such a visit, but was aware that any occasion that was manufactured to allow a visit 'might be considered as a precedent in other countries, which would embarrass him'. The only suggestion that was forthcoming from the ambassador was the celebration of de Valera's eightieth birthday in October 1963.[16] By February 1963 such an 'Irish only' visit was off the cards, and it became clear that Kennedy would visit Ireland only briefly during a larger multi-country European trip in the early summer of 1963. On 27 March 1963, de Valera issued a formal invitation to Kennedy.[17] Two weeks later a cable was sent from Washington to Dublin in which Kennedy accepted the invitation, proposed that the visit should take place on 26 and 27 June to allow him to visit Italy and Germany, and assured de Valera that 'there is no country I would rather visit'.[18] Despite an American request that the official announcement of the visit be made simultaneously by Washington and Dublin on 24 April, the Irish newspapers were carrying the story of the proposed visit within five days of Kennedy's acceptance cable.[19]

When news of Kennedy's visit began to circulate, the thorny question of whether a visit to Northern Ireland would feature on the president's itinerary emerged. British Prime Minister Harold Macmillan, on behalf of Terence O'Neill, the Stormont prime minister, invited Kennedy to travel north and open the Giant's Causeway both as a national park and as a symbolic feature of the province's topography. Kennedy declined the invitation, stating that there was not time in his itinerary.[20] The response was undoubtedly honest, as Kennedy's schedule in Europe was crowded, but it was also important for his tacit rejection of any contact with the North and the complexity of the partition question. Kennedy's trip was an Irish one, a visit that recognized the Irish Republic as a sovereign state, and that played a green card for the benefit of Irish-American voters in the United States in light of the upcoming 1964 presidential election. The language of his trip to Ireland is revealing in that the president, while reflecting regularly on the cause of Irish freedom, never publicly mentioned the partition of Ireland or the existence of Northern Ireland. He therefore can be seen to have embraced the ideal of an Irish Republic, as historically fought for by men like de Valera and Lemass, but by avoiding any explicit reference to the border, he diplomatically diffused any potential political conflict between Dublin, Belfast and London.

Once the decision had been made that Kennedy would indeed visit Ireland, a mass of planning and organization had to be undertaken by the government, including the setting of a schedule. From the time of acceptance to the moment of his arrival, the Irish had two months in which to prepare for its most important international visitor since the papal legate had attended the Eucharistic Congress in 1932.[21] The government formed an inter-departmental committee to plan the visit and liaise between the various parties that were involved. Its first meeting took place on 4 May under that chairmanship of Mr G. Woods, the chief of protocol.[22] Much of the work of the committee involved organizing events while Kennedy was in the country, ensuring the correct diplomatic protocols were followed, arranging for his safe arrival and transit around the country and liaising with the global media outlets that were expected to accompany Kennedy. One of the thorniest issues for the committee, and for the government generally, was setting Kennedy's route. Understandably, every town wanted to welcome the president, and many laid claim to some link with the Kennedy family lineage to reinforce their case or else offered to present him with some award of recognition or honorary title.

In planning for the Kennedy visit to Ireland, the Central Intelligence Agency (CIA) reported on the contemporary state of the host nation.

They concluded that Ireland was a country friendly to the United States, and largely supportive of its ideological beliefs. The only danger that the CIA foresaw for Kennedy was the reaction of the Irish crowd: '[they] will look upon President Kennedy's visit as a triumphal homecoming for one of their own and as a great compliment being paid to them by a world leader ... the police may underestimate the problems involved and the manpower needed to protect the Presidential party from such over-friendliness.'[23] To cope with the demands of such crowds, Garda Commissioner Daniel Costigan cancelled all leave for the duration of the Kennedy trip, and drafted extra men into those counties where the president would visit. In total there would be some 6,500 men on duty for the duration of the visit, and the president would also be accompanied by a special team of Federal Bureau of Investigation (FBI) officers.[24]

The images that would be associated with and projected by the media during Kennedy's visit were of great interest to Irish commentators. The impact of live satellite television and its ability to instantaneously open the visit to a mass audience in Ireland, the United States and beyond was, despite the innovative nature of the technology, well understood. Media coverage of the Kennedy visit was intense, and the planning had been carried out in great detail. It had been decided that the coverage of Kennedy's journey around Ireland would be undertaken by Telefís Éireann and the images provided by them to television companies from the United States and elsewhere. This was a huge test for Telefís Éireann. The service had only been on air since December 1961, and the provision of a constant stream of high-quality images of Kennedy in Ireland, to a large domestic and international audience, was of great importance in proving the technological competence of the Irish broadcasting company. In early June, Éamonn Andrews, chairman of the Radio Éireann board, travelled to the United States to meet with the White House press office to finalize all the details of the coverage.[25] The three major television companies in the United States screened twenty-two special reports during Kennedy's time in Europe, and pictures from the Irish leg of his trip were beamed back live via the Telstar II and Relay satellites.[26] To enable the Telefís Éireann pictures to be relayed to the satellite and onto the United States a special station was constructed at Crescent Quay in Wexford. This would relay the pictures to the BBC receiving station in the Goonhilly Downs in Cornwall, which was able to transmit them to the satellite. The pictures were then beamed down to the Andover station in Maine, which relayed them across the United States. In Ireland, or so one observer noted, 'Irish eyes were glued to television screens from the Aran Islands to the coal quay in Cork.'[27]

Effectively, the Kennedy visit was to be the single most important and biggest public spectacle to ever happen in Ireland. However, which Ireland would the president and the viewing public in the United States and elsewhere see? A *New York Times* feature that had been published shortly after the announcement that the visit would take place alarmed the *Irish Independent*. *The New York Times* reported that 'if all the leprechauns were tossed off their shamrocks this morning it was because of the arrival in Dublin of two advance agents of the White House'. Acknowledging that the dates for the presidential visit had been fixed, the paper felt that Kennedy's decision would lead to 'many an unearned smile and proffer of a Guinness or a Jameson that has been the reward of the American pilgrim'. The *Irish Independent* was appalled. Claiming that the Irish had not lost their sense of humour and could appreciate that the report was trying to be humorous, the paper questioned whether there was a danger that such paddywhackery would set the tone for the visit.[28] The paper was certain that the president would be properly welcomed in Ireland, a welcome 'consonant with his dignity and ours'. He would not, it made clear, be welcomed with 'waves of shillelaghs and caubeens, with shouts of "Erin go brágh" and "top o' the mornin'".[29] Expressing such clear opinions a month before the visit took place signalled the differences between American and domestic perceptions of what kind of country Ireland was. It remained to be seen however whether the Irish public would deliver the dignified welcome that the *Irish Independent* hoped for or whether it would play up to the American stereotype. The American vision of Ireland as both a place of nostalgic whimsy and a predominantly poor and rural country of high emigration had been powerfully reinforced in the 1950s and early 1960s through films such as John Ford's *The Quiet Man* and the 1960 CBS documentary on the contemporary state of the nation, 'Ireland: The Tear and the Smile'.[30]

THE SOCIO-ECONOMIC CONTEXT OF THE VISIT

Despite all the hyperbole and excitement that surrounded Kennedy's visit, what was the contemporary state of Ireland? Clearly it was a radically different one to that from which Kennedy's ancestors had left, but how had the country developed in the years since revolution and

in the period after Ireland's isolationism of the Second World War?
The post-war years and the decade of the 1950s were the most difficult since the founding of the state. As Europe emerged from war with
the job of rebuilding nations and economies, ably assisted by the funds
of the Marshall Plan and the steady advance towards the dropping of
trading restrictions, Ireland often remained inward-looking and
apparently locked into a vicious cycle of a weak economy, slow or non-
existent growth, and high emigration.[31] Between 1956 and 1961
emigration had risen to 14.8 per thousand annually. National income
rates in the 1950s had risen less than 1 per cent, industrial output had
only grown by 1.3 per cent in the same period and unemployment rose
accordingly. Most damning of all, in human terms, was the stark fact
that of the 502,000 10–19 year olds in Ireland at the time of the 1951
census, only 303,000 remained in the country a decade later. The
1950s were also symbolized by the continuation of censorship, a dominant church and near total lack of social modernization.[32]

While many of the socio-economic themes that had dominated the
1950s were still present when Kennedy visited in 1963, the country was,
in many ways, transformed. The global economy boomed during the late
1950s and early 1960s, and because of the development of the
European Economic Community (EEC) and the European Free Trade
Area, trade in Europe increased apace. Although excluded from the EEC,
Ireland benefited from the general upturn in conditions, and the policies
pursued by Lemass consolidated the improvement in the economy. T.K.
Whitaker's *Economic Development* and the publication of Fianna Fáil's
First Programme for Economic Expansion, both in 1958, encouraged the
development of the Irish economy and brought in a spirit of planning
and productive investment. The global and national economic developments and policy initiatives of the late 1950s and 1960s led to an upturn
in the Irish situation. Gross National Product (GNP) grew 4.5 per cent
each year between 1959 and 1963, national output grew by 25 per cent,
unemployment fell by a third and emigration slowed.

In the decade after 1958 other signs of prosperity were apparent:
the number of private cars rose from 143,000 to 330,000, while the
number of tractors grew from 34,000 to 59,000. Since 1953, the BBC
television service was available to certain areas of Ireland, and this was
joined by the Irish national service from 1961. As a result, by the mid-
1960s, there were 348,000 television sets in the country, the viewers
of which were exposed to a different world that moved beyond the
boundaries and expectations of that in which they had grown up,

exposing them to a diet of imported American and British program-
ming. Wider developments also underpinned Irish self-confidence and
brought about broader societal changes. The Second Vatican Council
under Pope John XXIII began its liberalizing agenda in 1962, while
Irish membership of the United Nations since 1955 and its concomitant
role in peace-keeping had improved Ireland's image in the arena of
foreign affairs. The Ireland that Kennedy visited was not then the
depressed nation of the 1950s, but rather one which was taking an
increased role in world affairs, was beginning to liberalize socially, and
whose economy was beginning to grow. While not an instantaneously
prosperous nation, the Ireland of the early 1960s was one that was full
of more self-confidence than had been evident in the 1950s and one
which, although still losing its young people to emigration, had stopped
the massive drain that had been evident in the previous decade.
Kennedy, as the leader of the world's most powerful and prosperous
nation, arrived in Ireland at a time of expectation. He came not only as
the descendant of an Irishman returning home, but as the symbol of
the hope and prosperity of what Ireland might become. For the first
time it seemed in the early 1960s that opportunity and potential wealth,
the very possibilities that had traditionally made emigration to the
United States and elsewhere palatable, might be achievable by remaining in Ireland. As Ronan Fanning commented on Kennedy's arrival, 'the
latter day Hero/Playboy of the Western World and the apotheosis of
the returned Yank who had made good, Kennedy personified the wider
ambitions of a new Ireland in which anything was possible'.[33]

THE VISIT

On the morning of the presidential arrival, the *Irish Press* carried a
special front page. It depicted Kennedy and de Valera, and under the
banner heading 'Welcome Mr President', read:

> Today visiting the homeland of your people you stand for almost
> two centuries of turbulent and always valiant endeavour. You join
> together, as no man has ever done before, the stories of this small
> country and this vast nation to which Ireland has made so many
> contributions, including that important one of the name of
> Kennedy.[34]

Such headlines summed up the complexities of the visit. Kennedy, the dynamic young modernizing president from the United States was returning home to Ireland by way of recognizing his heritage and the historic traditions of that country. He was met by de Valera, a frail and aged man who, although born in the United States, had grown up in Ireland, led the country through a period of revolutionary upheaval, and yet had clung to ideological dogma in the 1940s and 1950s to the detriment of his people. Given such dynamics of personal history, and the ideas that each man represented in their roles as head of state during a state visit, the physical comparisons between the two men and the countries that they embodied stood in stark contrast to each other. Kennedy praised the endeavour of the poor nineteenth-century Irish who had emigrated to prosperity in the United States. His visit coincided, however, with a series of societal and policy changes that sought to expunge forever the lack of opportunity in Ireland that had kept the stream of such emigration alive into the 1950s, and for whom his fellow president, de Valera, was partially responsible.

The arrival of Kennedy in Dublin on 26 June, after his success in Berlin, was keenly anticipated. While the business of his trip to West Germany and elsewhere in Europe was serious, his visit to Ireland was seen as entirely personal. *The New York Times*, while understanding that the visit was important for the Irish as Kennedy was 'one of our boys made good', highlighted the trip as 'one of the most publicized sentimental journeys in history'.[35] A crowd of 10,000 met Kennedy on his arrival at Dublin airport which was recorded by television cameras from around the world that beamed the pictures live to homes across Ireland and the United States.

On the tarmac, Kennedy and de Valera formally greeted each other, and their respective nations, in short speeches. De Valera's speech set the tone of the speeches for the whole trip. It began with a welcome in Irish, moved to a plea for the restoration of the language, and welcomed Kennedy, not only as the president of the United States but as 'the distinguished scion of our race who has won first place amongst his fellow countrymen'. The most important theme, however, was the journey of the Kennedy family as symbolic of the narrative of Irish history. Kennedy was located in de Valera's speech as the successful product of emigration, his family having been driven to the United States 'when people sought refuge [from] the misery of the tyrant laws that drove them from their Motherland'. In response Kennedy also advanced a series of themes that would become common throughout his visit. He echoed de Valera's reading of Ireland's history and its personal cost. In referring to the eight members of his family who had left Ireland in the 1840s, Kennedy concluded that 'no country in the world, in the history of the world, has endured haemorrhage which this island endured over a period of a few years for so many of her sons and daughters.' He claimed that his family, like all their fellow Irish emigrants around the world, kept a special place in their hearts for 'this green and misty island'. All returning emigrants and those Irish-Americans reared on ancestral memory like Kennedy himself who visited Ireland 'had come home'.[36] Beyond the personal and emigrant dimension of his speech that played to images of Ireland as home, Kennedy also highlighted the tradition of freedom in the Irish Republic. This did not refer simply to the struggle of national liberation, but offered an historic lineage for that tradition, and placed Ireland at the heart of the Western struggle in the face of the Eastern bloc countries.

As Kennedy drove into the city centre from the airport it was estimated that half a million people lined the streets to greet him.[37] Gardaí struggled to keep crowds behind the barriers, and at various points on the route, on George's Street and Arran Quay, the crowd broke through the lines to get closer to the presidential procession, as the CIA had predicted. Across Dublin, electrical retail shops had placed television sets in their windows, and these drew large crowds to watch Kennedy's journey across the city. On O'Connell Street cinemas had replaced their billing notices for the current films on show with the message 'Welcome President Kennedy'.[38] Kennedy's journey across the city ended at the American Ambassador's Residence in Phoenix Park, where he was to stay during his visit.

On 27 June, Kennedy undertook the most personal visit during his stay in Ireland. He travelled to New Ross and on to Dunganstown, County Wexford, to meet his Irish relatives. Both places, like all those that Kennedy visited, were completely redecorated. Platforms were erected for speeches, and all possible facilities made available to the press. Most pressing was the need for extra power and communications networks for the television coverage. Emergency phones to keep the president in touch with the White House were fitted everywhere he went, including four in the house of his relatives. The impact of Telefís Éireann's coverage of the Kennedy visit was also apparent on his distant Irish cousin, Mary Ryan. For the purpose of his visit she had installed in the family home in Dunganstown its first television so that she could watch every moment of his stay in the country.[39] It was a purchasing and viewing decision that was made by many of her fellow countrymen and women and ensured, as it was the first iconic national television moment, that everyone remembered Kennedy's visit even if they never saw him in the flesh.

The significance of New Ross, as the American papers reminded their readers, was that it was the departure point for Kennedy's great-grand-father, Patrick J. Kennedy, when he left Wexford in 1848 for a new life in the United States, impelled as he was 'by the potato famine and an urge to get ahead'.[40] In his speech to a crowd estimated at 10,000 at New Ross, Kennedy kept the emigration theme alive by remarking that he was glad to see in the crowd 'a few cousins who did not catch the boat'.[41] He was aware that if his great-grandfather had not been forced to leave Ireland, then rather than being president, he would 'be work-ing over at the Albatross Company or perhaps for John V. Kelly'.[42] The visit to Wexford was compared to his high-profile and politically tense trip to Berlin before he came to Ireland. Whereas Berlin had been about Cold War politics, Wexford was about coming home: this was a presi-dent who used his 'charm to work wonders on his own people'.[43]

His visit to the family in Dunganstown, the home of his great-grandfather, was viewed by the press as 'the great and most joyous moment of his Irish visit ... he captured the hearts of the people of the land whence his forefathers came'. In a similar vein, *The New York Times* referred to the event as 'a day of Irish sentiment'.[44] Although the president made no formal speeches at Dunganstown, he did raise his tea cup in a toast, declaring 'we will drink a cup of tea to all the Kennedys who have gone away and all the Kennedys who have remained at home'.[45] He was observed not as a visiting dignitary but as 'a neighbouring farmer [who] might have dropped in for an after-noon exchange of information about crops or the weather'.[46]

After leaving Dunganstown Kennedy travelled to Wexford town, where he placed a wreath at the statute of Commander John Barry and was made a freeman of the borough. Following the wreath-laying he made a short speech that compared the role of the Irish, including Barry, in the fight for American independence with the contemporary world of 1963. He stressed how central the Irish role had been, and continued to be, in the fight for freedom in the world. He spoke of how Ireland had, despite centuries of oppression, maintained her sense of national identity and strong faith. In this, the country offered itself as a model to all nations that were currently subjugated or those peo-ple who felt that freedom was on the run: 'Ireland and its experience has one special significance, and that is the peoples' fight.'[47]

After his return from County Wexford, Kennedy attended a garden party at the official home of President de Valera, Áras an Uachtaráin, and later a state dinner at Iveagh House in Dublin. It was a formal affair, attended by all the leading political and diplomatic figures in Ireland. In planning the event and drawing up the guest list, one problem was what the Irish government should do about inviting leading nationalist figures from Northern Ireland. The matter was discussed in the Dáil on 22 May 1963, and the government responded by assuring the chamber that 'in accordance with custom, the invitation list will extend to Northern Ireland.'[48] In the event, official invitations were issued by the taoiseach's office to all anti-partitionist MPs and senators from Stormont, the editor and manager of the *Irish News* and the president and vice-president of the Irish Association for Cultural and Economic Affairs.[49] The decision not to extend an invitation to the Stormont prime minister, members of his government or the Labour Party was seen by many commentators as a deliberate rebuke. The *Northern Whig and Belfast Post*, for example, led with the headline 'Kennedy Visit Snubs NI Government'.[50]

On 28 June Kennedy left Dublin by helicopter at nine in the morning and flew to Cork. He spent little over an hour in the city. From his landing site at Collins Barracks he was driven in a motorcade through packed streets to the city hall, where presentations were made. He returned to Dublin in mid-afternoon and went to Arbour Hill to lay a wreath on the graves of the executed leaders of the 1916 Rising. From there Kennedy travelled to the centre of Dublin to make the most important speech of his visit: an address to a joint session of the Irish parliament, the oireachtas. The occasion of his speech was the first time that television cameras had ever been allowed into the oireachtas, and the whole spectacle was organized so as to ensure maximum coverage by the various branches of the media.[51] The joint session took place even though the Attorney General's Office had advised the government that there was no provision in the Constitution for such a dual gathering. He did acknowledge, however, that, given the importance of the occasion, he could not see any legal or constitutional objection to the joint session taking place.[52]

In his speech Kennedy stressed again his Irish roots and talked about Ireland's historic role in the pursuit of freedom. In a reference to Ireland's role in the United Nations and on the Council of Europe, Kennedy argued that the nation's greatest function was as a 'defender of the weak and voice of the small'. In linking his trip to Berlin with his trip to Wexford, where he had listened to a performance of the local anthem, he said that 'those who suffer beyond that wall of shame I saw on Wednesday in Berlin must not despair. Let them remember, as I did yesterday, the "Boys of Wexford, who fought with heart and hand to burst in twain the galling chain and free our native land".'[53] He also used his speech to the oireachtas to again stress Ireland's contribution to the world despite its small size. He told the Dáil and Seanad members that no larger nation had managed to keep Christianity and Western culture alive during the Dark Ages, had contributed so much to the cause of American independence or provided the world with so much literary and artistic genius. Ireland, he told the gathering, had played a central role in censuring the Hungarian revolution, and was a model to those demanding freedom. Building on this theme, he asked: 'How many times was Ireland's quest for freedom suppressed, only to have that quest renewed by the succeeding generation?'[54]

On the same day as his oireachtas speech, Kennedy also became the forty-ninth freeman of the city of Dublin, and was awarded honorary degrees by both the National University of Ireland and Trinity College Dublin at Dublin Castle.[55] The evening was spent at a private dinner with President de Valera and leading members of government at Áras an Uachtaráin.

On his last day in Ireland, Kennedy travelled to Galway and Limerick before heading to Shannon airport for his departure from Ireland. In Galway, at a mass gathering in Eyre Square, he was granted the freedom of the city after a musical performance by local schoolchildren. In his speech he returned once more to the theme of emigration, and informed his crowd that 'if the day was clear enough and if you went down to the bay, and you looked west, and your sight was good enough, you would see Boston, Massachusetts. And if you did, you would see working on the docks those same Doughertys and Flahertys and Ryans and cousins of yours who have gone to Boston and made good.'[56]

At Shannon airport Kennedy made his final speech before departing. He told the gathered crowd and those watching on television that 'Ireland is a very special place. It is in a very real sense the mother of a great many people, a great many millions of people ... a great many nations.' His next stop was London, for a meeting with British Prime Minister Harold Macmillan. Playing up the theme of Irishness to the end, Kennedy, rather than referring explicitly to his destination, simply told the crowd that he was flying to 'another country'. His final words before leaving were: 'I am taking, as I go back to America, all of you with me.'[57]

REACTIONS AND MEANINGS

At the close of the Kennedy visit the *Irish Press* sought to understand the significance of what Ireland had witnessed in the preceding days. The paper's editorial took pride in the way that the president had applauded Ireland's role in its struggle for independence, and its subsequent role in the search for world peace. It acknowledged the harsh reality that had led him to Dunganstown to meet his relatives, a history of hunger and emigration. The editorial sought to give meaning to the welcome that Kennedy had received from the Irish people. It concluded that the enthusiastic crowds and the hearty greetings the president had received everywhere he went were a result of the Irish tradition of friendship, their respect for his position as the most powerful man in the West and his symbolic importance as the most successful Irish emigrant.[58] *The New York Times* recognized that Kennedy's European visit, which had been undertaken in the face of domestic press criticism, had been a success. The paper understood that Kennedy's impact in Ireland was such that, when he left, 'from Mizen Head to Fair Head in Antrim, there were sad hearts in Ireland'. For Kennedy himself, his trip 'home' had provided 'three days of sentiment, blarney and happy political going'.[59]

In retrospect it is surprising, considering Kennedy's place as a 'Cold Warrior' and the complexities of contemporary Ireland, how infrequently politics appeared as part of the visit. Especially striking was the complete absence of the partition issue from the public rhetoric. Neither was his visit, with one exception, the focus for any demonstrations on the issue. Only at the time of his arrival in Dublin was the partition issue raised. As Kennedy drove into the city a lone protestor held aloft a banner that proclaimed 'Undivided Ireland welcomes you – no partition for the Congo, why Ireland?' The press noted that most people out on the streets during the visit were 'willing to forget that the six Northern counties still are under British rule'.[60] The only explicitly political meeting of the visit was one conducted behind closed doors on Kennedy's first morning in Ireland. Before leaving to travel to other parts of the country, Kennedy had a morning meeting with Seán Lemass. This meeting, which took place at the American embassy and lasted an hour, was the only formal political discussion during Kennedy's time in Ireland. The two men discussed Ireland's future role in the European Economic Community, a prospect which Kennedy welcomed. However, he expressed a degree of scepticism over de

Gaulle's attitude towards Irish and British membership of the community. Unlike his public avoidance of the issue, Kennedy directly asked Lemass whether there was any progress being made on partition. Lemass outlined his belief that any solution had to be forged between Ireland and Britain, and that any international pressure, from the United States or other nations, would not alter the situation. Kennedy stated his belief that the prospects for a solution would be improved if Harold Wilson's Labour Party were to take control in Britain, but Lemass disagreed, saying that earlier experiences of Labour did not support this view. Kennedy moved the discussion on, and praised Ireland's role in the United Nations, and the Irish military presence in the Congo. The president also explained that he was less than optimistic about any nuclear test-ban treaty with the Soviet Union and that he feared the rise of China as a nuclear power by the 1970s. Despite these challenges, he considered that the state of global politics was less perilous than it had been even five years earlier.[61] While the minutes of this meeting are revealing of the mindset of the two leaders, it was a fleeting moment in a visit that has to be seen as celebratory rather than political, one which conforms to the ideals of state visits as outlined earlier, rather than one that sought to engender political controversy or division.

It is difficult to quantify what benefits were accrued by the Kennedy visit. Clearly the close Irish–American relationship was cemented further, and Ireland's transatlantic business balance, especially with respect to tourism, was boosted. The only directly tangible product of the visit was the agreement that an Irish American Foundation would be founded that would sponsor cultural exchanges between the two countries. The establishment of the foundation was encouraged by Dr Kiernan, the Irish ambassador in Washington. Kiernan was aware that Kennedy, following the announcement of the itinerary for his visit to Europe, had been criticized in the American press. The State Department, while acknowledging that Kennedy's visit to Ireland was always 'a sentimental journey', was keen to build up the visit so that it had an identifiable purpose and a context beyond the sentimental. The department identified the formal announcement of the establishment of the foundation as something that would give the Irish leg of his European tour a clear purpose.[62]

The Kennedy visit to Ireland has been seen by many commentators as a defining moment in Irish history. Immediately after Kennedy's time in Ireland, and especially in light of his subsequent assassination, commemorative books and films were issued that detailed his itinerary and brought together many of the photographs that had been taken.[63] In the years immediately following the event, works offering analysis of June 1963 began to emerge. Tony Gray wrote that the visit 'probably did more than any other single factor to boost Irish morale and destroy the last vestige of national self-consciousness', while Donald Connery argued that Kennedy's presence gave 'the essential business of creating and sustaining Irish self-confidence an historic boost'.[64] It is clear that the visit did coincide with a changing set of social and economic circumstances in Ireland and a heightened sense of national self-confidence.

Through the television and media coverage of the visit, Irish-Americans were given a greater sense of Ireland as a place where they would receive a friendly welcome. In Kennedy, the Irish national tourist agency, Bord Fáilte, had the best personal endorsement of Ireland as a holiday destination that they could ever have dreamt of. In the years following Kennedy's visit inward tourism from the United States grew, as did the number of American businesses choosing to invest in the country. Perhaps more important than such tangible economic benefits were the messages that were conveyed during the visit. The two great themes in all Kennedy's speeches were those of successful Irish emigration and the role of Ireland in the fight for freedom. To the Ireland of 1963, these themes were ones that most people hoped were products of yesteryear. While they understood the need for an Irish role in bodies such as the United Nations and on peacekeeping missions, the exploits of the revolutionary period belonged to popular memory, and while they could be applauded – as they were during the fiftieth anniversary celebrations of the 1916 Rising – Ireland was no longer a nation driven by the need for national revolutionary self-definition. Equally, when Kennedy spoke of successful emigration, it was hoped, especially after the experience of the 1950s, that no future generation would have to take the boat or plane to a foreign country. So, while Kennedy embraced two themes of which the Irish could be proud, they were perhaps products of Ireland's past that were in the process of being consigned to history. The thousands of people who cheered Kennedy did so because he was powerful and glamorous; he was one of them, and a success story. But he also spoke about and eulogized an old Ireland, the Ireland perhaps that belonged to the then 81-year-old de Valera rather than the new Ireland of Lemass.

CHAPTER EIGHT

Sex and the Archbishop: John Charles McQuaid and Social Change in 1960s Ireland

DIARMAID FERRITER

Few would dispute that John Charles McQuaid, appointed arch-bishop of Dublin in 1940, was the towering figure of twentieth-century Irish Catholicism. Born in Cootehill, County Cavan in 1895, McQuaid was educated at St Patrick's College in Cavan and later Blackrock College and Clongowes before he entered the Holy Ghost novitiate at Kimmage Manor in 1913. He went on to study at University College Dublin and completed a doctorate in Rome. Ordained in 1924, he was appointed dean of studies at Blackrock College in 1925 and served as a young president of the college from 1931 to '39 before being appointed as a relatively young member of the Irish Catholic hierarchy in 1940. It was an appointment that caused surprise, as it was the first time a priest from outside the ranks of the regular clergy had been appointed archbishop of Dublin since John Thomas Troy in 1786.

From his appointment, until his forced retirement in 1972, there were virtually no areas of Irish Catholic life that McQuaid did not influence, or at least attempt to influence. Clergy and politicians alike could ill-afford to ignore his views or defy his commands, as he kept abreast of developments in the spiritual and secular spheres. His interests, some would say obsessions, were meticulously recorded in his voluminous personal archive, held in the Dublin diocesan archives to which researchers were given access in 1997.

McQuaid was very much an enforcer of what today is often depicted as a suffocating, repressive and authoritarian church. By the end of the 1960s, the climate of international Catholicism was at odds with his pre-Vatican II outlook, and he looked askance at growing ecumenical trends; but in tandem, criticism of his style of leadership became more vocal. The perception of him, and perhaps Éamon de Valera, as having outstayed their welcome has led to hostile assessments in recent years, and their place in history has been castigated by those who in the 1960s began to experience intellectual disenchantment with 'traditional' Ireland. Novelist John Banville summed this attitude up well when he wrote in 1995 of an Ireland in the 1940s and 1950s that was 'a demilitarised totalitarian state in which the lives of its citizens were to be controlled, not by a system of coercive force and secret policing, but by a kind of applied spiritual paralysis maintained by an unofficial federation between the Catholic clergy, the judiciary, the civil service and politicians'.[1]

John Cooney, a veteran journalist who has admitted to being somewhat obsessed with McQuaid,[2] published his book *John Charles McQuaid: Ruler of Catholic Ireland* in 1999, having spent the previous few years researching in the archbishop's archive. According to Cooney, McQuaid was very conscious of his place in history: 'The very fact that he kept 700 boxes of detailed documentation is proof of that. He is a historian's dream because he has nice crisp assessments. His whole system was based on an espionage system, so he thinks like J. Edgar Hoover on whom he very much modelled himself. So in the whole of his archives you get the anatomy of the whole of Irish society, not just the Church.'

Cooney has been particularly vocal on what he regards as the most interesting and, indeed, unattractive of McQuaid's traits:

> Where things go off the rails a bit I think is that he's not just prepared to deal with the social issues, to make Ireland a better society. His weakness is that he's totally obsessed with sex, and it's the imposition of a very severe code of sexual conduct, the opposition to 'filthy' books and the opposition to the great writers, the snooping on people about their sexual mores, the obsession with purity, segregation of boys and girls, that girls have to be primarily trained in domestic education, to be housewives and so forth, the very fact that he's against mixed sports. His whole attitude to Irish society becomes therefore about him being 'the spy in the cab': he's almost like Ceausescu [former Romanian dictator] or any of these Eastern European leaders – he's bringing Ireland more and more under a kind of spiritual terrorism that is austere, that is

backward looking and which is also pretty strict theologically. By the late 1950s, he's pretty well taken on everyone in the state ... When you look at his archive, you can see he's got priests and laity, even people like Frank Duff of the Legion of Mary are effectively his spies.[3]

In contrast, Deirdre McMahon, in a perceptive overview of McQuaid's time as archbishop published in 2000, warned against the 'crude caricatures of hidebound Catholic reaction with which McQuaid has become identified since his death in 1973'.[4] As McMahon points out, many benefited from his public and private charity, and she argued that his life and career 'cannot be understood without encompassing this context of change in the life of his church and his country'.[5]

A phenomenally hard worker, McQuaid hand-wrote thousands of letters each year, and presided over a diocese that expanded during his archbishopric from 81 to 115 parishes, as well as co-ordinating a large number of welfare activities. He also forged close links with the English hierarchy through the establishment of an Emigrant Welfare Bureau and devoted much time to the physically and mentally handicapped and to the building of hospitals, as well as creating awareness about social problems such as alcoholism. He was absolutist about the interpretation and implementation of church teaching, and through various intermediaries he sought to monitor the activities of those regarded as dissident and a threat to his way of doing things.

In 2004, Tom Garvin returned to the fray with his assessment of McQuaid, describing him as 'an odd mixture of the progressive, the reactionary, the creative and the authoritarian'.[6] Garvin cites his determination to destroy the careers of those who were perceived to have stepped out of line in the conduct of their personal lives, including short story writer Frank O'Connor and his partner 'who were deprived of state employment in Irish radio on the grounds that they were giving public scandal by living together. Years later, in 1965, he ensured the dismissal of John McGahern ... from his job in the teaching profession. In both cases, the obsessively sexual nature of the archbishop's preoccupations was obvious.'[7]

Elsewhere in his work, Garvin drew attention to the changes of the 1960s and the fact that 'with the new freedoms (including the arrival of the contraceptive pill) came sexual openness and the end of the fear of powerful people', and he concluded that the collapse of clerical power in Ireland toward the very end of the twentieth century was directly related to the obsessional nature of the Catholic clergy's attitude towards people's sexual lives.[8] It is interesting to examine the extent to which the archive of McQuaid reflects these pressures and these battles. Arguably, it is on the issue of sex that McQuaid was finally defeated in the 1960s, and it is possible, by delving deep into his archive, to get a sense of an archbishop and a church under a degree of siege.

McQuaid was, more often than not, preoccupied with controlling discussion of religion. Sex was only one of the areas with which he was concerned, and he was sometimes preoccupied with it precisely because he realized there was a growing resistance to traditional Catholic teaching in relation to sexual morality. The determination of many people to make their own decisions about sexual activity and to seek out answers and information about sex meant that the labels applied to McQuaid by Cooney – 'ruler of Catholic Ireland' or 'undisputed champion of Catholic supremacy'[9] – actually ring somewhat hollow by the 1960s and the early 1970s, when he is 'brooding in his Victorian Gothic mansion in Killiney' having, it seems, been punished by Rome and deprived of the cardinal's hat for his failure to adapt to Vatican II. The truth is that Irish society, rather than McQuaid, had become obsessed with sex by the 1960s, and if it is true that you can find the whole anatomy of Irish society in his archives, then it is inevitable that much of McQuaid's archival material from the 1960s will be concerned with responding to the growing tide of liberalism.

More controversially, John Cooney was determined to link McQuaid to sexual abuse, directly, by relying on an anonymous and unreliable account of an alleged assault by McQuaid on a boy in a Drumcondra pub, and, indirectly, by asserting in 2003 that 'it is time for the present government to order the Gardaí to trawl the McQuaid archive and investigate the extent and the roots of clerical child sex abuse. Until this is done, the McQuaid legacy will continue to haunt the Irish Catholic Church.'[10] Following McQuaid's death, the Protestant archbishop of Dublin recalled not McQuaid's instilling of fear or his obsession with control but 'his wonderful care for the poor and his great concern for individuals',[11] which is supported by plenty of material in his archives. This points to one of the main weaknesses of Cooney's approach to McQuaid; he has been determined to blame McQuaid for the revelations that haunted the church twenty years after his death, but the attempt to make him a scapegoat for all that was wrong with the Catholic Church in the last century, and ignore all the other work he did, is a simplification too far. Undoubtedly, McQuaid had skeletons in his diocesan cupboard on the issue of sexual abuse. In 1960, Fr Paul McGennis, a priest of his diocese, sent pornographic photographs of children to be developed in England. The laboratory contacted the Gardaí. They in turn contacted McQuaid, who arranged for the priest to have 'treatment', but the priest continued to work and prey on children, and was eventually convicted in 1997.[12]

There is no doubt McQuaid and other bishops failed to protect children from paedophiles. But as the Ferns Report into clerical child sex abuse presented to the Irish government in October 2005 revealed, there was also a fundamental failure by the civil authorities to act, and completely inadequate social services.[13] True, McQuaid was dominant in his own archdiocese, but he did not control the others, and there is too much of a tendency to assume that he was the only bishop in twentieth-century Ireland. True, he won some of his political battles, but he also lost some (including, in the long run, the most celebrated of all – the issue of state intervention in the health services) and was challenged by de Valera and others, who were determined that he would not reduce the political class to subservience.

He also lost the war against social change and sexual liberalization in the 1960s. Although it is apparent from his archive that increased sexual permissiveness was not his only preoccupation – he acted on new social problems such as drug addiction and juvenile crime, adapted well to the communications age by setting up the Catholic Communications Office and encouraged training in television – he retained a deep distrust of social liberalization and ecumenism and was deeply unhappy with the changes introduced by the Vatican II Council.

In this sense he was a prisoner of his own upbringing and theological training and had a degree of paranoia that manifested itself in a personality that was intimidating and defensive. In April 1966, the theological journal *Herder Correspondence* editorialized scathingly about his failure to inspire the clergy and the laity and ascribed this to McQuaid's personality, with its 'unconquered shyness, the martyr complex, the dislike of public occasions and the penchant for the unnecessary harsh or humiliating phrase'.[14]

It is important to note that McQuaid's archive is not just about those who were in Dublin; it was also about those who left. Many women, in particular, had emigrated from Ireland in the 1940s and '50s. In conversation with renowned writer Sean O'Faolain, one woman summed it up succinctly: 'I saw what my mother went through

– not for me, thank you.'[15] Church leaders were often suspicious as to their motives for emigrating and seemed to believe that once outside of Ireland they would be sexually and socially compromised; that it would be much more difficult to tame them and hem them in – one of the reasons for McQuaid's decision to establish the Emigrant Welfare Bureau in 1942.

Change was also in the air in the 1960s for those who stayed at home. As June Levine recalled in her acclaimed book *Sisters*, 'It was female anger, subtle, veiled but there. It was an anger the cause of which was only partly recognised or understood. It was a hangover, an almighty international hangover. It was an anger which clearly said: "ok the awful 50s are gone; things were going right for a change." Going right for the boys. But what about us?'[16] Part of this female anger involved closely observing the previous generation of mothers and a determination not to repeat their mistakes. Nuala O'Faolain's mother, who had to cope with thirteen pregnancies, according to O'Faolain 'did not want anything to do with child-rearing or house-work. But she had to do it. Because she fell in love with my father and they married, she was condemned to spend her life as a mother and a homemaker. She was in the wrong job.'

More importantly for McQuaid, theological and legal arguments that supplanted the personal testimony of women with regard to contraception were being critically challenged. In the senate, Mary Robinson, first elected in 1969, highlighted the dilemma of women with many children who desired no more, but lived in a country with no contraception legally available.

Tom Garvin makes the point that McQuaid 'liked women, enjoyed their company and wished them to be good housewives and cooks, on the model of French women of the time'.[17] But it is also the case that many were rejecting that role, or were too impoverished in his diocese to afford that role or find it satisfying. In 1971, McQuaid's final pastoral as archbishop was on the issue of contraception, and entitled *Contraception and Conscience*. Perhaps there was an added urgency to this message, given that so many women were now defying church teaching in the aftermath of the issuing of the encyclical *Humane Vitae* (1968) that reiterated the Catholic Church's opposition to contraception, and because feminism was one of the movements with which McQuaid was uncomfortable.

But contraception was only one challenging subject for him in the 1960s; others included the behaviour of Irish Catholics abroad, television, new perspectives on marriage, new publications with sexual content, and the fact that the church was being more closely scrutinized than ever before.

These challenges ultimately led to a siege mentality, summed up in McQuaid's exasperated response to yet another query from the media. In March 1970 he wrote to Osmund (Ossie) Dowling, his faithful and often fawning press secretary: 'I am very tired of RTÉ's attention to Bishops and priests. I do not understand why they do not pay attention to the Army, the Law, Medicine and especially journalism; fruitful fields for investigators. They are not anxious to promote the Kingdom of God.'[18]

Herein lay the weakness of McQuaid in the face of the changes of the 1960s – he was still refusing to grasp or accept the fact that sex sold, and one of the reasons so many journalists wanted to ask so many questions was that the church (and McQuaid) were struggling with sexual issues, if not delusional about them. In April 1965, journalist Tim Pat Coogan requested replies from McQuaid to a questionnaire he had asked him to fill in for a forthcoming book. McQuaid wrote to Dowling: 'I shall not meet Mr Coogan; the questions are impertinent intrusions with my personal life or tendentious misrepresentations in several cases. Only yesterday the Bishops warned me that this man is going to write a flaming book of criticism.'[19]

Nonetheless, McQuaid did draft replies to the questions (which were never sent to Coogan), including the boldest one which read: 'Is it fair to say that the Irish church is obsessed with sex and fails to concern itself sufficiently with things like poverty, lack of equal educational opportunity for all, the level of widows and orphans pensions?' McQuaid's reply was as follows: 'No. There is probably a saner attitude to sex in this country than almost anywhere else. Family life is stable, women are respected, and vocations are esteemed. Sex, in the sense used here – illicit sex – is a sin and is the concern of the church. The other comparatives are not sins.'[20]

Coogan and others were well aware, of course, that this was a complete fallacy. The myth that the Irish were the most sexually pure race on earth was beginning to wear thin. McQuaid was aware of this façade too, particularly in view of the anger and disbelief with which *Humane Vitae* was greeted in certain quarters by those who had expected the church to show more flexibility in relation to contraception. In November 1968 McQuaid wrote to the principal of the Irish School of Administration, objecting to a proposed debate with the motion 'That

the people of Ireland should reject *Humanae Vitae*': 'While it is unde-
niable that for some persons this teaching will involve great difficulty,
it is for me a matter for amazement that your school could, in such
terms, propose to deal with an encyclical letter that is deliberately
meant to safeguard the sanctity of marriage.' To add insult to injury,
Ossie Dowling had been asked to chair the meeting. McQuaid
regarded this invitation as 'provocative and hurtful'.[21]

The previous year, Peter Lennon had written to McQuaid seeking
help with his film, which eventually became *Rocky Road to Dublin*.
McQuaid accused Lennon of previous 'gross misrepresentations', a
reference to Lennon's articles in British newspapers about Irish
Catholicism, but Ossie Dowling encouraged McQuaid to help him on
the grounds that 'he, too, has a soul to save'. Lennon wanted to use Fr
Michael Cleary in the film, to which McQuaid tetchily responded: 'I
shall pick the priest.'[22] But it was in fact Cleary who was used, pranc-
ing about and singing in a maternity ward and advising a young
married couple about their future together.

In reacting to the likes of Lennon, McQuaid's main preoccupation
was to control discussion of religion and prevent the use of religion for
entertainment, but he could do little to prevent Lennon's film from
confronting the difficult issues. One of the most powerful moments in
the film is when a young woman talks anonymously off-camera about
the issue of contraception: As Angela Bourke recorded: 'Only one
woman speaks in this film ... she tells of yearly pregnancies since her
marriage at 21, followed by a miserable three-year effort at birth control. The words *coitus interruptus* roll off her tongue more than once,
"I felt all the time guilty," she says, "and I hated it."' She sounds like a
person with resources; she had access to doctors, but she went to confession and she told the priest:

> And do you know what he told me to do?' 'Go home like a good
> child and move into another room, because as long as you're
> sleeping with him, you're the occasion of his sin.' 'Anyway,' she
> concludes with resignation, they're always on the men's side in
> this country, and so are the doctors. They think women should
> grin and bear it, and put up with it, because, you know, we're
> Catholics and we shouldn't be making it harder for the men.[23]

This woman, perhaps, was unlucky with her priest. Ireland's best-known
agony aunt, Angela Macnamara, who wrote for the *Sunday Press*,
found that after the *Humanae Vitae* encyclical her postbag began to

bulge with letters from people having difficulties with it (she herself was 'gob smacked by the encyclical'): 'At first my responses swung somewhere in between. Suggesting that couples speak to their own priest in the privacy of the confessional brought me to realise that "shopping around" for an understanding priest had begun. There was an unseemly, but understandable, rush for the "easy man". Even from the early stage the public were not taking this encyclical lying down. (If I may pun on it).'[24]

A further challenge to the church was the appearance of family planning clinics, the first of which opened in Merrion Square, Dublin, in April 1967. It was open three evenings weekly; as *Hibernia* put it, 'a quiet start has been made to a scheme with considerable significance'. It was formed by five doctors and two housewives, including journalist, broadcaster and mother of eleven Marie Mullarney, and the clinic was aimed at all income groups.[25]

McQuaid was made well aware that not all his priests were toeing the line. Although an article in the *Irish Press* had noted in September 1966 that 'marriage guidance is scarce in Ireland. Scarce, that is, outside the doctor's surgery – and sometimes within also',[26] McQuaid appointed thirty marriage guidance counsellors for the diocese in the same year. He commented pointedly and defensively two years later, lest people thought it was just a modern response to fertility issues, that 'It would be a serious error to think that a marriage advisory service has not been utilised until recently. Such assistance has been the normal work of the church since the very beginning.'[27] As he put to Barrett in 1956, 'the idea of putting the marriage counselling into the [Catholic Social Welfare] Bureau as a separate section is excellent, if I may say it, because it was my idea'.[28]

But as Fr Peter Cunningham, a priest working in the marriage counselling centre, explained to him in 1967, 'During 1966, there were 6,559 marriages in the archdiocese and only 972 couples passed through our course. It is hoped that many more would be willing to take part in shorter, improved courses.'[29] Another priest involved in this work, Fr Michael Browne, made it clear to McQuaid in April 1970:

> In Dublin there are only a small number of doctors who are genuinely interested in the temperature method of family planning; a smaller number again recommend it to their patients and help them with it … one has good reason to believe that the majority

of doctors regard the method as too time consuming for them as well as being too complicated and too restrictive for the average person. In very many cases the easy way out for the doctor is to prescribe the pill.[30]

It was not just the doctors McQuaid had to worry about. It was also some priests. In November 1971 he received a letter from a young couple in the Dublin suburb of Crumlin. They were engaged to be married and had attended lectures of the pre-marriage course in the College of Industrial Relations. The letter writer's uncle had encouraged them to go; he was essentially, in a move McQuaid would have been proud of, using them as spies, as he and his wife were members of the Right to Life and Nazareth Family Movements. A few comments from the lecturer Fr Reynolds were recorded as follows:

> 'The pope has not condemned the use of the pill' and 'It was up to your own conscience': Fr Reynolds then made his reply by stating that a cardinal had given permission to nuns in the Congo to take the pill as precaution against being raped, and he then continued to say that if a cardinal could give permission it was good enough for him.

But worse was to follow. They complained to another lecturer, Fr Baggott, who asserted that *Humanae Vitae*

> ... was only an opinion of the Pope which he did not agree with. We pointed out that this was against the natural law and Fr Baggot then said that shaving and cutting one's nails was also against the natural law and he then went on to give an example of Philip II of Spain refusing to change the direction of a river for the betterment of the community because he considered this to be against the natural law. We then asked him was he intending to express his opinion to the class and he stated that he would give a balance which in our opinion he had no right to do. We feel that it is a sad reflection in the Catholic city of Dublin that these personal opinions were being put forward at a pre-marriage course in this diocese.[31]

McQuaid had always concerned himself with the poverty of Dublin, and he was well aware of the difficulties large families gave rise to. Some of the most extraordinary and heart-rending documents in his archive are contained in the Catholic Social Welfare Bureau family welfare section, containing letters of distress mostly from mothers with fathers imprisoned or unemployed, some facing eviction, many living on the eldest daughters' earnings, trying to rear nine, ten, eleven, twelve or even thirteen children on a pittance. It would be a simplification to reduce all these problems to the issue of contraception, but of course it was relevant.

A typical letter came on behalf of a family of nine children in Raheny, ranging in age from 16 to 9 weeks: 'the birth of their ninth child and was in hospital for longer than usual. During this time the eldest girl, the only wage earner at present, was kept at home to run the house.'[32] These people, of course, were not going to challenge McQuaid or his teaching; these were, after all, essentially distressing begging letters, with the authors stressing their impeccable Catholic credentials, but there is the occasional hint of resentment that they were so resigned to their situations. In December 1968 the brother of a mother of ten children, ranging in age from 6 months to 16 years, wrote to McQuaid on her behalf, after the family had been evicted from their home in Ballyfermot:

> My sister's devotion is such that when I touched the subject of her distress, she merely replied: 'Blessed Martin will not let us down and God is good.' She also said there are plenty of others just as badly off. Well, your Lordship, while such remarks are very complimentary to the teaching of the church, I think you'll agree that in this particular case, a slightly more realistic approach is called for on the part of my sister.[33]

The author of this letter was now residing in England, which was significant. Many in the Irish Catholic Church, including McQuaid, were conscious that Irish Catholics in England could sometimes begin to question the faith in a more detached way. This detachment was one of the reasons he had established the Emigrant Welfare Bureau in June 1942. Some of those working for the bureau, or on its behalf, sent McQuaid detailed reports of the moral challenge facing Irish emigrants, and the bureau was still active during the period covered by this chapter.

In 1963, for example, it dealt with 9,923 cases, of which 31 per cent of males and 14 per cent of females had no accommodation before they travelled to England.[34] 'Moral welfare' topped the list of problem cases, and many young women were repatriated from the London area (136 in 1963), it being noted by the director, Cecil Barrett, that 'not one of these 136 girls sought help in Ireland before leaving' due to 'anxiety and need for secrecy in a small country with a small population'.[35]

In truth, McQuaid wanted these issues to remain secret. He castigated Richard Hauser, from the Centre of Group Studies in London, who had conducted research into the activities of Irish prostitutes in England and who subsequently addressed the Irish Association of Social Workers (IASW) in Dublin, dismissing him as 'an Austrian Jew' and a 'chancer' and, with Cecil Barrett, succeeded in persuading Brian Lenihan, then junior minister for lands, not to share a platform with Hauser.[36] But he was not able to censor Hauser's message, which was reported, to Barrett's disgust, in the national press. Hauser pointed out that one sixth of the prostitutes coming before the courts in London were Irish and suggested no-one cared 'a hoot about them'. He was also anxious to investigate conditions at Artane Industrial School, which McQuaid did not like: 'Hauser's evident determination to educate and train us is as puzzling as it is unsought. But then he is a difficult bird and quite aggressive.'[37]

It was not true that no-one cared 'a hoot about' Irish prostitutes in England and emigrants who had fallen on hard times – the church did; it just did not want this side of the emigrant experience explored by others and it was hostile to social workers. (In 1963, McQuaid defiantly boasted that he would continue to spy on them and maintained, 'I will give no approval to the IASW'.)[38] It also historically had a very simplistic attitude as to why some Irish emigrants' behaviour changed once they were abroad, arguing that Britain was a pagan, unwholesome country where standards of public morality had degenerated.

As far back as 1943, the honorary secretary of the Emigrant section, Henry Gray, had sent back many reports to McQuaid which included the observation that 'an Irish girl who is foolish enough to seek to be as "modern" as her English compeers renders herself open to grave abuse ... many of them are innocent victims in that they have practically no knowledge of sex matters when they arrive in Britain. England's non-Catholic youth is, by contrast, saturated with unwholesome knowledge and it would seem to be essential that our Irish emigrant youth should be equipped to safeguard themselves by a Christian and normal understanding of sexual matters.' Beside these final two words, McQuaid placed a disapproving, or perhaps curious, 'x'.[39]

McQuaid remained very defensive about this portrayal of Irish emigrants for the next twenty years, complaining to the archbishop of Westminster in 1960: 'that we must still endure the old misunderstandings is now evident'.[40] But there was another uncomfortable reality that McQuaid struggled to accept: Hubert Daly of the Legion of Mary sent McQuaid reports in the 1950s which suggested Irish people in England did not want contact with priests. As Daly was told by a priest in England, 'The Irish have no real love for their priests; it is only a sort of superstitious fear … their only idea of an outlet when they need relaxation is over-indulgence in drink and women.'[41] The simple truth, reiterated many times, is that many Irish had abandoned the Ireland of McQuaid; but also, as was pointed out in the *Standard* newspaper by an Irish contributor in 1953, the idea of the sexual purity of the Irish was a myth: 'The self-righteousness of the Irish is the cause of the trouble. Our people at home do not face the fact that there is original sin in Ireland as much as in any other part of the world. A girl who goes wrong in England was restrained only at home by outward devotion, not by faith.'[42] Five years later, the Catholic Rescue and Protection Society informed the Irish government that in the previous year they had repatriated eighty-five girls, but noted that there were 'many times that number who refused to return to Ireland'.[43]

There were other reasons for McQuaid and his agents to be worried about new ideas and more frank discussion of things sexual, including the arrival of television to Ireland. McQuaid and others wanted to exploit the potential of television to spread the faith, but they were also well aware of its dangers. In June 1962, the report of the Catholic Television Committee made it clear that its aim was that 'religion may have a central and honoured place in Irish television from the outset'.[44] They saw few causes for complaints in the initial years and were very satisfied with the 'moral tone', hardly diminished by the 'occasional lapse', but believed 'direct teaching on TV is still the unsolved problem'.[45] In truth, the real problem was the failure to agree on debate, which became more pronounced from the mid-1960s onwards.

As Fr Joe Dunn, one of the priests whom McQuaid had sent to the United States to be trained in television techniques, wrote to McQuaid: 'It seems to me the greater of two evils for religious leaders to protest about this kind of programme [those with a sexual content] … Of course, the "clean up TV" campaign in England was laughed at a lot, but it seems clear that it had some effect. I wouldn't like to say that it has reached the situation here where such a campaign is called for, but if it has, I think it is important that there are no clerics involved in it. It must be remembered that because of the nature of television production one can't keep a close censorship over producers.' McQuaid's reply, as was so often the case, was succinct and withering. Dunn's letter, he maintained, 'seems to ask that a cleric as such is to apologise himself out of existence, or hide himself permanently'.[46]

In the meantime, McQuaid's agents kept tabs on the personal lives of the Radio Telefís Éireann (RTÉ) personnel, partly through the efforts of Dermot O'Flynn, Supreme Knight of Columbanus. A report sent by O'Flynn in March 1962 revealed that of the sixteen RTÉ producers, only four were Catholics, including 'Miss Chloe Gibson, an English convert, but separated from her husband' and 'Shelah Richards – Producer of Religious Programmes! – A divorced actress who has been associated with numerous left-wing groups for many years' [emphasis in original].[47] McQuaid courted the senior RTÉ Catholics, including the director general, Edward Roth (who wrote in January 1962: 'May I say your Grace's selection of cigars is excellent'[48]) and the chairman of the TV Authority, Éamonn Andrews.

Perhaps not surprisingly, there was no question of Gay Byrne, the presenter of the Saturday night programme 'The Late Late Show', puffing on cigars in McQuaid's company. Inevitably, because of its regular determination to facilitate discussion of previously taboo subjects, the complaints came thick and fast about his show. In November 1966, a diocesan of McQuaid summed it up by writing that 'The Late Late Show' 'seems to be taken up with sex, pornography and obscene films. These "frank discussions" never contain a single reference to any religion, much less the Ten Commandments ... as a direct result of this terrible state of affairs, it would be interesting to know the number of teenage "shot-gun" marriages in Dublin over the past five years.'[49]

But an interesting aspect of 'The Late Late Show' controversies is that they again revealed that there was nothing McQuaid could do. As an anonymous letter writer pointed out to him, 'The Late Late Show has developed into a sex orgy. The fact is that You have all fallen down on your job and raising a family in a Christian atmosphere is an impossibility' [emphasis in original]. Then came the real sting in the tail: 'we are no better than all the other countries of the world. No longer Christian, just masquerading under the name. Over to you.'

In response to the first of these letters, McQuaid suggested that viewers had to publicly protest, as television 'is sensitive to public criticism' and that 'I have my own way of reaching these offenders.'[50] But the truth was that he did not have as much power as he claimed. As director general of RTÉ, Kevin McCourt admitted to McQuaid in

February 1966: 'Not infrequently to my frustration, I cannot be the policeman of all I want.'[51]

Neither could McQuaid, and neither could another of his confidants, Thomas Coyne, secretary of the Department of Justice, who had frequently discussed the issue of censorship with him. Enclosed in the correspondence between them in 1960 was an advertisement from the *Observer* Newspaper on 3 April 1960, in which a proud mother and her daughter, wearing just her new bra, were beaming at each other, under the heading: 'Delightful news for the understanding mother: New bras and girdles specially designed for 11–16 year olds'. McQuaid was disappointed that the state was not doing more to prevent the circulation of such advertisements, and was not satisfied with Coyne insisting that 'if the state is encouraged or even allowed to become an arbiter of morals, it may be tempted to usurp the functions of the church'. Coyne wrote about the variety of 'unwholesome trash' now in existence in Ireland, 'which have a demoralising effect not merely on the weak-minded but on the weak-willed as well and are a greater menace because they are retailed at a price which is low enough to give them a relatively wide circulation', but it was difficult to name and shame because of the 'practical impossibility of specifying all such publications and the risk that those left unspecified might be wrongfully presumed to have ecclesiastical approval'.

But Coyne maintained it was still a task for the priest, not the state, nor the police, to 'check the false emphasis on sex ... the moral flabbiness and the false philosophies that are so much in vogue. This, as I see it, is a task for the priest, not for the policeman.' He then referred to the advertisement, which although certainly not obscene in the eyes of the law, 'shows quite plainly how small girls and their parents are being systematically indoctrinated with the idea that sex appeal (to use the jargon) consists in a provocative display of secondary sexual characteristics. This is the sort of thing that cannot possibly be suppressed by the State without the State's appearing to make itself ridiculous, which the civil authority is always unwilling to do.'[52]

It was also clear over the next few years that some politicians were not content to leave the old systems and the old personnel unchanged with regard to the policing of morality. Brian Lenihan, when he was minister for justice in 1964, made it clear to McQuaid that he was determined to reconstitute the Censorship of Films Appeal Board: 'I am aware that some of the members are very advanced in years, some hard of hearing, some evidently do not understand the import of some of the film scenes at all, some have been noticed to doze during film-showing and finally, decisions have been made with only a small number of members present at appeals.'[53] Lenihan went on, two years later, to plan a change in the censorship laws because the definitions of 'obscenity' had changed so dramatically.

McQuaid had won some small battles but he was losing the big ones, partly because he refused point blank to engage with journalists, or to agree to interviews, despite establishing a press office in 1965 and encouraging other clerics to become involved in attempting to control the media's agenda. From the beginning of the 1960s his message was reiterated many times regarding journalists – they were to be kept 'off me'.[54] This contributed to the image of McQuaid as forbidding and out of touch, or as he put it to journalists in 1965, 'the ogre in his den'.[55] He justified his refusal to be interviewed again in 1966 when responding to an *Irish Independent* journalist: 'You will have an ample opportunity to put me into focus after my death.'[56] June Levine, who wanted to interview him in April 1971, was also refused, even though 'she believes that she, being of the Jewish faith, could write an article which would have even more impact than one by a Catholic'.[57]

McQuaid was also conscious that material aimed specifically at women and their sexuality and fertility was becoming much more prevalent. The magazine *Woman's Way* attracted particular attention and criticism. One of its advertisements that infuriated McQuaid and others was published in 1965: 'Family Planning: Science and Nature go hand in hand: THE ONLY METHOD APPROVED BY ALL CHURCHES' [emphasis in original]. 'Nature's pattern of the rhythm of fertility can now be pinpointed for each individual woman by using the C.D. indicator.' The magazine defied the archbishop's wishes in publishing it, despite McQuaid's stern rebuke that 'I never approve of any device and I do not approve of this.' Ossie Dowling did, however, manage to persuade the advertising manager of *The Irish Times*, Arthur Rhys Thomas, not to publish the advertisement, Dowling noting that 'Arthur is an old friend of mine'.[58]

On 21 December 1967, McQuaid's secretary recorded a memo for McQuaid after Dr Michael Browne, bishop of Galway, had called to see him to discuss the nature and trend of *Woman's Way*:

> In regard to the editorial staff of *Woman's Way*, Dr Browne instanced Mrs Caroline Mitchell, the wife of Charles Mitchell of Telefís Éireann. Mrs Mitchell is a Protestant ... some of the other

members of the editorial staff may be lapsed Catholics ... Dr Browne understands that the magazine has a wide circulation, particularly among teenagers who read the magazines in hairdressers and factories. Often this is the only journal that they read. Angela Macnamara contributes weekly to this magazine. Apart from her articles, the other articles dealing with matters of sex are very much astray morally. Dr Browne stated that some mothers are very perturbed by the whole tone of these sex articles and have said that while they read the magazine themselves they would not like to see their daughters reading it.

Interestingly, McQuaid's secretary, J.A. MacMahon, also introduced a note of caution in his comment attached to the letter:

These magazines contain articles by some serious people like Angela Macnamara. They also contain regular features from such well-known personalities as Charles Mitchell and Terry Wogan ... these magazines are dealing with questions which are very widely discussed. They might well reply that they are catering for a demand. It is possible that an appeal to women to exercise caution and moral judgement in regard to women's magazines might be better than a condemnation of these magazines as such.

It is not clear what, if any, action McQuaid took. In truth, he was powerless to stop these articles, despite pressure exerted informally or in private. In October 1971, a free sex information booklet was included in the magazine, which included a passage on masturbation.[59] Earlier that year, McQuaid had been informed that a group of activists in the Irish Women's Liberation Movement (IWLM) were planning to protest about contraception at the laying and blessing of the foundation stone for a new church in his diocese. 'Let them all come!' McQuaid wrote defiantly in the margin.[60] He may have been defiant, but the fact the women were prepared to confront him publicly was yet another sign that his domination and unquestioned obedience to his church's teaching was coming to an end.

In assessing the challenges facing McQuaid at this juncture, historian and Dominican nun Margaret MacCurtain has suggested: 'I think he was too old at that stage even to grasp the significance of what he was issuing – that the subject of contraception had become so uncontainable that this final pastoral is almost lip-service.'[61]

John Cooney has rejected this analysis and surmised that if there had been no *Humane Vitae*, McQuaid would have slipped from view at an earlier stage:

> I just don't agree with that. I think the whole passage of *Humane Vitae* in 1968 gives him a new lease of life. He thinks that Pope Paul VI is beginning to see sense again and that the Council's aberrations are now a thing of the past and that we can go back to the real uniformity. He's becoming a hard-hitter again – he stops any attempts by Mary Robinson, John Horgan and Trevor West in the Senate from mobilising Jack Lynch to bring in a full contraception bill.[62]

MacCurtain, however, maintains that the game was up at that stage, that a momentum had developed that McQuaid was not in a position to resist:

> But he's overtaken by history. In a sense, we're on the verge of European union ... and the whole tenure of the Commission on the Status of Women, parts one and two, had the effect of bringing Catholic and Protestant women together in a united stand. He was up against too much.[63]

The material in McQuaid's archives confirms the veracity of MacCurtain's assessment. To a certain extent, McQuaid's Ireland was dead and buried before he vacated his post.

CHAPTER NINE

Turmoil in the Sea of Faith: The Secularization of Irish Social Culture, 1960–2007

TOM GARVIN

Monsignor Paddy Browne (Pádraig de Brún), a much-loved president of University College Galway, was asked two generations ago what the beliefs concerning the afterlife of the Connemara fisher folk and peasantry were. These people were Irish-speaking and held by nationalists to be close to the pure and spiritually loyal Gaelic and Catholic tradition. Browne replied that they had three incompatible theories about life after death: firstly, they accepted the Catholic orthodoxy that told them that if they were just in this life, they would see God, and if unjust, they would go elsewhere. Secondly, they believed that when you die, you die like a dog in a ditch, and that's the end of you. Thirdly, they believed sometimes that you hung around after death and took a mainly malicious interest in the lives of the living. They were Christians, atheists and pagans, all depending, I suppose, on the time of day or night. Like Brendan Behan, they were only daylight atheists.[1]

A JESUIT IN IRELAND

An American Jesuit, Fr B.F. Biever, pioneered the study of political attitudes in Ireland in the early 1960s, at the behest of the redoubtable archbishop of Dublin of the time, John Charles McQuaid. Biever was trained in the techniques of in-depth survey research, a set of skills woefully absent in the Ireland of the time. The survey sample was of Dublin city and county, and confined to Catholics. This was the first scientific study of its type in the Republic of Ireland, and is, for that reason, of great value as an historical artifact and as a milestone against which subsequent work can be compared and judged. The study was mainly concentrated on attitudes toward religion and clerical authority, but did deal necessarily with political attitudes, opinion about church and state relationships and attitudes toward democratic governance. At that time, Irish democracy had been functioning in an independent nation-state for forty years. Irish democratic legitimacy seemed secure, although the memory of a bitter Civil War that had accompanied the state's foundation was still fairly fresh.[2]

The portrait of Dublin Catholic political culture revealed by this 1962 survey is quite startling. Attitudes to the Catholic Church varied little by class or region of birth. Almost 90 per cent of the sample agreed that the Catholic Church was the greatest force for good in Ireland and over two-thirds endorsed the proposition that if one followed a priest's advice, one could scarcely go wrong. Priests were seen as the natural social, economic and political leaders of the country, and their status was so high that the democratically elected politicians of Leinster House, the Irish parliament's home, were quite overshadowed. Cynicism about politicians and about any attempt at lay leadership independent of clerical backing was very prevalent and had deep historical and cultural roots. One respondent conceded that the clergy might 'make mistakes' occasionally, but felt that they were not just out for themselves and that he would rather be wrong with his priests than 'right with those damn crooks in Dublin'. Another remarked: 'you can't trust anyone in this country except the priest; he *has* to be honest!' while another respondent commented forcefully that 'people gripe about the censorship in the press and say that the priests are too powerful. No priest can be too powerful. If we had followed what the priests have been telling us for years, we would be content with what we have, and not getting all excited about being like the rest of Europe.'[3]

At the time, education was generally controlled by the churches and financed by the state, and there was controversy about extending the lay and technical sectors. Mass education of the modern type scarcely existed. One respondent was openly scornful about secularizing the educational system: 'You know, there are some people who think the government should run education. Imagine that!' The Catholic Church had done a 'good job', he felt. Having listened to 'them fools' in Leinster House shouting, insulting each other, and 'doing nothing', he thought that clerical influence should actually be increased. Another said bluntly, and perhaps accurately, that priests were better educated than were politicians. He therefore argued that it would be stupid of the public not to accept their leadership. One man remarked: 'We are simple people, sir … child-like, maybe child-ish, in many ways. We cannot behave ourselves without help; no-one can. That's what I like about the church; if you are wrong, by God you'll hear about it!' When asked which side they would take in the event of an outright clash between church and state, a massive 87 per cent said they would back the church.

Biever was describing the democratically elected politicians of the Republic of Ireland as being quite helpless in the face of this cultural climate; by a simple, popularly imposed iron political necessity, most important legislation was routinely cleared by clerical authorities in advance of government enactment. The Irish democratic process was heavily tinged with theocracy, for the overwhelming reason that the majority wished it to be that way. Recent tensions between clerical and lay authorities over medical care for expectant or adoptive moth-ers had been resolved in favour of the priorities of the clergy amid great controversy, reflecting the great prestige which priests and nuns enjoyed in the Ireland of the time. It should be remembered that because of clerical control of the educational system, the clerical authorities could ensure that the majority were persuaded to support church power. The virtues and near-infallibility of the Catholic ecclesiastical machine and the goodness and wisdom of its priests, nuns and brothers were extolled in classes on religious knowledge and church history in schools, articles, books and pamphlets, in sermons from the pulpit, and in programmes on the new electronic media. Opinions expressing contrary views were downplayed or even censored, officially or unofficially. Furthermore, given the very inadequate Irish welfare state of the time, the Catholic Church was looked to gratefully for sustenance by an impoverished electorate, and was rewarded by the poor man's payment: political, and even electoral, support. As Biever put it, the Irish were indeed 'priest-ridden', but they liked it that way.

Again, the clergy like to wield their power; Catholic political leaders were forbidden to attend the funeral services of their non-Catholic colleagues, friends and constituents, and they generally abided by this prohibition, albeit with some murmuring. Public figures genuflected and kissed the ring of a bishop when encountering one in public. The archbishop did not wait on the prime minister of the country; the prime minister went to the archbishop's palace, cap in hand. The church did not provide education – and often an excellent education supplied by dedicated and sometimes brilliant teachers – merely out of the goodness of its heart. It did so because it wished to recruit faithful and dedicated servants, 'soldiers of Christ', missionaries to the English-speaking world; and Catholic leaders of a Catholic people: priests, nuns, trade union leaders, middle-class professionals and businessmen. Some Catholic orders, the Christian Brothers in particular, imparted a potent mixture of authoritarian Christianity, a sometimes rabid patriotism, and a rigid and puritan lifestyle. An instantly recognizable political style, combining a bullying form of argument with holier-than-thou postures, characterized some of the products of their schools.

Lay Catholic organizations, most conspicuously the Knights of Columbanus, controlled official and unofficial censorship systems and acted as what might best be termed para-clerics. Many secret unbelievers kept their opinions strictly to themselves and even joined the Knights or similar organizations for safety's sake. Sending a child to a non-Catholic school was punishable by excommunication, entailing an imagined eternal damnation if one were to die before reconciliation with the church was effected. A similar rule applied in the Dublin archdiocese to Catholics wishing to go to the traditionally Protestant Trinity College rather than to the mainly Catholic University College Dublin (UCD), the latter being referred to by Biever as 'obviously second best'. It must be remembered that most Irish people received little education beyond the age of 13 or so, and only a small minority achieved a high school Leaving Certificate, earned by taking a quite searching examination at age 18. Even fewer went on to third-level education. Irish religious culture was much as it had been in the nineteenth century: one of literal belief in God, Christ, the Resurrection, the Virgin birth, miracles, miraculous cures, good and evil angels, saints, heaven, hell, purgatory, limbo and all the rest of it. Even quite educated people half-believed in cures by faith healing, holy wells, and pilgrimages to sites associated with real or even imaginary saints. Fairies, banshees, pookas and leprechauns were not quite disbelieved in. This was an elaborate syncretic system of beliefs partly rooted in pre-Christian paganism and partly non-Christian in psychological texture. Catholic schoolchildren and their parents were conscripts in a compulsory system driven by spiritual threats and promises backed up by a politically powerful and popular church. A version of what the great English social historian E.P. Thompson termed 'spiritual terrorism' kept Catholic Ireland in line for an entire century; Alexis de Tocqueville's warnings about the dangers of majority tyranny in democracies were apposite.

However, there was a sense even at the time – and hindsight wisdom amply confirms that sense – that the public belief system that Fr Biever was documenting so vividly at the beginning of the 1960s was already becoming the past, rather than the future. Even in 1962, incipient change was visible and more change was seen as inevitable. Those few who had completed second-level education to age 18 were far more willing to question clerical prerogatives and formed a small, isolated and clearly alienated group; they were alienated not so much from the priests as from the popular culture which endorsed the power of priests. Irish democracy was clericalized and the newly educated and inexperienced Catholic middle class was denied political and cultural power by the mass of their fellow citizens and many of the clergy, although by no means all of the clergy. There were dissident priests and nuns as well. Whereas an extraordinary 88 per cent endorsed the proposition that the Catholic Church was the greatest force for good in the country, an equally striking 83 per cent of those who had stayed in school to age 18 or older flatly disagreed with that proposition.[4]

Biever warned that these young, educated and newly middle-class people were the greatest challenge facing the Catholic Church in the Ireland of the 1960s and 1970s. Their attitudes are uncompromising, he wrote; they pointed sharply at weaknesses in clerical leadership, and they deeply resented clerical claims to authority in non-religious policy areas. They were, however, mainly talking to themselves, and not many listened to them. 'Helplessly they face the overwhelming majority complacency and the staggering lack of educational potential which the church-oriented school system has produced.' They were not going to emigrate, and did not have to in the context of a new, if partial, prosperity. One of the educated minority expressed himself as follows:

> No, I don't think the church is the greatest force for good, and do you want to know why? She doesn't let us speak here … The clergy make all the decisions, and all we have to do is obey … I am sick and tired of being looked upon with suspicion simply

because I have an education. Priests aren't the only ones with brains, you know, although you couldn't tell it to hear them speak or see them act ... The church censors the press, it censors the magazines, it censors the televisions ... what doesn't it censor? Is this the greatest force for good? Not to me, it isn't! It seems to me that the church is more interested in keeping a stranglehold on the people than in making us better as a nation, and that I don't buy ...

Biever juxtaposes this opinion quite neatly with a defence of the church by some members of the clergy. The church, one cleric said, was 'the only force [for good] left'. Some of 'your smart intellectuals' had forgotten that the priests never deserted the people in times of want and suffering. Another said: 'We have more education, thank God, and with that education comes the responsibility to lead. I think we are [leading].' One cleric said thoughtfully, and evidently with some self-doubt: 'The politicians are new to the game; we have few economists, our professional people leave. Who stays? We do.'

DECADES OF SLOW CHANGE

In the early 1960s, then, an undercurrent of nascent anti-clericalism ran through the tiny, newly educated upper stratum of a relatively modestly educated culture. It must be remembered that the Republic was a post-revolutionary society, and it had lost most of its old upper class, mainly Protestant and unionist in tradition, either through partition, emigration or simple cultural marginalization. Catholic middle-class anti-clericalism may date back to the fall of Parnell, but more immediately it derived from resentment at clerical power and recent crude attempts to interfere in public policy matters. In the post-war period, a small but vocal group of public dissidents such as Hubert Butler, Owen Sheehy-Skeffington, Sean O'Faolain and Michael Sheehy bore witness to a mainly Catholic liberal tradition, one that was commonly covertly admired and vaguely feared. As early as 1944, a UCD economist, James Meenan, had confided to his diary that he foresaw a wave of Catholic anti-clericalism in about twenty years. He was writing in the context of the archbishop taking over a large chunk of UCD's educational mission at that time. His prophecy was confirmed, although, as waves go, the wave of change of the 1960s and after was a fairly gentle one.[5]

As late as 1971, an opinion poll reported that only 22 per cent of the adult population favoured the legalization of divorce in the Republic. Irish legal prohibitions on divorce were *more* stringent than those of Catholic canon law. Even young people opposed divorce, although by smaller majorities; of people under 25 years of age, 39 per cent of men and 28 per cent of women favoured divorce; scarcely a revolt of flaming youth. However, contraception, illegal in theory at the time, was clearly favoured by the young. The cut-off for liberal views in terms of age was around the early 1930s; those born after 1939 were clearly post-British in mentality and therefore less constrained to think 'my church, right or wrong', as was the attitude of many older people. Much of this shift was strengthened by the pope's unexpected veto on contraception in 1968, which provoked a quiet but very general rebellion among women. In 1971, however, Catholic Ireland was alive and well, if showing her age somewhat. Rather worried liberal Catholics urged church leaders to be less uncompromising, sensing an inevitable collision between generations.[6] Ten years on, in 1981, clear, if small, majorities favoured anti-traditional stances toward divorce, religious pluralism and contraception, at least in principle. Individual liberal priests made slightly frantic attempts to repair the alienation that was occurring in a quiet, unspoken and even polite way between the educated laity and the clerical apparatus. Sean O'Faolain had begged the church to cease to rule by command rather than by argument and persuasion; in the end, a paralyzed church failed to hitch young men and women to its star, to use O'Faolain's own phrase; it was incapable of doing so, for cultural and intellectual reasons.

In fact, in the 1980s, neo-traditional forces attempted to turn back the clock in a period of economic regression reminiscent of the poverty-stricken '50s. Victories were won by traditionalists on the issues of divorce and abortion. Large majorities were racked up against both threats to the moral consensus in national referendums which demonstrated that the old, popular, pro-clerical collective opinion was alive, if not exactly well. The calculation was that the Catholic position on abortion in particular would have to be nailed into the Constitution if the process of secularization was to be stemmed, and a time of economic depression was the right time to do it. The anti-abortion amendment succeeded in 1986, but was to backfire spectacularly in 1992 because of a statutory rape case, ironically forcing a softening in the official line on abortion. The referendum campaigns on divorce and abortion of the 1980s and '90s were very bad tempered and vicious, and were also felt to be irrelevant to a small country whose fragile economy seemed to many to be going down the tubes as emigration of the young resumed in quantities reminiscent of the 1950s. In that strange period, incoherent episodes such as the spate of moving statue sightings in 1982–3 were symptomatic of an embattled popular traditionalism trying to fight back against unbelief, scepticism and satire.

However, much of this new resistance to change actually came as much from the Vatican as from native Catholic leadership. Irish church leaders found themselves being forced to take up positions which they might have soft-pedalled were their elbows not being jostled by out-of-touch potentates in Rome. Even within the country, neo-traditionalism characterized lay Catholic leaders more than the clergy. As the clergy grew older and its ranks thinned, lay traditionalist leaders became more outspoken and conspicuous. The end result was an eventual, and total, loss of intellectual leadership by the ecclesiastics and their replacement by politicians, academics, civil servants, technical experts and journalists.

Secularization is a general cultural characteristic of modern societies; this is particularly true of Europe, where the sea of faith is far smaller than it once was. France, Scandinavia and England are essentially post-Christian societies. The contrast with the United States is quite striking; the United States is a very modern and very religious country, and this indicates that there is no necessary relationship between modernization and the death of faith, but that there is one between secularization, social structure and political power. In particular, faith seems to be endangered when there is a perceived unduly close relationship between church organizations and the secular state; clerical political power comes to be seen as undemocratic and illegitimate, particularly in a democratic, modernizing society which has become educated. Jesus did say, after all, 'render unto Caesar the things that are Caesar's, and unto God the things that are God's'. This sounds very much like an enunciation of the doctrine of separation of church and state. Arguably, the rather extreme version of this doctrine installed in the Constitution of 1789 has, ironically, saved American Christianity from a European fate; a similar doctrine has not saved French Catholicism, perhaps because the church fought against separation tooth and nail for two centuries. After all, unlike in America, the French state actually tried to take over the Catholic

Church after the Revolution of 1789, echoing a French tradition of caesaropapism that goes back to Philip the Fair and the Babylonian captivity of the papacy in Avignon.

Although belief in Catholic dogmas is far weaker than it was a generation or two ago, most Irish people are still religiously minded and love their faith. But deference to priests has disappeared, and attention to the teachings of clerics has weakened. Many people who ignore the church's instructions and who rarely go to church see themselves as perfectly good Catholics, and see no contradiction in their point of view. This is an almost 'Protestant' stance that would have been quite impossible forty years ago, but now is probably mainstream. Since the mid-1960s, education in Ireland has expanded enormously, and nowadays everyone stays in school to Leaving Certificate, while 50 per cent of each age cohort gets some kind of third-level education or training. Ireland has been participating, with some delay, in a general process of cultural change associated with higher levels of education, affluence and urbanization everywhere in the West.

Despite dramatic cultural change, Ireland is nowhere near as godless as England or France. It took the clerical scandals of the 1990s, a series of self-inflicted wounds on the Catholic Church, to wreak serious and probably irreversible damage to the church's previously central position in Irish society and culture. Child molestation, the extra-legal imprisonment of girls and young women suspected of immorality, the illegal shielding of clerical wrong-doers by senior ecclesiastics, the hypocrisy of preaching a strict sexual code while secretly transgressing it oneself, and cover cynicism allied with power-seeking, started to be publicized in an unprecedented way. These scandals only became conceivable in a context where secularization was affecting the minds of priests and nuns themselves, so that traditional beliefs and discipline were weakening. The stigma on non-marital relationships disappeared, as did the taboos on homosexuality and illegitimacy. However, acceptance of Catholic teaching on abortion is still general, although somewhat conditional.[7]

END OF AN EXPERIMENT

An American political scientist, Harry Eckstein, argued back in the 1960s that liberal democracies find it difficult to operate if there are large, popular, non-democratic organizations within them which wield considerable cultural power. He was thinking of mainland European countries of that period in which strong, popular, Catholic, national churches faced large popular communist parties with deep roots in the electorate. Authoritarian, top-down organizations would tend, he argued, to impart their authoritarianism to the state itself. Certainly, Irish democracy was marked from the beginning by a noticeable tendency toward high-handedness which contrasted with the rather slapdash and easy-going social style generally characteristic of the Irish people. It could be argued, however, that in the long run – and we do live in Keynes's long run – democracy eats away at authoritarian institutions and habits of behaviour, and certainly something like this has happened in Ireland. Irish journalists are far more outspoken about the misdeeds of the powerful than they were a generation ago, constrained as they were by harsh libel laws and a willingness of the powerful to intimidate their opponents. Oracular styles of authority were increasingly challenged in Ireland, and with the coming of television and mass education, the old passivity faded away.[8]

Furthermore, secularization in Ireland, together with the concomitant collective humbling of the Irish clergy, marked the end of an ambitious social experiment on the part of the Catholic Church, one which was prefigured by Cardinal Paul Cullen's modernization of the church in Ireland decades after the Great Famine. This was the project of building a Catholic society that fully realized Catholic social and moral values within the framework of an independent and genuinely democratic new country. Tridentine social and ethical values were to be reconciled with the practices and institutions of Anglo-American democracy. But Caesar was to cede power to God where God claimed precedence. Ireland was also to be a guinea pig for ideas of reorganizing society along what were termed vocational lines. Vocationalism was very much a fashionable idea during the years after the First World War, and attracted thinkers on both the right and left of society. The central idea was that territorial democracy was incomplete on its own, and needed to be supplemented, or even supplanted, by economic representation. Fascist countries often set up just such schemes of organization; Salazar's Portugal was touted as an ideal to which governments should aspire.

Another related ideological strand was *distributivism*, and Hilaire Belloc's condemnation of capitalism as dividing humanity into the possessing few and the dispossessed many had impressed numerous young revolutionaries who helped set up the Irish state in the early twentieth century. Many priests were also attracted to it. Ireland had evolved into a society of smallholders, and fear of both big business and of big labour characterized this society. Distributivism was a kind of Christian democracy, the central idea being the redistribution of property by the state to ensure that all households owned property, and therefore had a stakehold in the system; there were to be no proletarians and no fat cats either. Distributivist and vocationalist ideas seemed to promise stabilization and a static society, something that certainly attracted the consensual centre of the Irish democracy. However, in the long run, such an institutionalized stasis began to be perceived as anti-democratic and as a mask for vested interests, already powerful enough in the tiny democracy that was independent Ireland. By the late 1940s, interest in vocationalism was on the wane. The ideology faded, but collective bargaining between government, labour and employers became institutionalized from 1946 on, as Ireland gradually became Ireland, Inc. and slowly turned itself into an export economy.

Ireland's experiment with Catholic democracy is over. Furthermore, the Ireland which was subjected to the experiment scarcely even exists anymore. At the time of independence in 1922, some 60 per cent of the population was engaged in agriculture, and most of the rest worked in services linked directly or indirectly to agriculture; essentially the Ireland that seceded from the old United Kingdom was the agrarian sector of that kingdom. The new country was 95 per cent practising and believing Catholic at that time. In 2006, eighty-four years later, only about 7 per cent worked on the land, and the small, self-sufficient owner-occupier yeoman farmer was no more. Ireland went from being a peasant society to being a suburban information technology country with no intervening stage of smoke-stack industry. Perhaps 50 per cent of the population go rarely or never to religious services. Furthermore, recent waves of immigration have given a traditionally emigrant society a new challenge: how to absorb immigrants, many of whom are not Catholic or even Christian. Ironically, some of them are more Catholic than the average Irish person. The closed little country beloved of de Valera and McQuaid is as remote from modern Ireland as is the Gaelic-speaking Ireland of the sixteenth century, and as irrecoverable. It is not clear what role, if any, Catholicism is to play in this new country; if it gets another chance, the Catholic Church could again play a central, if humbler, role. It remains to be seen whether it is actually capable of meeting such a challenge.

CHAPTER TEN

The Irish Catholic Narrative: Reflections on Milestones

LOUISE FULLER

The change in the role and influence of the Catholic Church is central in any assessment of twentieth-century Irish history, and in this chapter the intention is to chart some of the key turning points in the course of that change. From the 1950s this influence was being challenged and it had declined radically by the end of the century

Socio-political developments in the course of the nineteenth century hold the key to understanding the dominant position of Catholicism in Irish society, which lasted well into the latter half of the twentieth century. Following Catholic emancipation in 1829, the Irish bishops and clergy became increasingly politicized. The Catholic bishops agreed to back Parnell and the Irish Parliamentary Party in their agitation for a resolution of the land issue and for home rule in return for the party's commitment to represent their interests in securing third-level education rights for Catholics. The majority of the bishops in early 1917 still supported the Parliamentary Party and were wary of Sinn Féin.[1] Their decision to lead the popular resistance to conscription in 1918 was a major turning point for the church in Ireland. Traditional Catholic theology held that it was morally wrong to contravene the law of the existing government. But Murray's research has rightly highlighted 'the capacity of the Church to accommodate itself to successful or popular revolt'.[2] Writing of how the anti-conscription movement had galvanized the country, Bishop Foley of Kildare and Leighlin pointed out that 'no mission that was ever held so profoundly affected the lives of the whole Catholic people, and the Sinn Féiners were second to no others'.[3] The election of December

1918 made it even clearer who now held the political mandate, and the bishops weighed in accordingly.

When Sinn Féin split after the Treaty was signed by the Irish delegation in London in the early hours of 6 December 1921 and ratified by the Dáil on 7 January 1922 by sixty-four votes to fifty-seven, the bishops threw their weight behind the pro-Treaty side. The latter had won the Dáil vote and the June election – thus representing the democratic wishes of the people. In a joint pastoral letter in October 1922 the bishops formally declared themselves against de Valera and his republican followers.[4] The church's place in the political consensus was, by now, guaranteed by a hundred years of history. With the founding of the Free State the Catholic Church, too, had arrived. It had fought a long, hard battle to consolidate its position during the course of the nineteenth century, and freedom now served to strengthen further its power and dominance. A close alliance was formed between the Catholic church authorities and the Free State government during the Civil War years, and W.T. Cosgrave looked to the church to reinforce the authority of his government; he sought to protect what he saw as the distinctive Irish Catholic tradition by means of legislation and censorship. De Valera, when he came to power in 1932, was equally zealous in this regard. By means of several pieces of legislation through the 1920s and 1930s the Catholic moral code became enshrined in the law of the land. The prevailing discourse which dominated political, cultural and social life in the Republic was that of the Catholic church. The process culminated in the drawing up of a new Constitution in 1937, deeply influenced by Catholic teaching and in which Article 44 recognized the 'special position' of the Catholic church.[5]

The narrative of twentieth-century Irish Catholicism is the narrative not only of the development of the close relationship between church and state during the early years, whereby politicians in their public lives and by means of legislation legitimized the Catholic ethos, but also the challenges to this status quo that arose gradually through the 1950s and 1960s and gained momentum from the 1970s. Several factors influenced these developments, individually and collectively, throughout the period in focus, 1918–1998. Most notable were the changes in political thinking from the late 1950s, which led to new directions in economic thinking, changes in educational ideology and also changes in communications policy, which led in due course to the establishment of an Irish television station. On a macro level, the single most important event was the election of Pope John XXIII in 1958. His convocation of the Second Vatican Council, 1962–5, led to fundamental reappraisals in the Catholic church, which had profound implications for a country like Ireland, which was, and is, overwhelmingly Catholic in population. From the late 1950s to the 1990s, Irish governments/ politicians distanced themselves gradually from church influence and began to adopt a more independent line in many policy areas that involved 'taking on' the church. Whereas deference characterized their approach to the church authorities initially, by the latter stages politicians had become more assertive and independent in their relations with church figures; the lines of demarcation between what was the business and responsibility of church and state became more defined. Distinctions were made between matters of church, state, morality and the law, but these clarifications did not come to pass without hard battles. By the end of the period under review, legislative and constitutional provisions which reinforced the Catholic ethos had been challenged and dismantled. But the church defended what it saw as its legitimate territory at every stage, and the milestones along the way are precisely what I wish to highlight in the course of this chapter.

De Valera's Fianna Fáil government remained in power from 1932 to 1948, when it was replaced by the Inter-Party government. It was during the tenure of office of this government that the first major challenge to the power of the Catholic church was mounted. The so-called Mother and Child crisis has been well documented and many would say over-rehearsed, but there is no gainsaying its impact. The Catholic bishops vehemently opposed the efforts of minister for health Noël Browne to provide free medical care for mothers and children up to the age of 16, seeing them as state interference in the area of motherhood and sexuality, on which the church had very definite teaching. The ins and outs of the controversy is not of concern here, rather the dogmatic tone and manner of the bishops' interference, which, combined with the objections of the Irish Medical Association, led to the downfall of the government in 1951. This, along with the deferential tone of the politicians who discussed the crisis in the subsequent Dáil debate, indicated the enormous power of the hierarchy at that time. Dr Browne himself in his resignation speech declared: 'I as a Catholic accept unequivocally and unreservedly the views of the hierarchy on this matter.'[6] That said, the fact that he sent the correspondence that had passed between himself and the hierarchy to the newspapers, thus airing the controversy in public, meant that the church was placed under scrutiny and exposed to criticism for the first time. It is this writer's considered view that this public airing sowed a culture of disaffection that would come back to haunt the church down the line.

The church won the battle and lost the war, but this was hardly appreciated by the church authorities at the time, if subsequent remarks by Archbishop D'Alton of Armagh and Bishop Lucey of Cork are anything to go by. In October 1951 Archbishop D'Alton, addressing a Catholic Truth Society of Ireland (CTSI) conference, gave his view that 'we have a right to expect that our social legislation will not be in conflict with Catholic principles'.[7] A few years later, in 1955, addressing a Christus Rex congress in Killarney, Bishop Lucey gave his view that the bishops were in fact 'the final arbiters of right and wrong even in political matters'.[8] He added that the state might, in other areas, ignore the experts but in matters of 'faith and morals it might not'. The tone of these remarks gives a sense of how the bishops viewed their position in Irish society at that time – they saw themselves as having the right to have a final say in certain areas in which they believed they had rights and an expertise that superseded that of the state. In a matter of twenty years or so they would be couching their statements – or backtracking on their position, depending on how one wishes to see it.

Ireland had been neutral during the Second World War and the changes that took place in education and social welfare in Britain and continental Europe in the post-war era did not happen in Ireland. Such reforms required state intervention, and bishops' pastorals railed against such interference, which was seen as smacking of communism. However, at a time when there was a haemorrhage of people leaving the country, there were those in the civil service and even in the church who were beginning to realize that state intervention in the economy was necessary if Ireland was to meet even minimum standards of being able to sustain its own population. In 1958, T.K. Whitaker's paper *Economic Development* spelt out what was necessary to turn the economy around,[9] and the *Programme for Economic Expansion*[10] (often referred to as the First Programme) that followed has always been seen as a key turning point in economic and social history. It signalled a decisive shift in economic thinking that would have a ripple effect right through Irish society. Increasingly from then on, economic imperatives would guide political thinking, in view of the success of the First Programme after its implementation in 1958.

The necessity to be open to foreign trade and investment, advocated by economists and politicians, did not confine itself to economic policy, but rather was underpinned by a general attitude that was more accepting of foreign influences. It gradually led to a lessening of the insular mood that had characterized past Irish experience. Irish Catholicism, in terms of its presentation by the bishops and its expression in the devotional lives of the people, had changed little since the late nineteenth century, but by the early 1960s it could no longer be insulated from developments at home and abroad. In the 1950s, the main thrust of the bishops' pronouncements was that Ireland should be shielded, at all costs, from the corrupting influences emanating from continental Europe. The apprehensiveness felt in relation to changes on the horizon are reflected in the words of Archbishop D'Alton writing in *The Furrow* in 1950:

> We have to face the fact that with the rise of the new inventions such as the cinema and the radio, we no longer enjoy our former comparative isolation. Our people are constantly being brought into contact with a civilization for the most part alien and materialistic in outlook.[11]

From the late 1950s, protecting people from these corrupting influences would prove increasingly difficult and, in the course of time, impossible.

A new generation of political leaders was emerging in Ireland in the late 1950s. De Valera had repeatedly expounded a vision of Irishness that upheld spiritual values and eschewed the materialistic and secularistic attitudes seen to be developing in mainland Europe. His guiding principle had been to create an Ireland that would be culturally and economically insulated from these corrupting influences. In this endeavour he was very much in tune with the bishops' views as expounded in their pastoral letters. He retired from active politics on 17 June 1959 and was subsequently elected president. He was replaced as taoiseach by Seán Lemass, who was more pragmatic and interested in people's material welfare. Throughout the 1950s the bishops had successfully fought off demands for change in the licensing laws. The Lemass decision in 1959 to ignore their trenchant warnings regarding the dangers and consequences that would result from a relaxation of legislation was the most concrete development to usher in the new era – it marked a total change from the tentative approach of past governments.

Henceforth politicians began to adopt a more independent,

assertive approach to policy-making. One area that had always been seen as the unquestionable domain of the church was education. The importance of education for the transmission of the cultural heritage had long been understood by the church, and the battle for control had been hard-fought in the nineteenth century. Successive ministers for education were in no doubt as to their place vis-à-vis the church. In 1956, Richard Mulcahy had famously construed his role as that of a 'plumber', who would not presume to pontificate on the deeper philosophical issues of education, which he would leave to the teachers, managers and churches.[12] The Council of Education, set up by Mulcahy, reported on primary education in 1954 that 'our primary schools today are essentially religious and denominational in character ... and their purpose is religious'.[13] Regarding secondary schooling, in 1962 the report team saw its purpose as the 'inculcation of religious ideals and values'.[14] The church's structural hold over education ensured that the classical, liberal, curricular tradition with its literary academic bias was seen as more prestigious than vocational education provided in the 'techs'. In 1956 John J. O'Meara, professor of Classical Languages in UCD, criticized the 'snobbery' that led to pupils in secondary schools 'learning pass Irish and pass Latin and profiting from neither' when they might have benefited from vocational education were it not for 'social prejudice'.[15] In an article in the *Sunday Press* in 1959 he complained that the extensive reforms that were urgently needed in education were neglected as a result of over-caution on the part of the state, because of its respect for the church's interest in education.[16]

But this was about to change. In 1962, the then Minister for Education, Patrick Hillery, announced that Ireland was to participate in an Organisation for Economic Cooperation and Development (OECD) study of the education system. The report, a root and branch analysis, published as *Investment in Education* in 1966, represented a fundamental ground shift in educational thinking which was set to have profound implications for Irish society.[17] Essentially, it had the effect of consigning the ideas propounded in the Council of Education report to the dust. Whereas religious imperatives had been seen as central to educational thinking up to then, the education enterprise began to be seen in a radically new light – as an investment in human capital, which was vital for the success of a country's economic well-being. The report highlighted the importance of vocational education, seen hitherto as the poor relation. This was a landmark report. The key planks of the changed direction of educational policy – investment in the economy and the promotion of equality of educational opportunity – led to quantitative and qualitative changes. The first comprehensive schools were built in the mid-1960s. The decision by Donogh O'Malley to introduce free post-primary schooling from 1967 and a third-level grants scheme in 1968 has rightly been viewed as a watershed in Irish life.

While the system, based on meritocracy, is by no means perfect, these changes gave a generation of school children access to second- and third-level education that was, until then, beyond their reach. The educational infrastructure as it then existed – traditional religious-run secondary schools – could not cope with the influx of pupils, and state entry into the educational sphere to provide comprehensive schooling became an inevitable flashpoint. The autumn 1968 issue of *Studies* was devoted to a symposium on the new developments. The mood of the moment was captured in a seminal article by Sean O'Connor, assistant secretary of the Department of Education, in which he set out the new directions of educational policy. He wrote that 'no one wants to push the religious out of education ... but I want them in it as partners, not always as masters'.[18] Church personnel were defensive, and a submission from the Teaching Brothers' Association described the government's reform proposals as 'nationalisation by stealth'.[19] The Irish system of education had been bedevilled by rote learning and an examination system that gave little impetus to creative thinking or independent-mindedness. Gradually these issues began to be addressed by changes in pedagogy that placed the learner at the centre of the education process and encouraged a more questioning approach to knowledge. This had implications for Irish society and for the influence of the Catholic church, which began to be more open to question in due course.

Another key development that in time would change the Irish cultural landscape beyond recognition was the cabinet decision in July 1959, on foot of the *Report of the Television Commission* published in the same year, to set up an Irish television station.[20] The communications media – radio and press – played a key role in legitimizing the Catholic ethos in the 1950s. Ceremonial coverage of church events, as opposed to critical commentary, characterized Radio Éireann's approach at that time. The *Irish Independent*, the largest-selling daily newspaper, marketed itself as a Catholic newspaper well into the 1950s and published bishops' pastoral letters verbatim.[21] The arrival of television spelt the death knell of the church's power over the media.

Radio Telefís Éireann (RTÉ) was launched on New Year's Eve 1961 and the bishops' apprehensiveness in relation to the new medium can be gleaned from a statement issued after their October 1961 meeting, when, while acknowledging its potential for good, they went on to observe that it

> ... can also do great harm, not merely in the diffusion of the erroneous ideas of those who are lacking in deep or accurate knowledge of religious truth, but also in the broadcasting of programmes which offend all reasonable standards of morals and decency.[22]

The same kind of apprehensiveness was echoed by President de Valera in his address at the inauguration ceremony of the national television service, when he said:

> I must admit that sometimes when I think of TV and radio and their immense power, I feel somewhat afraid ... Never before was there in the hands of man an instrument so powerful to influence the thoughts and actions of the multitude.[23]

The early years of television coincided with the reappraisals taking place in the Catholic Church as a result of the Vatican Council, 1962–5. In 1958 Pope Pius XII had been succeeded by Pope John XXIII, whose short few years in the papacy revolutionized Catholicism. Pope Pius XII had carried on in the defensive mould of popes of the nineteenth century, which could trace its origins back to the Council of Trent. His attitude to change was defensive, and he was wary of modern developments. Pope John XXIII, on the other hand, was determined that the church should come to terms with modernity. His pontificate and announcement of the Second Vatican Council was set to have repercussions in Ireland and throughout the Catholic world. The fact that there were dissenting views at the Vatican Council, as represented by the so-called progressive and conservative elements, demonstrated clearly that the church was not the monolithic structure that many people in Ireland construed it to be. Whereas emphasis on authority and certainty had typified the mood of the church heretofore, there was now a growing realization of the importance of dialogue; a more horizontal conceptualization of church replaced the traditional hierarchical model. Irish Catholics had been accustomed to being told what to do by the hierarchy and clergy. The façade that there were definite black and white answers to all the complex questions of life was exposed as simplistic: the church could certainly give guidance, but it was up to people to inform their consciences and to come to decisions accordingly. The primacy of conscience was now emphasized in a way that it had not been formerly. Patterns of worship that had been set in stone for centuries were revised and a 'new' theology conceptualized the person's place in the world in a far more dynamic way than had scholastic philosophy, which had been the basis for Catholic theology since the thirteenth century.

Long before the era of spin and the spin doctor the council had its own slogan, which captured the essence of its mission – '*aggiorna-mento*' or updating. It was a huge media event. Exposure to, and questioning by, the media allowed the church to be seen as fallible. Pope John set the tone with his media-friendly presence. His more relaxed attitude to modern life served to reinforce the more open climate that was developing in Ireland both socially and politically. In Ireland, while Cardinal Conway was essentially an old-school cleric, he was pragmatic, and realizing that the winds of change were blowing, took his cue from Rome, despite the more wary attitudes and conservatism of some of the prominent Irish bishops of the time, for example Archbishop McQuaid of Dublin, and Bishops Browne of Galway and Lucey of Cork.

As it happened, the bishops' worst fears in relation to television were realized within a very short few years. One show in particular has been seen as significant in terms of its impact. Hosted by Gay Byrne, it was typically 1960s, bold and brash and was true to its signature tune 'it started on The Late Late Show'. The chat show was a very new genre in Ireland, and in a society where open and frank discussion was an entirely new phenomenon it was understandable that the show should become popular almost overnight. Cherished ideals could be demolished in the course of casual discussion, and television was no respecter of egos or reputations. In a society such as 1960s Ireland, its capacity to be subversive was endless. A spin-off from church reform was that many of the younger clergy embraced the new mood and became regular panellists on the show. They were open-minded and at ease with discussing all manner of hitherto delicate and taboo topics, often having to do with sexual matters, an area in which the church saw itself as having the main expertise and in which very definitive rules and regulations were laid down that were not to be questioned, let alone contravened. Boundaries were a key feature of Irish society at that time, and they were to be respected. Certain areas

were beyond the pale – not open to discussion. Now these same areas
were being aired live on television, which from the mid-1960s reached
into ever-increasing numbers of homes throughout the country.

In February 1966 an important boundary was pushed back – and
things would never be quite the same again. A female participant in
the show, when questioned about her night attire on her wedding
night, proclaimed that she had not worn any. Bishop Thomas Ryan of
Clonfert, recently returned from Rome where he had been secretary to
Pope John XXIII, scandalized by the discussion and not knowing that
he was about to make history and become infamous overnight,
contacted RTÉ to complain about the incident, saying that he would
be preaching about it in his cathedral church in Loughrea the following day.[24] It became a *cause célèbre*, and whereas a bishop's authority
would not have been questioned heretofore, this time the bishop had
the worst of it; and not alone that, but it was played out in public and
in the media. Just when it appeared that things could get no worse, on
the same show a few weeks later, in the course of a discussion relating
to the new cathedral in Galway, Bishop Browne of Galway was
referred to as a 'moron' for commissioning it.[25] Such public insults to
a bishop were hitherto unheard of, and anybody alert to the signs of
the times might have sensed that things would never be the same again
for the church in Ireland. The fact that RTÉ stood its ground and
defended the show, alluding to the Television Audience Measurement
(TAM) ratings, was an indication that there were new priorities in Irish
society. The bishop's position had been undermined. The mystique of
his office had been shattered. People power had entered the equation.
It was a signal that the media would in time replace the influence of the
hierarchy in Irish society. Television would replace the church as
taskmaster in due course. There was a certain prophetic ring to the
Irish Times lead writer's comments in relation to these matters on 29
March 1966, when he wrote:

> People in public life must accept the rigours of public life … In so
> far as people who are not politicians take part in public life, or
> comment on public affairs, they must expect to suffer the same
> attentions – adulation and abuse – as other public men.[26]

Bishops had been accustomed to making pronouncements, and to
command and expect obedience – this independent thinking, as it
gradually gained currency, signalled a new era for the Irish bishops.
They were no longer above reproach or beyond the reach of demands

for accountability. Though these events in themselves were trivial, they truly represented an important turning point in Irish life; television very quickly led to the democratization of Irish society.

This of course was the swinging sixties – a time of liberation, and in the media age Ireland would experience the same liberating forces. The gloomy post-war era had well and truly passed. The Kennedy visit in 1963 fed into the optimism of the times. A native son and Catholic had reached the White House. It was the era of The Beatles and 'flower-power'. The song proclaimed that 'all you need is love'. The Woodstock rock music festival in 1969 captured the optimistic mood of the times. Everything seemed possible – there were those who began to use drugs to push out the boundaries of experience. The anovulant pill appeared on the scene in 1960. It was an easy method for women to control their bodies and fertility and to extend their freedom of choice to avail of the many new experiences and lifestyle opportunities that began to present themselves from the 1960s. The women's liberation movement began in Ireland in the late '60s. Increasingly, the rigid censorship that had operated since the early years of the state was being challenged, and far-reaching reforms took place in the mid-to late '60s, which further added to the more liberal climate that was evolving in Irish society. While this relaxation applied to books and films, it did not extend to literature that offered advice on or promoted birth control or abortion, issues that would force themselves more and more on to the political agenda in a short space of time, and on which the Catholic Church had very definite teaching.

The birth control issue had already forced itself on to the agenda at the Vatican Council. Pope John XXIII had 'kicked for touch' by appointing a papal commission to investigate this area. This was later expanded by Pope Paul VI. In the wake of the council, the church appeared to be in tune with the mood of the times. There was a climate of expectancy abroad that the church's longstanding opposition to artificial birth control would be modified. Thus when Pope Paul VI made his pronouncement in July 1968, via his encyclical *Humanae Vitae*, reiterating the church's traditional teaching,[27] it was a definitive moment for Catholics in Ireland and throughout the world. It was a major turning point because it was an issue that went right to the heart of people's lives. By this time society was more open as a result of television, travel opportunities and the impact of the women's liberation movement, and the pronouncement, for many, fell on deaf ears in a way that would have been unimaginable ten years earlier. The

Catholic Church's authority, weakened at the time of the council, now suffered a body blow.

A further catalyst for change was the situation developing in Northern Ireland from the late 1960s. After his historic 1965 visit to the North to meet with Prime Minister Terence O'Neill, Taoiseach Seán Lemass set up an all-party Dáil committee to study the 1937 Constitution to examine whether there were aspects of the Constitution that would preclude the cultivation of good relations with the unionist population in Northern Ireland. The committee's report was published in 1967 and a number of its recommendations were to have profound implications for Irish society. The 'special position' of the Catholic Church was raised, as was the constitutional ban on divorce.[28] The outbreak of the 'Troubles' in 1969 lent a new urgency to the deliberations of the committee. In the course of a radio interview in September 1969 Jack Lynch (who succeeded Lemass as taoiseach) suggested that Article 44 might be amended.[29] Cardinal Conway reacted by saying that he 'personally would not shed a tear' were the 'special position' clause to go,[30] and on the basis of a referendum poll in 1972 it was deleted from the Constitution. Despite the fact that it had no force in law, its insertion in the Constitution, as well as its deletion, was of course very symbolic. Regarding the article banning divorce, Cardinal Conway and the hierarchy were fiercely opposed to any reversal of this position, and while it could be consigned to the background for now, it was an issue that would cause church–state confrontation in the 1980s and '90s.

The battleground in the 1970s was dominated by the issue of contraception. The two pieces of legislation governing contraceptives in Ireland were the 1929 Censorship of Publications Act, prohibiting the publication, distribution or selling of literature advocating birth control, and the 1935 Criminal Law (Amendment) Act, Section 17, which prohibited the importation, manufacture and sale of contraceptives. The women's movement played a central role in the campaign to change the law relating to contraception. The ban on artificial contraceptives was challenged by a group of women from the movement who travelled to Belfast on 22 May 1971 and purchased contraceptives.[31] It was a highly publicized media event and on their return to Connolly station, when they were allowed to pass through customs unimpeded, the law had been flouted and was seen to be obsolete. Nonetheless, attempts to change the law in 1971, 1973 and 1974 were unsuccessful. It was clear that the Catholic bishops were against any attempts to change the status quo; therefore there was little appetite among politicians to promote liberalizing measures. However, several other developments around this time would force them to confront the issue before too long more.

The *Report of the Commission on the Status of Women* in 1972 declared that parents had a right to 'regulate the number and spacing of their family' and that the methods they chose 'must remain a matter for their mutual selection and be influenced by their moral conscience'.[32] In the following year, in the McGee case, the Supreme Court ruled that Mrs McGee had a right to import contraceptives for her private use.[33] Also, the fact that the Family Planning Clinic had found a way to get around the legislation and dispense contraceptives, while not technically selling them, meant that it was only a matter of time before the law would have to be changed in line with practice. In 1979 Charles Haughey, minister for health in a Fianna Fáil government, introduced a very restrictive measure of contraception,[34] which he dubbed an 'Irish solution for an Irish problem'. While very limited in its provision, nonetheless it was a major breakthrough in the Irish context and marked the beginning of the dismantling of legislation that supported the Catholic ethos in Ireland.

During the 1970s the Catholic bishops were forced to come to terms with the fact that the era when they could rely on state law to bolster Catholic morality was about to disappear. While never changing their position in principle, by means of a series of statements, the first of which was in 1973, they refined it and developed a consistent line on where they stood on issues relating to church, state, morality and the law. In their statement in 1973, the bishops argued that no change in state law could make something right that was wrong in itself.[35] Contraception, they argued, remains wrong regardless of changes in the law, but they then allowed that it did not follow that the state is bound to prohibit the importation and sale of contraceptives. They continued, somewhat disingenuously, that 'no one has ever suggested, least of all the church herself, that they should be prohibited by the State'.[36]

The Second Vatican Council's *Declaration on Religious Freedom* had marked a decisive shift in Catholic understanding on the relations between church, state, morality and law, recognizing as fundamental the right to religious and moral freedom in society.[37] However, in a country where such close relations had existed between church and state since its very foundation, and in which legislation had propped up Catholic teaching, it was understandable, if not very wise, for the church authorities to think that this situation could continue indefinitely in a society that was experiencing profound changes. Aspects of what was a key debate on the merits or otherwise of the secular state were played out in the media between politicians like Conor Cruise O'Brien and Garret FitzGerald and Bishop Newman of Limerick who, in 1976, in the course of a speech made in Carlow, maintained that his personal view was that 'the Catholic people of our State have a right – a political right – to the provision of the kind of social framework that supports them in the living out of their moral and religious principles'.[38] The generality of the bishops through the 1970s were distancing themselves from Newman's position and were accommodating, if unwillingly, to the changed times. Their position heretofore, however, would not have been too far removed from that of Newman. Significantly, in an article in the Dominican publication *Doctrine and Life* in early 1979, Bishop McNamara of Kerry, who was most vocal against any relaxation of the law, observed that it was 'not the State's duty to make better Christians, still less better Catholics'.[39] Coming from McNamara, an influential church figure who was very conservative in his views, this was an important recognition and could be construed as a significant turning point.

In September 1979 a major event for Catholic Ireland took place – the visit of the newly elected Pope John Paul II, who made it his business from the time of his election as pope in 1978 to reverse the more liberal direction Catholicism had taken since Vatican II. His election as pope has had a crucial impact on Catholic culture worldwide over the past thirty years. Ironically, the Haughey bill passed in July 1979, some two months before John Paul's visit, was far more representative of Irish society at that time, notwithstanding the approximately one million people who turned out to greet the pope. John Paul picked up the mood of Irish society and the path it was likely to follow, and in his speeches railed against consumerism, materialism and the permissive society.[40] But Ireland was already on course to go headlong down that road, irrespective of any warnings the pope might sound. His visit signalled the beginning and end of an era, although it did, however, act as a spur to galvanize conservative Catholics to band together to lobby and resist the liberalizing developments in Irish society.

Throughout all this time the situation in Northern Ireland continued to deteriorate. Hunger strikes in which ten republican prisoners died, before they were called off on 3 October 1981, had further polarized the unionist and nationalist communities. Taoiseach Garret FitzGerald in the course of a radio interview in September 1981 had announced his intention to pursue a 'crusade' for constitutional reform, pointing out in relation to the Republic that 'our laws and our constitution, our practices, our attitudes reflect those of a majority ethos and are not acceptable to Protestants in Northern Ireland'.[41] Since the Anglo-Irish summit, which had taken place in 1980, there was a recognition that any possibility of peace and stability in Northern Ireland would require a development of the unique relationship between Britain and Ireland. The New Ireland Forum, which began in Dublin Castle in May 1983, was conceived by John Hume, leader of the Social Democratic and Labour Party (SDLP) and Garret FitzGerald and was designed to explore the nature of Irish society, with a view to bringing about the kind of social and cultural changes that would allow all traditions to live in peace and harmony.

In any such efforts, FitzGerald was going to be pitted against various elements of right-wing groups who had emerged in the early 1980s – groups like the Society for the Protection of the Unborn Child (SPUC), the Pro-Life Amendment Campaign (PLAC), the Irish Catholic Doctors' Guild, the Council of Social Concern and many others. Their emergence made for a highly charged and conflicted atmosphere, as these groups were fiercely opposed to FitzGerald's campaign to reform the confessional aspects of the Constitution. The Pro-Life Amendment Campaign, an anti-abortion lay pressure group, was formed in 1981. Its purpose was to have a clause inserted into the Irish Constitution that would preclude any change in the law that might allow abortion to be introduced by the 'back door'. In 1981–2 there were three elections, and the instability of the political situation meant that this group was able to extract promises from politicians, sometimes against their better judgment. The campaign, led in the main by lay Catholics, was a new development in itself. The Episcopal Conference issued a statement recognizing the right of each person to vote according to conscience, but added that it was the bishops' view 'that a clear majority in favour of the amendment will greatly contribute to the continued protection of unborn human life in the laws of our country'.[42] A pro-life amendment to the Constitution, voted on in referendum in September 1983, was passed by a margin of 66.45 per cent in favour, to 32.87 per cent against, after a particularly divisive campaign.[43] The result reflected a new and deep urban/rural divide in Irish society, with predominantly rural constituencies overwhelmingly voting Yes, while urban, largely middle-class areas provided the strongest resistance to the amendment. In Dublin, for instance, where the result was 51.6 per cent Yes, and 48.3 per cent No, five constituencies opposed the amendment. The apparently seamless Catholic culture of the past was well and truly gone.

When the Catholic bishops appeared in a public session at the New Ireland Forum on 9 February 1984, led by Bishop Cahal Daly of Down and Connor, it provided a platform for them to reiterate their position on church teaching vis-à-vis state law. Bishop Daly declared categorically that 'we in no way seek to have the moral teaching of the Catholic Church become the criterion of constitutional change or to have the principles of Catholic Faith enshrined in civil law'.[44] He was questioned as to whether the bishops would seek to influence the outcome, if a government sought to remove the constitutional ban on divorce by a referendum. The response, which had become a formula by this time, was that it was up to legislators to draft legislation and if the bishops considered there to be adverse consequences for society, they would state their views accordingly. Essentially the bishops' role and influence was gradually becoming that of one of several vested interest groups who had a right to influence public affairs, whereas formerly they constituted the main, and sometimes the only, power broker.

The proceedings of the New Ireland Forum gave Garret FitzGerald some confidence to press on with his 'crusade' for constitutional reform. In due course, he announced details of his coalition government's intention to hold a referendum to remove the constitutional ban on divorce on 26 June 1986. He presented the proposed change in the context of his crusade for a more pluralist Ireland, which would improve relations with Northern Ireland and also relations between the nationalists and unionists north of the border. Until about a week before the referendum, opinion polls indicated that increasing numbers supported the introduction of divorce. But results on the day reflected the resilience of traditional values – 63 per cent of those who voted rejected the government's proposal. The result was a repeat of the 1983 abortion referendum outcome. In this instance the majority of rural constituencies voted overwhelmingly against the amendment.[45] An atmosphere of resentment and intolerance surrounded the campaign, which prompted Bishop Laurence Ryan of Kildare and Leighlin to comment that it was 'doubtful if a democratic decision by the electorate ever before met with such resentment ... a resentment which amounted to rejection of the people's right to make the decision they made'.[46] To the extent that these issues were seen as a battle of strength between church and state for the hearts and minds of Irish people, in the 1980s, despite setbacks, the church was viewed by many as having won out. However, on all of these social/moral issues on which the church held strong views, the situation had changed totally by the mid-1990s.

In 1992 and 1993 there were several developments that would alter Irish society almost beyond recognition. Family planning legislation extended in 1985 was further liberalized in 1992, after which contraceptive devices became freely available throughout the country.[47] In the same year, a Supreme Court judgment in the so-called X Case ruled that abortion was legal in limited cases in which there was a real danger that the woman was liable to commit suicide.[48] In 1993 legislation was passed that legalized homosexual practices, as a result of a European Court of Human Rights directive which called for the decriminalization of homosexual acts between consenting adults.[49] The bill, as passed by the oireachtas, defined adults as people aged 17 and over.[50] In all instances, these developments were against the expressed wishes of the Catholic hierarchy. May 1992 saw the most ground-breaking development in Irish life to date: the early morning news broke the story that Bishop Eamonn Casey of Galway had an affair with an American divorcée during his time as Bishop of Kerry (1969–76), that they had a son, that he had denied the mother and child, and the impression was that he had used diocesan funds to pay off the mother's claims, lest the secret be found out.[51]

This was followed by a spate of clerical scandals involving child abuse by individual clergy and in institutions, homes and industrial schools run by clergy, and religious brothers and sisters. Such revelations were coming to light at precisely the time when the church needed all the moral authority that could be mustered in trying to defend Catholic moral principles, which had been enshrined in the Constitution and in legislation but were being increasingly eroded. Whereas heretofore the church was its own moral guardian according to the principles laid down in canon law, repeated allegations led to the government setting up the Laffoy Commission to inquire into Child Abuse in Religious Institutions on 23 May 2000.[52] This was an ironic turn of events, because previously the church monitored the moral behaviour of the state. Now there was a reversal of roles, and the state was acting as moral policeman in areas that were the church's own domain and in which formerly it would have brooked no interference from the state.

The next milestone was the divorce referendum in 1995. On this occasion, the leaders of all the political parties – the coalition government of Fine Gael, Labour and Democratic Left and the opposition parties Fianna Fáil and the Progressive Democrats – campaigned for a Yes vote. The bishops made a statement outlining their arguments against divorce, but most of the lobbying was done by anti-divorce lay groups. By this time the hierarchy had an official line that they kept to, but there were also clerics who did not toe the official line and were prepared to speak their minds. The referendum proposal was carried, but by a very narrow margin of less than 1 per cent – 50.28 per cent voted in favour and 49.72 per cent voted against the proposal;[53] once again the urban–rural divide was reflected in the voting pattern, with rural constituencies voting along traditional lines.

The result was of huge significance. When the all-party committee which reviewed the Constitution reported in 1967 and raised the lack of availability of divorce as being prejudicial to the interests of certain sections of the community, whose religion did not preclude them from availing of divorce facilities, the mere mention of the possibility of divorce produced a very strong adverse reaction from the Catholic bishops, several of them devoting sections of their Lenten pastoral letters to the matter.[54] A sense of the kind of authority wielded by the bishops at that time can be gleaned from the tone of Bishop Hanly of Elphin's remarks in the course of a pastoral letter which he devoted entirely to the subject. He pointed out that 'the State has no authority to dissolve any marriage, even the marriage of pagans' and observed that 'it is the solemn duty of every Catholic voter to register his vote against the provision of divorce facilities by the Oireachtas'.[55] This kind of specific 'advice' delivered in a very prescriptive tone was typical of bishops at that time. But by now there were plenty of indications that it was becoming less and less acceptable and that many were ignoring such advice. A key concept in the course of the Vatican Council deliberations was the importance of the church taking note of the 'signs of the times' – but the bishops were slow to recognize that the times were changing, despite the many indications that were clearly in evidence.

The last line of defence in terms of Catholic sexual morality was the issue of abortion. The purpose of the 1983 amendment to the Constitution was to ensure that abortion would not be available in Ireland. However, a case in which a 14-year-old alleged rape victim became pregnant and was prevented by court injunction from travelling to Britain for an abortion led to the Supreme Court ruling on 5 March

1992 that abortion was legal in limited cases in which there was a real danger that the pregnant woman was liable to commit suicide.[56] In a referendum the following November the electorate voted in favour of the right to information on abortion services and the right to travel to avail of such services, but rejected the wording of the substantive issue relating to the circumstances under which abortion is permissible.[57] So the matter was left unresolved. Because it was so emotive and divisive an issue, it was almost ten years before the government was able to re-visit it.

In late 2001, the then taoiseach, Bertie Ahern, announced that a further referendum was to be held on the issue in the following year. Voters would be asked to vote Yes or No to the terms of the Protection of Human Life in Pregnancy Bill, 2002. If approved in referendum, and subsequently enacted by the oireachtas, this would outlaw suicide as a ground for abortion, found to be constitutional by the Supreme Court in 1992.[58] Even though the new proposal fell short of what the church authorities would have wished for, in that it gave legal protection for the unborn only after implantation in the womb, as opposed to from the moment of conception, and thus was seen as 'a limited or imperfect measure', they still recommended Catholic voters to 'support this measure, even if it is viewed as less than might have been desired'.[59] This pragmatic compromise, on such a central cornerstone of Catholic morality, indicated in no uncertain terms the change in the bishops' position in Irish society. However, despite the bishops' advice and their issuing of twenty-four pastoral letters to recommend acceptance, the referendum proposal was defeated by a margin of less than 1 per cent – 50.42 per cent voted No, while 49.58 per cent voted Yes.[60] What was interesting was that the most extreme wing of the pro-life movement had urged a No vote, because it was considered that the amendment did not go far enough in protecting the unborn from the moment of conception, and this contributed to the defeat of the referendum. The Catholic lay right were now to the right of the bishops and, unlike the bishops, they were not prepared to compromise – an interesting development in itself.

The failure of the 2002 referendum marked the culmination of the dismantling of legislative and constitutional provisions that enshrined Catholic morality – a process that had continued unabated since the 1970s. Challenges had begun in the 1950s – change happened slowly but surely from the '50s and accelerated from the early '70s. Reacting to the result of the 2002 referendum on the evening news, Fr Martin

Clarke, spokesperson for the hierarchy, expressed disappointment, but went on to say that we must 'accept with serenity the people's will'.[61] This was a very far cry from the dogmatism of clerical statements in the past – both the result and his reaction spoke volumes about the change in the power and influence of the Catholic Church in Irish society by the turn of the twentieth century.

CHAPTER ELEVEN

Some Fitting and Adequate Recognition: A New Direction for Civic Portraiture in Nineteenth-Century Ireland's Industrial Capital

GILLIAN MCINTOSH

B elfast City Hall's corridors are lined with portraits of its mayors and lord mayors, and prominent in its grounds are freestanding public statues of the same subjects, the providers of Belfast's civic culture. According to Marcia Pointon:

> Objects like paintings which symbolize the ownership of a particular class or institution, enshrining the sense of identity of that group, tend to have a longer and less disturbed life than other kinds of household objects. And this is particularly true of portraits.[1]

Belfast's civic memorials provide an extant, largely unbroken narrative of the city's civic identity dating back to the second half of the nineteenth century, apparently 'marking continuity in a world of discontinuity'.[2] Their layers of meaning can be understood within the context of the social, political and cultural concerns of the period in which they were produced and presented. These are complex and coded works of art, and an exploration of them reveals aspects of Victorian Belfast's intricate political landscape, its tensions and personalities. In particular, this chapter looks at the first two civic portraits commissioned and presented in Belfast by the council to two former mayors. Through them it charts the progression from the private to the public sphere in the representation of the town's civic identity.

Belfast initially made its fortune from linen, but by the latter half of the nineteenth century shipbuilding was the dominant industry and, in combination with the export business of the town, the source of its fortune. The population rose rapidly to meet the needs of the shipyards and the factories filling the townscape. In terms of local government, Belfast had had a corporation since 1613, when the town received its first charter from James I. It was significantly reformed in 1840, as part of the broader move to improve municipal government in the United Kingdom, and after that sat for the first time in 1842, occupying a building in Victoria Square. In 1871 Belfast Town Hall opened in nearby Victoria Street. In a rapidly expanding town, which was granted city status in 1888, this building was soon considered too modest for the citizens of Belfast and more significantly for its municipal fathers.[3] These men began to plan for the creation of a new and grander municipal home, which culminated in 1906 in the opening of Belfast City Hall in Donegall Square.[4] As Kate Hill has argued, 'Members of the middle-class male elite used civic institutions as an extension of their own social arena, for mutual appreciation and convenience, and to consolidate their own class or group identity.'[5] The expansion of Belfast was further evidenced in the 1890s, when Queen Victoria conferred the title of lord mayor on the mayor of Belfast in 1892 and the boundary of the city was extended, with the city's wards expanding from five to fifteen, in 1896.

The symbolic ownership of these new civic spaces rested with the middle-class élite who built them; it is predominantly the images of local notables (with the exception of Queen Victoria's statue, which dominates the front of City Hall) that fill the corridors and grounds, in the form of paintings, busts and statues. According to Simon Gunn, 'The most spectacular organised manifestations of provincial culture in Victorian industrial cities were the public pageants that punctuated the urban year.'[6] In common with other industrial urban centres such as Liverpool, Birmingham, Manchester and Leeds, civic buildings such as the Town Hall and the City Hall gave Belfast's political élite a suitable stage on which to perform civic ceremonials – secular rituals – with formal procedures, speeches, dress and dinners, all reported in the local press.[7] Such civic rituals were concerned with the 'performity of power', making authority in the industrial city publicly visible.[8]

While Belfast's civic landscape was dominated by the local political élite and primarily represented its vision, the interpretation of this landscape by others was not always predictable or homogeneous. In the period in which the portraits here were commissioned and presented to the council, the Conservatives dominated the local political scene in Belfast. Indeed, apart from a brief resurgence by the Liberals in the 1860s (a large number having been co-opted onto the council in 1857 as part of Conservative attempts to settle the Chancery case), which peaked with the election of Edward Coey as mayor in 1861, Belfast was a Conservative town. The extension of the franchise in 1868 may have brought in a new body of Belfast voters in the form of skilled workers, but this expansion did not alter the town's political landscape. These workers, who in England may have supported the Liberals, 'in Belfast espoused Toryism or a populist Orangeism – working class, democratic and sectarian – which opposed a Liberalism that embraced Catholic voters'.[9]

Belfast Town and City Halls, linked as they were by pragmatic function, share the position of fora for the symbolic expression, in the form of civic portraiture and statuary, of Belfast's political élite. Moreover, these architectural developments were part of the physical embodiment of civic pride also evidenced (although, in Belfast, often in an inadequate way) in 'the improvement of public health, the demolition of slums, the acquisition of public utilities, the promotion of new civic buildings and the provision of libraries and museums'.[10] The townscape of Belfast was changing exponentially. Progress was literally apparent at street level. In addition to the creation of new streets (most significantly, Victoria Street) there were also improvements in the surface of the roads and footpaths of the town, which while slow and often the subject of complaints to the local papers, was an ongoing process. As Gerard Slater argues:

> It was not surprising that a Corporation of businessmen should be interested in the construction of new wide streets. A prospering commercial and industrial centre, supplying a substantial hinterland and extensively engaged in exporting and importing, could no longer function efficiently with a labyrinth of narrow and congested streets.[11]

By the 1840s street lighting in the town was being fuelled by Belfast's own gas. The Belfast Improvement Act of 1845 allowed for the widening of streets, improved lighting and management of livestock in the town.[12] This made the town centre an aesthetically more pleasing place, and one in which the genteel citizen would feel more comfortable shopping and promenading. Better street lighting also gave a feeling of added security, however real that was in practice. In the second half of the nineteenth century the issue of cleanliness dominated in Belfast, and focused on the foul-smelling Blackstaff River (colloquially known as the 'Blackstaff nuisance') and the town's overworked and underperforming sewers. Under the Belfast Improvement Act of 1878 the 'Blackstaff nuisance' was addressed, while Ormeau Avenue and the streets between it and Donegall Square were completed. Under the Belfast Improvement Act of 1884 Queen's Bridge was widened, St George's Market was enlarged and improved, and Arthur Square, Rosemary Street, North Street, University Road and Stranmillis Road were improved. Almost 857 private streets were handed over to be sewered and paved between 1878 and 1896. As Bill Maguire has described it, 'This fury of paving and sewering continued into the 1890s as more and more houses were built and as action on the grounds of public health became ever more necessary and unavoidable.'[13]

This drive to create more aesthetically pleasing urban centres, manifested in the Improvement Act of 1878, was articulated most prominently in Belfast with the construction of Royal Avenue in the 1880s and, later, in the civic pride expressed through the building of the Free Public Library (1888) and the City Hall (1906). Such developments, however, have to be offset by the contribution made by a more popular urban dynamic. These urban developments required labour, and Belfast had plenty of willing hands. Drawn to the urban centre by the employment opportunities offered in the linen industry, shipbuilding and trading, the influx of rural inhabitants to Belfast was impressive. Its population more than quadrupled between 1800 and 1851, from 20,000 to 87,000. That rate of increase did not slow down, and by 1901 its population stood at 349,000. In terms of Belfast's contribution to the evolution of civic government, John Beckett has argued that it was this combination of 'commercial and manufacturing greatness as well as [population] size and municipal achievement' that Belfast councillors used to support their argument that the town should be granted city status in the late 1880s.[14]

Civic portraits can be read as political statements, and in examining them this chapter explores the political culture that spawned them and which they were meant to serve. According to Simon Gunn, such portrait presentations represent the drama of civic ritual contained within it, simultaneously the imaginary constitution of a united urban community and a symbolic claim to authority over that community on the part of a civic leadership.[15]

In the mid-nineteenth century Belfast was marked by controversy, not merely that associated with the infamous (and drawn-out) Chancery suit. In 1854 John Rea, a Liberal solicitor, brought a case against Belfast Town Council, naming as special respondents the town clerk John Bates, the treasurer John Thomson and sixteen leading councillors as a means of attacking Bates and the Conservatives who had a stranglehold on local political power in Belfast. The corporation was accused of borrowing more than was allowed by the Belfast Improvement Acts between 1845 and 1850; buying the May's Fields rather than the gasworks; and fraudulently borrowing £84,000. After the original hearing, the case was found against the town council and all the named respondents. Following an enquiry by a Royal Commission, which reported in 1859, the corporation was absolved of many of the original charges against it. Unfortunately for them, the special respondents were still held personally responsible for £273,000. The question of the special respondents continued to be debated, as the Conservatives tried (and the Liberals refused to support them) to have the special respondents cleared through several Indemnity Bills into the early 1860s. This context should be borne in mind in any reading of the portraits of William Mullan and Philip Johnston, the former who acted as a witness to the Royal Commission and the latter who was named as a special respondent.

More generally, in the years which followed the municipal reforms of the 1840s, the council was characterized (according to Budge and O'Leary) by 'one-party dominance and a penchant for corrupt practices':

> The general impression is an unpleasant one – of one party securing control over the Corporation by questionable means and maintaining itself in power without scruple, while the opposing party's respectability is matched by its impotence.[16]

With many of the leading industrialists and merchant princes viewing the council as corrupt and choosing to serve instead on the harbour board or chamber of commerce (although many served simultaneously on more than one), there was a clear need publicly to reinforce, albeit symbolically, the legitimacy of the council to govern.

Civic portraiture (and later statuary) contributed to this effort by the council to make its authority visible and create the impression of local government constituting a united, respectable political body. In most urban centres the mayoralty played a significant role in the civic landscape as the focus of 'almost every public ritual from "mayoral Sunday" ... to grand civic events'.[17] Mayoral portraits were therefore particularly important, representing not merely the individual but the council and indeed the town itself. This chapter is particularly concerned with the first two civic portraits presented to the town council in the 1870s, those of former mayors William Mullan and Philip Johnston. It also reflects on the significance of the siting of these civic memorials. There was, for instance, an evolution in the presentation of portraits in Belfast in terms of the public and the private spheres. In October 1874 former mayor William Mullan's portrait was presented to his wife at home, albeit in the presence of a large number of the council. Two months later Philip Johnston's portrait was presented to the corporation, for display in the council chamber.[18] Marcia Pointon has argued that 'the ordering of civic spaces could also be achieved at a symbolic level via the strategic placing of portraits'.[19] Thus, Johnston's portrait was hung in a prestigious position in the chamber, over the mayoral chair, in full view of all who sat in the council chamber. The importance of the placing of Belfast's civic portraits in the council chamber of the Town Hall was highlighted in the *Belfast Street Directory* of 1884, which described the position of the portraits of Philip Johnston (hung at the top of the chamber), James Alex Henderson (hung at the north end), Dr Samuel Browne (on the east wall), Sir Robert Boag (left of the main entrance) and Sir John Savage (right of the main entrance).[20] Over a decade later the *Street Directory* of 1895 prioritized the portrait of Queen Victoria, by Sir Thomas A. Jones, unveiled in 1884: 'The portrait occupies the most prominent position in the Council Chamber on the north side wall, right behind the Lord Mayor's chair, so that as each member addresses the chair he faces the Queen's picture.'[21] By 1895 there were fifteen civic portraits in the Town Hall, but not all could be accommodated in the council chamber and were instead displayed on the walls of the principal hall and staircase.[22]

There are few earlier portraits, or portraits of earlier Belfast mayors.[23] The majority of those sitters who were mayors in the 1860s had their portraits (a notable exception is Mullan) presented to the council in the late 1880s; for instance, Sir William Ewart's was presented in October

1886 and (three-time mayor) John Lytle's in December 1887. Lytle's was, therefore, presented some twenty years after he held the office of mayor, and sixteen years after his death. Collectively these portraits argued for civic continuity. It is possible too that the presentation of these particular portraits was part of the campaign, gaining momentum in the mid-1880s, for Belfast to be granted city status, reminding the audience of the town's civic heritage and lineage.[24] Such portraits aimed to represent noble, civic-minded individuals who could unite across party and religion in a town where politics had a distinctly sectarian hue and where cross-party harmony was not a major feature of the political sphere,[25] and not merely in the dynamic between Catholics and Protestants. Relations between Presbyterians and Episcopalians in the town were historically fractious; in the pre-Famine period 'relations between [them] were soured by disagreements over national education, the Scottish Church and Presbyterian marriages'.[26] In general, in the period under discussion, there remained a deeply held belief among many Presbyterians that Conservatives failed to defend their interests when it was believed that they conflicted with those of Episcopalians.

To return to the mayors of the 1870s and their 'visual biographies': these portraits' sitters are universally male, Protestant and wealthy.[27] When its corporation was reformed in 1841 Belfast was a Protestant town whose government was dominated by a Conservative élite. This seeming uniformity was not, however, a monolithic Protestant identity, but one that was marked by some fluidity. 'The first reformed Belfast Town Council consisted of 18 Presbyterians, 15 Episcopalians, 6 Methodists and 1 Quaker.'[28] One can further reveal this complexity through a brief examination of the religion of Belfast's mayors in the 1870s. Philip Johnston was a Methodist (although born into the Church of Ireland and then brought up a Moravian), Sir John Savage was a Presbyterian (although previously a Methodist), James A. Henderson was an Episcopalian, Thomas Lindsay a Methodist, Robert Boag a Presbyterian, Sir John Preston was a member of the Church of Ireland, while John Browne was a Presbyterian.[29] Thus, while the Conservatives dominated local government, the religious identity of the political élite in Belfast was characterized by a degree of movement rather than rigidity.

The men the 1870s portraits represent were in the latter stages of their municipal careers, holding the position of mayor as a reward for past civic duty. In their iconography the portraits represent aspects of the town's civic culture, but also symbolize the dominance of Belfast's merchant class – a dominance that had existed since the reformed council of 1842.[30] They were nearly all presented to the council by the subjects' 'friends', and all while the subjects were living. These portraits hung originally in the Town Hall in Victoria Street. Such works of art thus can be said to 'define the history of the institution which they decorate and have both a material and an historical presence, depicting the people who once worked within the walls on which their portraits hang'.[31] As Pointon has argued, it is not only 'what is possessed that is significant but where and how it is made visible'.[32]

These half-dozen 1870s portraits, executed in oils, portray the fathers and capitalists who formed the first town council in Belfast following the opening of the new municipal home and who were hailed as those who had improved Belfast as a town.[33] The first two portraits were presented to the man who had overseen the creation of Belfast's first Town Hall, William Mullan, and to the first mayor to preside in it, Philip Johnston. Johnston was a Methodist, born in Ballinderry in 1804, and the *Belfast Newsletter* paid this tribute to him when he died: 'his was one of the first of the handsome portraits which now contribute towards making our Council Chamber one of the finest in the United Kingdom'.[34] While all were councillors and mayors of Belfast, not all Belfast mayors in the 1870s had their portrait presented to the council.[35] The majority of these portraits were by Richard Hooke, a native of County Down who moved to Manchester in the 1850s 'where he established a considerable reputation, painting many of [that] city's leading figures'.[36] He returned to Belfast annually, exhibiting his work and gathering commissions from local citizens. Two portraits, those of James Alex Henderson and Robert Boag, differ from the rest of the 1870s collection, as they are full length and by Sir Thomas A. Jones, president of the Royal Hibernian Academy.[37] The rest of the portraits are of the head and shoulders. Two of the portraits are of individuals still well known to those interested in the history of Belfast: James Alex Henderson, proprietor of the *Belfast Newsletter*, and Dr Samuel Browne, who became Belfast's first medical superintendent officer of health.[38] The others are less well known, if at all. All were principally members of the mercantile class; John Browne, for instance, was a timber merchant, an importer and property owner.[39] Of the other subjects, several were connected to linen, which had continued to expand as an industry into the 1870s.[40] Robert Boag, for example, was a linen merchant.[41] Born in Scotland, the son of the Congregationalist minister and lexicographer John Boag (1775–1863), he moved to Belfast in the first half of the nineteenth century. Thus the social and economic power in the first decade of the new Town Hall in Belfast rested both literally and symbolically with the merchant class. However, the subjects of these civic portraits derived their fame and their enduring part of the memory of Belfast from their civic office rather than from their personal accomplishments.

Civic portraits not only acknowledged the individual subject, but reinforced the institution their subjects worked in and for, and reinforced the positions of those involved in the presentation and the council in general. In making claims for the legitimacy of the local political élite to rule, such portraits underlined and elevated the civic trappings of the mayoral office; John Browne's (1879–80) portrait, for instance, depicts him holding paper, an icon of civic work, or learning, and represents the symbols of office, with the mace on the table and the robes of office on a chair. Philip Johnston (1871) is represented wearing the mayoral robe and chain, reflecting the dignity of his office, and also holding paper. Some portraits drew attention to Belfast's civic progress, and thus they embodied the civic pride of the town as well as expressing it. In 1872 Belfast Council had taken powers to purchase the gas undertakings and Sir John Savage (1872), as chairman of the gas committee, was a leading figure in this enterprise; his portrait thus represents him with his hand on the *Journal of Gas Lighting*. James Alex Henderson's (1873–4) portrait represents him in the robes of his office, wearing the new mayoral chain which was created during his tenure as mayor. On a table near him, in addition to the two maces, is a copy of the Corporation Gas Bill as well as the 1874 report of the British Association for the Advancement of Science, which held its conference in Belfast that year.[42] Only one of the portraits indicates the subject's occupation outside of the civic sphere: Dr Samuel Browne's (1870) represents him with his hand on a book entitled *Sanitary Science*, indicating his medical profession (understandable given that the portrait was the gift of his past pupils at the Royal Victoria Hospital) while at the same time alluding to the attempts (with varying degrees of success) at improving the sanitation of the town, which continued throughout the latter half of the nineteenth century and into the twentieth. While civic portraits thus make reference to the individual, the biographical is clearly not the full scope of their reference.

These portraits of soberly dressed men were not meant to reflect primarily the identity of the sitters but their status as civic officials. In this capacity they go beyond the individuals to their roles in the community. The majority of the sitters are dressed in dark colours, reflecting civic rectitude rather than any display of personal wealth or fame. And despite the wealth of these men (and some were very wealthy indeed) there are generally no urban signifiers (warehouses, trading ships, factories) behind them.[43] Again, while symbolically this indicates the primacy of the message – that the viewer should focus on the serious, sober, solitary civic worthies – it also pragmatically indicates a restraint in the cost of the portrait. Belfast's council was expanding its role in the 1860s. In a town that featured periodic civil unrest, where partisan (and at times corrupt) politics had been prominently before the public, the borough officials needed to express and represent their authority, and did so increasingly in a symbolic form. The creation of a new Town Hall presented the opportunity for new manifestations of civic pride by providing a dedicated forum for civic ritual and was both a symbol and locus of civic legitimacy. This increased emphasis on civic authority and continuity was symbolized in 1874 by the creation of a new mayoral chain that featured the arms and crests of former mayors, thus highlighting the lineage and pedigree of the highest civic office.[44] This year, 1874, was, additionally, when the first civic portrait was presented to an ex-mayor, Philip Johnston, for display in the council chamber.[45]

While this presentation is clearly significant, Johnston's portrait was not the first civic portrait of a Belfast mayor to be commissioned. In October 1874 former mayor William Mullan was presented with his portrait (or rather Mrs Mullan was) in his home at Willowfield on the Woodstock Road. On 22 October eighty 'leading inhabitants and merchants of Belfast' gathered at Mullan's home for the presentation of the portrait executed by Philip R. Morris. Mullan is represented sitting in the mayor's office, wearing the chain and robes of the mayoralty, 'transacting business'.[46] A committee to collect subscriptions (170) for the portrait was chaired by Sir John Savage (mayor himself in 1872). At the presentation Savage explained, 'It was felt that the time had come when service, long and faithful, given to the town should receive some fitting and adequate recognition.'[47] Significantly, although not the first mayor in the new Town Hall, William Mullan chaired the committee that had overseen its erection.[48] In addition to his 'integrity and honour' as a merchant, his 'impartiality, forbearance and dignity' as a magistrate and his 'usefulness and activity' as a member of the town council and harbour board, Mullan was praised for his role in the 1854 Chancery suit. And it was this damaging episode in Belfast's civic history that was the focal point of Savage's presentation speech, and provides a context in which to interpret the Mullan portrait.

While William Mullan was not a named special respondent in the Chancery suit, his civic role was bound up with it. Mullan, a prominent merchant and Liberal, was elected to the corporation in 1856 as part of the efforts by the Conservatives to reach a compromise with the Liberals over the Chancery case.[49] He became alderman for St Anne's ward as part of one of the Conservatives' failed attempts to have the case settled; in an effort to achieve this they 'were willing to loosen their grip on the Corporation' and make concessions to the Liberals.[50] Despite these efforts the Liberals did not manage to maintain a presence on the corporation, although Edward Coey (a Liberal) and Mullan were elected mayor for 1861 and 1866 respectively.[51] A 'Whig ally of the Conservatives', he 'was one of the first to align himself with the Conservatives on the generality of municipal questions' and tried (but failed) in 1857 to secure the passage of an Indemnity Bill.[52] Moreover, he gave evidence to the Royal Commission in 1859, when he condemned Rea's suit as 'a piratical exercise'.[53] Thus, at the presentation of his portrait Sir John Savage described how Mullan had thrown 'himself heart and soul into the breach, and many a valuable hour was given and many a long journey undertaken, to promote a settlement of that unhappy business'.[54] More generally, Mullan was acknowledged as being a good public servant to Belfast, and his subscribers were described as being of 'all shades of politics, and of all sects ... in religion – of Conservatives and Liberals, of Protestants and Catholics alike'.[55] The presentation of this portrait was, in one reading, a means of symbolically uniting the civic body in a public way against the background of the divisive case. In response, Mullan paid compliments to the assembly of 'gentlemen of such standing'.[56] He was the first of the 1860s mayors to be honoured with a portrait, and the manner in which his was subscribed to and presented would be repeated throughout the following decades. What differentiated Mullan's from the others was that it was presented with the intention of being displayed in a private space, not in the new Town Hall.[57] That honour went to Philip Johnston, and Johnston's portrait thus symbolized the move in Belfast's civic space from the private to the public sphere.

Like Mullan's, Johnston's portrait also spoke to the drama of the Chancery controversy. According to James A. Henderson, Belfast's mayor at the time, Johnston had seen the town in 'evil times' and now in 'more prosperous times'.[58] Johnston had also, Henderson told the assembly, been one of 'that small band, who were so much harassed by proceedings' about which the mayor said he would say no more. Unlike Mullan, Johnston was one of the named special respondents in the Chancery case. Concluding his speech, James Alex Henderson said, 'I am sure no matter how many portraits may afterwards be placed in this building to none more worthy can a position be assigned.'[59] Presented by his 'many friends', the portrait was placed in the 'place d'honneur in the Council Chamber; it rests immediately behind and above the civic chair, and is distinctly, and almost necessarily, observable from every municipal seat'.[60] Johnston, responding, looked to the future when he hoped Henderson's portrait, and those of future mayors, would adorn the walls. It was because he was the new Town Hall's *first* mayor that he was so honoured, he claimed modestly, rather than by any achievement as mayor. And, some twenty years after legal proceedings were taken, he chose to use his speech to defend his erstwhile colleagues against Rea's claims and the Chancery suit:

> I may be permitted to say that my connection with the Corporation commenced in 1845, the second election after it was a corporate body. Nearly all those who composed the Council at that time have passed away. Whatever mistakes they may have made I fearlessly assert that they had the well-being of Belfast deeply at heart (Hear, hear).[61]

One of the claims in the case had been that the council had borrowed money to buy the gasworks, but instead had bought May's Fields. Johnston stood behind this development of Belfast's markets, an area previously known he said as the 'dingy swamp'.[62] There was a sense, then, in this portrait presentation of old scores being settled. In addition, although the Liberals had experienced a brief resurgence in their fortunes in the town following the Chancery case, by the period of the new Town Hall their fortunes had slipped fatally, never to recover. As well as symbolizing that the local civic body could rise above controversy and dissent, this pair of mayoral portraits was part of a much-needed effort to draw attention to the dignity and respect due to (and legitimacy of) the municipal government (which, as the

Chancery case and the subsequent Royal Commission had revealed, was not without blame in Belfast) and the growth of a (perhaps more respectable) civic identity. And, arguably, to draw a line under the matter finally. These early portraits were, however, also partisan attempts to endorse publicly those perceived to have been wronged, or who had supported the Conservatives in the long-running Chancery case.

As in many other industrial urban centres, the memorialization of local political élites in Victorian Belfast was manifested initially in civic portraits and later, portrait statuary. As James Vernon argues:

> Then, as now, the civic landscape represented the town to itself through public buildings and amenities, street names, statues, and memorials – it articulated not only the competing narratives of the community's historical purpose and destiny, but also the roles of the different individuals and groups within those narratives.[63]

Through both these civic portraits the aspirations, values and agendas of Belfast's local political élites can be explored. These acts of commemoration can effectively be related to ongoing local political tensions in Belfast, revealing the enduring and detrimental legacy of the 1854 Chancery suit. Through celebrations of local individuals who had achieved the highest civic honour of mayor, the civic body was legitimized in a symbolic way. In the mechanisms that surrounded the commissioning and presentation of these memorials, members of the local government could be seen uniting for a common cause, which ostensibly raised them above party politics. This was often (as in the case of the portraits of Mullan and Johnston) against the background of perceived attacks upon the council or serious dissent within it. In terms of the siting of the memorials, there was a move from private to public space once the Town Hall was completed on Victoria Street. Thus, as much as the creation of Belfast's new municipal home, these portraits both embodied civic pride (by celebrating the position of mayor, for instance) and were materially part of the process of expressing it. With the creation of the City Hall in Donegall Square in 1906, another civic space was opened up, one that offered the opportunity for the display of portrait statuary.[64] At the start of the twentieth century this availability marked a perceptible change in the approach to and use of civic space in Belfast. The appetite for portrait statuary declined in Belfast as it did elsewhere, with Robert McMordie being the last of the city's lord mayors to be memorialized in this way in 1919.

The tradition of civic portraiture in Belfast, however, continues to flourish into the twenty-first century.[65]

CHAPTER TWELVE

The Origins of the Peace Process

THOMAS HENNESSEY

The Belfast Agreement, or Good Friday Agreement as it is more commonly known, is the most significant political development in the history of the island of Ireland since partition and the granting of independence in 1920–2. The Agreement of 1998 effectively ended the 'Troubles' in Northern Ireland – although this remained unclear for some years afterwards. At one level the conflict was between states: the United Kingdom of Great Britain and Northern Ireland, on the one hand, and the Republic of Ireland – or Éire to give that state its correct legal title. The constitutional dispute between these states arose because Éire's Constitution, Bunreacht na hÉireann, declared, in Article 2, that 'The national territory consists of the whole island of Ireland, its islands and the territorial seas.' Article 3 stated that pending the 're-integration of the national territory', the Irish parliament and government had the right to exercise jurisdiction over the whole of the island although it chose, voluntarily, not to apply this to Northern Ireland (Bunreacht na hÉireann). This was a territorial claim. According to the Irish Constitution, Northern Ireland was a part of both the Irish *nation* and the independent Irish *state* – it was *not part* of the United Kingdom. According to British constitutional legislation – to the Acts of Union 1800 – Northern Ireland was part of the United Kingdom – and had been since the Union came into existence on 1 January 1801. It was the representatives of the unionist population in Northern Ireland that objected most strongly to Éire's territorial claim on the grounds that it did not recognize their right to be separate from the rest of the island politically. In effect, the Irish state formally challenged the right of British sovereignty in Northern Ireland. The legitimacy – or lack –

of British sovereignty in Ireland manifested itself in the debate over the principle of consent, also known as the 'unionist veto' and a denial of Irish national self-determination: should the entity of Northern Ireland have the final say over whether that territory should remain in the United Kingdom or become part of a united Ireland?

The Anglo-Irish Agreement (AIA), signed between the British and Irish governments in 1985, was the major political initiative of the 1980s. Its origins lay in the electoral rise of Sinn Féin following the Hunger Strikes of 1980–1. The British offered the Irish government a consultative role in Northern Ireland's affairs but not the executive role Dublin sought. This formed the basis of the Anglo-Irish Agreement signed on 15 November 1985. Unionist opposition to the AIA was total. However, the problem for the unionist community was that, unlike a power-sharing Executive that required their participation, they had no institutional entity to attack and undermine. The AIA was between two sovereign governments and did not require their participation or consent.

With the new Anglo-Irish relationship progressing, the late 1980s saw the development of two separate processes which eventually evolved into the Northern Ireland Peace Process. One involved the British and Irish governments and the constitutional parties in Northern Ireland; the other involved an intra-nationalist dialogue between the Irish government, the Social Democratic and Labour Party (SDLP) and the republican movement with secret British–IRA contacts. The first of these – the inter-party talks process – began in 1989 with an initiative by Peter Brooke, the secretary of state for Northern Ireland, and continued under his successor, Sir Patrick Mayhew. The talks were divided into three strands. Strand 1 concerned the internal government of Northern Ireland; Strand 2 'North–South' relations between Northern Ireland and the Irish Republic; and Strand 3 'East–West' relations between the United Kingdom and the Republic. The negotiations never got beyond any meaningful discussion in Strand 1.[1] The talks collapsed in 1992. But an important line had been crossed and all the main constitutional participants had engaged with one another for the first time since the 1970s.

In 1989–90, Peter Brooke initiated contacts between the British government and the republican movement. He began this with a speech in which he recognized that there could be no military defeat of the Provisional IRA (PIRA). He followed this up with a second speech in which he emphasized that Britain had 'no selfish strategic or economic interests in Northern Ireland'. Britain stayed in Northern Ireland because the majority of people there wanted it to do so. His successor, Sir Patrick Mayhew, added that no-one but republicans excluded themselves from negotiations. To enter the political mainstream they needed to abandon violence for good. There was also some evidence of movement on the part of republicans. In 1991, Sinn Féin published *Towards a Lasting Peace*, which urged the British government to become persuaders for Irish unity. This quite clearly illustrated the influence of Hume. Then, in 1992, at the annual republican commemoration of the father of Irish republicanism, Wolfe Tone, a senior member of Sinn Féin admitted that there would have to be a sustained period of peace before British withdrawal. The demand for immediate unity had been abandoned. Secret contacts between the British government and the PIRA had begun in 1990. The contacts between the two parties took the form of an exchange of position papers but no negotiation. Sinn Féin wanted the British to recognize all-Ireland national self-determination and to become persuaders for a united Ireland. The British refused point blank to become persuaders and instead emphasized the consent principle. They also demanded a permanent end to PIRA violence.[2] The gulf between the two sides was enormous and the contacts ended quite quickly.

HUME–ADAMS TO THE JOINT DECLARATION

It was at this stage that it became public knowledge that John Hume, the leader of the SDLP, and Gerry Adams, the president of Sinn Féin, had continued their negotiations. They now agreed a common position known as 'Hume–Adams'. This stemmed from Hume's desire to produce a declaration which could be made by the British and Irish governments and which would end IRA violence. A 'Hume–Adams' declaration was produced and given to the Irish government to be passed on the British government. Hume was convinced that the principles enshrined within it would end the IRA's war against the British. The crucial parts, relating to self-determination, read:

> The British Prime Minister reiterates, on behalf of the British Government, that they have no selfish, strategic, political or economic interest in Northern Ireland, and that their sole interest is to see peace, stability and reconciliation established by agreement amongst the people who inhabit the island. The British Govern-

ment accepts the principle that the Irish people have a right collectively to self-determination, and that the exercise of this right could take the form of agreed independent structures for the island as a whole. They affirm their readiness to introduce the measures to give legislative effect on their side to this right (within a specified period to be agreed) and allowing sufficient time for the building of consent and the beginning of a process of national reconciliation. The British Government will use all its influence and energy to win the consent of a majority in Northern Ireland for these measures. They acknowledge that it is the will of a majority of the people of Britain to see the people of Ireland live together in unity and harmony, with respect for their diverse traditions, independent, but with the full recognition of the special links and the unique relationship which exists between the peoples of Britain and Ireland.[3]

This version contained all of the main republicans demands – a declaration of British withdrawal within a given time period; that the desired outcome of negotiations was an independent Ireland; and that the British government would adopt the role of persuaders for a united Ireland. The opening line of Hume–Adams also asked the British prime minister to address the concerns of republicans as to why the British remained in Ireland and to reassure them that they no longer had any wish to remain except to see peace. Albert Reynolds, the taoiseach, presented the document to the British prime minister, John Major. But the taoiseach's instinct told him that Major would find the document unacceptable; furthermore he considered it unbalanced – 'it was a nationalist document, and there was no balance whatsoever in it in relation to the Unionist position'.[4] Major did, indeed, find it unacceptable and an attempt to bypass the consent principle. The result was the Downing Street Declaration in December 1993.

In the Declaration, the British government, in an effort to remove the main republican justification for violence, namely British imperialism in Ireland, declared that it had 'no selfish strategic or economic interest in Northern Ireland'. This was a crucial statement, for it differed from Hume–Adams in a fundamental way: the British were saying that they had no *selfish* strategic or economic interest in Northern Ireland – but they did have *unselfish* strategic and economic interests. Furthermore, they admitted – by its absence in the Joint Declaration that which was in Hume–Adams – that they did have a *political* interest in Northern Ireland. After this the British declared that their primary interest was to see 'peace, stability and reconciliation established by agreement among all the people who inhabit the island'. The role of the British government was to 'encourage, facilitate and enable' the achievement of such agreement over a period of time, through a process of dialogue and co-operation, based upon the 'full respect for the rights and identities of both traditions in Ireland'. In this, the British government accepted that such agreement might take the form of a united Ireland, but crucially stated that it agreed that

> ... it is for the people of the island of Ireland alone, by agreement between the two parts respectively, to exercise the right of self-determination on the basis of consent, freely and concurrently given, North and South, to bring about a united Ireland, if that is their wish.

The British government thus rejected the republican demand that the unit of self-determination should be the island of Ireland; concurrent referenda, North and South, still permitted Northern Ireland to self-determine its constitutional future, and consent, or not consent, to a change in its status, regardless of how the rest of the island voted. Nevertheless, the section on self-determination was couched in 'Green', nationalistic language: although it reiterated the principle of consent and the self-determination of Northern Ireland, it offered the potential of both parts of Ireland agreeing to – albeit separately – a solution that could be interpreted as all-Ireland national self-determination. For the Irish government, the taoiseach, Albert Reynolds, agreed that it would be wrong to attempt to impose a united Ireland in the 'absence of the freely given consent of a majority of the people of Northern Ireland', and he accepted, on behalf of the Irish government, that the 'democratic right of self-determination by the people of Ireland as a whole must be achieved and exercised with and subject to the agreement and consent of a majority of the people of Northern Ireland and must, consistent with justice and equity, respect the democratic dignity and the civil rights and religious liberties of both communities'. Thus the Irish government now also recognized consent. The taoiseach then confirmed for the first time that, in the event of an overall political settlement, the Irish government would, not could, put forward and support proposals for changing the Irish Constitution which would fully represent the principle of consent in Northern Ireland. Both governments confirmed that democratically mandated parties which 'establish a commitment to exclusively peaceful methods and which have shown that they abide by the democratic process, are free to participate fully in democratic politics and to join in dialogue in due course between the governments and the political parties on the way ahead'.[5]

This closed the door on Hume–Adams and left the republican movement in a quandary. They were faced with a common British–Irish position which, in addition, both the Ulster Unionist Party (UUP) and the SDLP now accepted. In response, they developed the Tactical Use of Armed Struggle (TUAS) doctrine. This envisaged the creation of a pan-nationalist alliance based on building a common negotiating position among Sinn Féin, the SDLP, the Irish government and Irish-Americans influencing President Bill Clinton. This would force the British to abandon the unionists and agree terms acceptable to the republican movement. It was on this basis that the PIRA announced a cessation of military operations on 31 August 1994. But the PIRA refused to say that its cessation was permanent (it could not, as this would have contradicted the TUAS strategy as presented to the grass-roots). The ceasefire caused uncertainty in some unionist circles. There were fears that the cessation was tactical based on the refusal of re-publicans to declare it permanent. Loyalist paramilitaries were more confident. The Combined Loyalist Military Command (CLMC), an umbrella loyalist paramilitary grouping, declared their own ceasefire in October 1994 on the basis that the 'Union is Safe'. In response to unionist anxieties, John Major and Mayhew introduced the concept of the dismantling of paramilitary arsenals – decommissioning – as evidence that the PIRA's war was over. The PIRA rejected this as an attempt to force an admission of surrender from it. As a consequence, Sinn Féin was refused entry to all-party talks.

As the impasse persisted, the British and Irish governments pushed ahead with their discussions and produced, in February 1995, the Frame-works Document as a basis for all-party discussions. Alongside a North-ern Ireland Assembly there would be a North–South institution with consultative, executive and harmonizing powers.[6] The unionist parties were forthright in their rejection of the contents of the Frameworks Document, which reminded them of Sunningdale and the Council of Ireland, fearful that they encompassed a process whereby an all-Ireland government – the North–South body with *executive* powers – could evolve by stealth without a formal transfer of sovereignty from the United Kingdom to the Republic of Ireland. All unionists rejected this out of hand as a return to the Sunningdale model. The governments appointed an international commission, under the chairmanship of a former US senator, George Mitchell, to break the impasse on decommissioning. It produced a set of principles committing all participants in negotiations to non-violence. It also recommended that decommissioning should progress alongside, instead of before, political negotiations.[7] While John Major accepted the report, he also proposed elections to a forum as unionists refused to engage with Sinn Féin outside such a mechanism. The IRA took this as yet another stalling tactic and ended their ceasefire, in February 1996, with a massive bomb in London's Docklands, killing two people.

The PIRA's renewed campaign was mainly directed at British mainland targets, such as the bomb which destroyed Manchester city centre injuring over 200 people; apart from sniper attacks on the border, the campaign aimed to avoid alienating Sinn Féin's increasing electoral support which stemmed from its role in the peace process. In 1997 a new Fianna Fáil government, now led by Bertie Ahern, came to power in the Republic, as did Tony Blair's New Labour government in Britain. With the Conservatives, in particular, out of the equation, the republican movement calculated that this was the time to restore its ceasefire. They duly did this and were admitted to all-party talks. They joined the Ulster Democratic Party, associated with the UDA, and the Progressive Unionist Party, associated with the UVF, who were already there. As the republicans walked in, Paisley's Democratic Unionist Party (DUP) walked out. But the UUP, led by David Trimble, did not. Trimble's leadership of the UUP was a key turning point: unlike his predecessors, he was prepared to accept a North–South institutional arrangement so long as this was not on the Sunningdale/Frameworks model which envisaged a central executive body. The scene was set for historic negotiations.

The talks format followed the now familiar Stands 1, 2 and 3. In Strand 1 – the internal government of Northern Ireland – the divide between the UUP and the SDLP centred on power-sharing in a Northern Ireland Assembly once again. The SDLP wanted a power-sharing cabinet; the UUP did not want a cabinet and instead offered a committee system. The UUP wanted the Assembly to make decisions on the basis of majority rule; the SDLP wanted a nationalist veto. The UUP offered a bill of rights to protect minority rights; the SDLP wanted 'sufficient consensus' inscribed into the Assembly's standing orders – that is, that there should be a majority of unionists and nationalists *separately* for legislation to pass. Sinn Féin did not accept the need for an assembly, instead arguing for stand-alone all-Ireland institutions.

In Strands 2 and 3 the centre of gravity rested between the Irish government and the UUP. The Irish wanted a North–South institution with executive powers; the UUP would only accept a consultative body. There was, however, movement in other areas. Trimble proposed, and the Irish government accepted, the principle of a consultative Council of the British Isles – this reflected the unionist belief that East–West, or Britannic, links were more important than North–South relationships. The Irish made the substantial offer of the removal of the territorial claim in Articles 2 and 3; in return they expected the British government to repeal the Government of Ireland Act, 1920 which they mistakenly saw as a British territorial claim over Northern Ireland.

NEGOTIATIONS

In an effort to demonstrate to the UUP that they were serious about a deal, the Irish government passed – through Martin Mansergh (the taoiseach's special advisor on Northern Ireland) to one of Trimble's advisors, Austin Morgan – a copy of a revised Articles 2 and 3 that would be the Republic's claim to Northern Ireland. The new Article 2, rather than, as before, claiming that all of the territory of the island of Ireland constituted the national territory, stated: 'It is the entitlement and birthright of every person born in the island of Ireland, which includes its islands and seas, to be part of the Irish nation.' The new Article 3 enshrined the consent principle, 'recognising that a united Ireland shall be brought about only by peaceful means with the consent of a majority of the people, democratically expressed, in both jurisdictions in the island'. The phrase 'both jurisdictions in the island' recognized that *two* states existed in Ireland – Éire and the United Kingdom of Great Britain and Northern Ireland – rather than one, as the 1937 Constitution had. The Irish, in return, had secured from the British a commitment to repeal the Government of Ireland Act, 1920. Mansergh believed that the Government of Ireland Act was the equivalent of a British territorial claim to Northern Ireland. Now it would be removed. The British, in turn, committed themselves to a united Ireland if a majority of people in Northern Ireland voted to cease to be part of the United Kingdom and form part of a united Ireland. Constitutional issues, then, had been resolved outside of the formal talks process. Trimble, on the other hand, was comfortable with all of this: he realized that the British 'territorial claim' to Northern Ireland rested upon the 1800 Act of Union, *not* the Government of Ireland Act. The Irish had backed the wrong horse.

THE MITCHELL DOCUMENT

On 25 March, Senator George Mitchell, the independent chair of the talks, made a dramatic announcement: 9 April 1998 was the deadline by which an agreement would have to be concluded. Mitchell was determined to get to the first landmark in his schedule – an initial draft of a comprehensive agreement by 3 April, based on the discussions and papers submitted by the talks participants. In most of the areas – changes in the Irish Constitution and British constitutional law; prisoners; policing; criminal justice; and a new British-Irish Council – there was a common British–Irish government position. By 3 April, however, there was no draft document for the political parties to consider. The main area of discussion between the British and Irish governments centred on Strand 2 and what was required to keep Sinn Féin on board without alienating the unionists.

In London the prime minister and taoiseach met, in an attempt to resolve the North–South differences. Tony Blair and Bertie Ahern instructed their officials to bring an agreed document to Mitchell in Belfast on 5 April. The governments' officials now requested, on behalf of the premiers, that Mitchell present a composite document to the parties – including the section relating to Strand 2 agreed in London – with the remainder composed by the chairman's team in Belfast, as the chairman's document. A reluctant Mitchell agreed, although the final draft of Strand 2, containing a number of annexes, was not available for the parties until late on 6 April. The unionist parties were aware that the document which would eventually emerge would be most unpleasant in Strand 2.

When the misnamed 'Mitchell Document' was finally revealed to the parties, later that night, the talks almost collapsed. Most of the constitutional aspects appeared satisfactory to the UUP – the recognition of consent; the recognition of the territorial integrity of the United Kingdom of Great Britain and Northern Ireland; and options including the SDLP and UUP models, for consideration in Strand 1 – the internal government of Northern Ireland. It was Strand 2 which produced the crisis. Here there were no options – everything had been decided for the unionists. Together with an outline of the envisaged North–South Ministerial Council (NSMC) the document contained a series of annexes outlining the areas in which the council would decide common North–South policies, specific areas where decisions would be taken on action for North–South implementation and a series of North–South implementation bodies. The council's authority and functions were to be derived directly from London and Dublin. Effectively, the Northern Ireland Assembly was bypassed. It was not Belfast, but London and Dublin that determined the remit of the council. There were pages and pages of areas containing proposed North–South co-operation that would be carried out by the NSMC.

Blair embarked for Belfast in an effort to save the talks. When Trimble arrived at Hillsborough Castle, to greet Blair, he appeared to the London team to be calm and lucid and said simply – and repeatedly – that he could not do a deal on the basis of what was on offer in Strand 2. Blair 'said effectively that he would negotiate for him'.[8] He had no choice for he feared that Trimble would walk out of the talks.[9]

Bertie Ahern then flew to Belfast the day of his mother's funeral. There Blair had to tell Ahern that if the talks were not to collapse there had to be a complete rewrite of the North–South part of the agreement.[10] As Ahern put it, the unionists wanted the consent principle enshrined, an Assembly, the Irish constitutional claim on the North gone, 'and they want to give fuck all in return'.[11] Despite this, Ahern did not rule out making amendments because, he realized, they were essential to get the UUP back on board. Later Blair reassured Trimble that he told the Irish that they had to amend the text on North–South matters radically and that there could be no progress elsewhere until this was unblocked. But to do this he needed a clear commitment from the UUP that if he unblocked this issue, they would be prepared to move on other matters, particularly Strand 1. When a tripartite meeting was convened involving the British, the Irish and the UUP, Ahern agreed that the Irish would agree to radical changes to Strand 2.[12] The governments were surprised when the UUP accepted that there was room for manoeuvre on their part.[13] The UUP claimed they had a solution that would 'do the trick'.[14] This was that the North–South Ministerial Council would not have any functions up front but the Northern Ireland Assembly was committed to agreeing at least six matters for future co-operation and implementation. Thus it would be the Northern Ireland Assembly deciding North–South co-operation rather than the governments or the North–South Ministerial Council.

Authority in North–South co-operation would spring from Northern Ireland. The broad agreement in Strand 2 was the catalyst for movement in Strand 1. With the Irish having broken nationalist ranks and given up the agreed NSMC, John Hume and the SDLP had to focus their aims on Strand 1. And, after securing their objectives in Strand 2, Trimble felt that he had to abandon any hope of a weak series of committees, in Strand 1, and concede to the SDLP their model of a power-sharing Executive – including a nationalist veto. Constitutional issues (repeal of the Government of Ireland Act and Articles 2 and 3), as well as Strands 1, 2 and 3 (where both governments and the UUP and SDLP accepted the creation of a British–Irish Council and the replacement of the Anglo-Irish Agreement by an inclusive British–Irish Agreement), the main legal difficulties that dogged Anglo-Irish relations and North–South relations for decades, had been solved.

But what did Sinn Féin have to show? Their whole strategy appeared to have been based on Dublin securing a powerful North–South arrangement on their behalf. But Ahern had done the deal with Trimble. By 12.15 a.m. – Good Friday – the British became aware that the Irish were being 'spooked' by Sinn Féin during a meeting between officials. Blair, at this stage, believed Sinn Féin 'didn't want a deal at all. They were holding the whole thing to ransom.' At 12.30 a.m. Blair spoke to Ahern. Sinn Féin were stuck on three years for prisoner releases. As arguments went on about the size of the Assembly, Blair, at 2.15 a.m., asked Hume and Mallon what Sinn Féin were up to. Hume replied that 'it was all about prisoners'. They wanted them out in one year 'and think they will end up with two'.[15] In the second of two meetings with Adams and Martin McGuinness, the republicans produced a list of their concerns – containing seventy-eight points on which they wanted answers from the two governments. It was 4 a.m. on Good Friday. Ahern believed that Sinn Féin were not going to sign up to an agreement. He sat down with Adams and McGuinness, talking through all the points they had raised, and recalled: 'I painfully went though every single one of those with them, arguing as passionately as I could for the benefits of doing a comprehensive deal.' The British stuck to three years. Sinn Féin rejected this outright. Adams argued that 'released prisoners are the best ambassadors for the peace process'.[16]

Blair enlisted the help of the president of the United States, phoning him in Washington and suggesting that Bill Clinton call Adams and explain that there was no way the British could do a deal on prisoners unless Sinn Féin signed up to a wider agreement. British public opinion would only accept the release of prisoners if the republicans signed up to the whole agreement.[17] When Clinton phoned Adams he said: 'Gerry you gotta understand this is a nightmare for Blair, because if there's any act of violence after any of these guys get out, he'll be accused of basically being made a dupe for murderers. And so it's hard for him, and the longer it gets to wait, the more he can point to acts of good faith which justify this clemency.' In the end Blair agreed to give Adams a private oral assurance that if Sinn Féin signed up to a deal, 'we would bring forward release from two years to one'. The final thing that seemed to reassure Adams was Blair promising that he would not turn his back on the process once an agreement was signed.[18]

Then the final crisis blew up. Around midday on Good Friday the parties to the talks got the new text of the agreement. Then 'all hell broke loose'.[19] Alongside prisoner releases and a commission to look at the future of the RUC was the fact that the agreement did not link decommissioning with Sinn Féin serving in the Assembly's power-sharing Executive. Trimble found that parts of his negotiating team were in open revolt. But Blair was determined that the talks would not collapse at this late stage. He came up with the idea of a letter[20] that suggested that 'if people did go back to violence, and there were insufficient ways of getting rid of people in those circumstances from the democratic process once they had shown that they were not prepared to abide by the democratic process, then we would review the rules for that. So I gave them that assurance. Then we dictated the letter, basically giving them the assurance that they needed, and perfectly justifiably needed.' Trimble and his deputy leader, John Taylor, accepted the letter – but another key UUP member did not: Jeffrey Donaldson was not satisfied – the letter was not part of the final agreement but a separate document to which no-one else had signed up. He left the talks venue and would become the focus of dissension, within the UUP, to the terms of sharing power with Sinn Féin before decommissioning occurred. At 5 p.m., Good Friday, 10 April 1998, George Mitchell announced to the final plenary session that an agreement had been reached.

In Strand 1 there was to be a Northern Ireland Assembly, at the core of which was to be a power-sharing Executive. The Executive and Assembly were to be governed by 'sufficient consensus' or a double veto. This meant that for a decision to be ratified by the Assembly there would have to be a majority of unionists and nationalists separately. Although there was a first minister (unionist) and a deputy first minister (nationalist), they were co-equal and neither was subordinate to the other.[21]

In Strand 2 there was to be a North–South Ministerial Council that would be a consultative body with no executive powers: 'To exchange information, discuss and consult with a view to co-operating on maters of mutual interest within the competence of Administrations, North and South.' The Assembly, however, was committed to agreeing six areas of North–South co-operation so that nationalists were reassured that the NSMC would not be a mere talking shop. All decisions would be by consensus: therefore both unionists and nationalists had a veto over all decisions.[22]

Strand 3 saw a British–Irish Council established. It too was a consultative body. It was to be made up of all devolved administrations within the United Kingdom, Crown dependencies within the British Isles and the sovereign governments in London and Dublin.[23] A British–Irish Intergovernmental Conference replaced the Anglo-Irish Intergovernmental Conference set up by the AIA. British and Irish ministers and officials would be unable to discuss matters devolved to the Assembly, while Northern Irish ministers would be allowed to attend conference meetings as observers.[24]

In terms of 'constitutional issues', the principle of consent was enshrined at the heart of the agreement: all parties agreed that there would not be a united Ireland without the consent of a majority of the people in Northern Ireland voting for it.

(1) It is hereby declared that Northern Ireland in its entirety remains part of the United Kingdom and shall not cease to be so without the consent of a majority of the people of Northern Ireland voting in a poll.

(2) But if the wish expressed by a majority in such a poll is that Northern Ireland should cease to be part of the United Kingdom and form part of a united Ireland, the Secretary of State shall lay before Parliament such proposals to give effect to that wish as may be agreed between Her Majesty's government in the United Kingdom and the government of Ireland.

Articles 2 and 3 of the Irish Constitution were redrawn to separate nation and state in Irish constitutional law.

The Government of Ireland Act, 1920[25] was repealed but was replaced by the Northern Ireland Act, 1998 which reasserted the sovereignty of the Westminster parliament over Northern Ireland.[26] A

Human Rights Commission was established to monitor and safeguard human rights in the province, while the European Convention on Human Rights was incorporated into Northern Irish law.[27] There was to be an end of Emergency Powers legislation, combined with a reform of policing and the criminal justice system.[28]

The most controversial aspects of the agreement – alongside the possibility of Sinn Féin serving in the Executive – centred on decommissioning and prisoners. All paramilitary prisoners were to be released on licence within two years.[29] For the Protestant community in particular this represented the release of murderers back on to the streets. It highlighted the essential difference between the Belfast Agreement and Sunningdale: in 1974 the unionist community rejected the North–South constitutional arrangements; in 1998 the Protestant reaction was an emotional one against the freeing of prisoners and the prospect of sharing power with Sinn Féin, particularly in the absence of decommissioning. As for decommissioning, the agreement stated that parties to the agreement were to use their influence with paramilitaries to achieve disarmament.[30] Sinn Féin declared that they were an ordinary political party and not the PIRA. Therefore if the IRA did not decommission, Sinn Féin should not be excluded from participating in the Executive. Trimble's UUP, however, took the view that the IRA and Sinn Féin overlapped to such an extent as to be indistinguishable. Consequently, they would refuse to participate in the Executive with Sinn Féin until the IRA began decommissioning.

Years of stalemate followed. The moderate unionists (the UUP) and nationalists (the SDLP) who negotiated the Strand 1 and Strand 2 elements of the Belfast Agreement were, ultimately, displaced in electoral terms by the 'extremes' of Northern Ireland politics: Ian Paisley's DUP and Sinn Féin. A relatively stable power-sharing Executive was eventually formed after the IRA finally decommissioned their weapons allied with a tinkering with the Belfast Agreement to satisfy the DUP; but in fundamentals it remained the agreement negotiated by the Blair–Ahern–Trimble–Hume axis. The successive agreements negotiated by the DUP and Sinn Féin remain the progeny of the UUP and the SDLP. In that sense Paisley and Adams may have won the electoral peace but they lost the war of ideas to Trimble and Hume. And that is what counts in the long run.

Notes

INTRODUCTION

1. For recent assessments of the revisionist debates, see John M. Regan, 'Southern Irish Nationalism as a Historical Problem', *The Historical Journal*, vol. 1 (2007), pp.197–223; and Evi Gkotzaridis, *Trials of Irish History: Genesis and Evolution of a Reappraisal, 1938–2000* (London, 2006).
2. Tom Garvin, *1922: The Birth of Irish Democracy* (Dublin, 1996).

CHAPTER 1 WHAT DID THE EASTER RISING REALLY CHANGE?

1. Charles Townshend, *Easter 1916: The Irish Rebellion* (London, 2005), pp.270. This is the first full scholarly account of the Rising, and the starting point for future discussion.
2. Jonathan Githens-Mazer, *Myths and Memories of the Easter Rising: Cultural and Political Nationalism in Ireland* (Dublin, 2006), p.212.
3. Peter Hart, *The IRA at War, 1916–1923* (Oxford, 2003), pp.88–109.
4. Charles Townshend, *Political Violence in Ireland: Government and Resistance Since 1848* (Oxford, 1983), p.277.
5. Donal Nunan, 'Price Trends for Agricultural Land in Ireland, 1901–1986', *Irish Journal of Agricultural Economics and Rural Sociology*, vol. 12 (1987), pp.71–2.
6. Over the course of 1918, for example, the Munster and Leinster Bank's account holdings rose by an astonishing 40 per cent. *Cork Examiner*, 11 January 1919.
7. Nunan, 'Price Trends for Agricultural Land', p.69.
8. Ibid., p.70.
9. David Fitzpatrick, *Politics and Irish Life: Provincial Experience of War and Revolution* (Dublin, 1977), p.246.
10. David Fitzpatrick, 'Strikes in Ireland, 1914–21', *Saothar*, no. 6 (1980), p.36.
11. Hart, *The IRA at War*, pp.50–1.
12. W.E. Vaughan and A.J. Fitzpatrick (eds), *Irish Historical Statistics: Population, 1821–1971* (Dublin, 1978), p.263.
13. Michael Wheatley, *Nationalism and the Irish Party: Provincial Ireland, 1910–1916* (Oxford, 2005), pp.221–2, 231.
14. David Fitzpatrick, 'The Logic of Collective Sacrifice: Ireland and the British Army, 1914–1918', *Historical Journal*, 38, 4 (1995), pp.1017–30.
15. Patrick Callan, 'Voluntary Recruiting for the British Army in Ireland During the First World War', unpublished PhD thesis, University College Dublin, 1984, p.175.
16. Wheatley, *Nationalism and the Irish Party*, pp.227–42. See also Dermot Lucey, 'Cork Public Opinion and the First World War', unpublished MA thesis, University College Cork, 1972, pp.73–88.
17. *Irish Rebellion Handbook* (Dublin, 1998 [1916]), p.164.
18. *Irish Volunteer*, 24 July 1915.
19. *Irish Volunteer*, 8 April 1916.
20. *1916 Rebellion Handbook*, pp.175–6.
21. Alvin Jackson, *Home Rule: An Irish History, 1800–2000* (London, 2003), pp.155–74.

22. David W. Miller, *Church, State and Nation in Ireland, 1898–1921* (Dublin, 1973), p.337.
23. K. Alix Anttila, 'Irish Public Opinion in the Aftermath of the Easter Rising', unpublished MA thesis, Memorial University of Newfoundland, 2006, pp.15–36. See also J.J. Lee, *Ireland, 1912–85* (Cambridge, 1989), pp.29–36 for a wider sampling of press reactions in the immediate aftermath of the Rising.
24. Patrick Maume, *The Long Gestation: Irish Nationalist Life, 1891–1918* (Dublin, 1999), p.184.
25. Fergus Campbell, *Land and Revolution: Nationalist Politics in the West of Ireland, 1891–1921* (Oxford, 2005), pp.238–9.
26. Sinn Féin membership numbers are taken from RIC County Inspectors' Reports from every county in Ireland (PRO CO 904/103–5). The figures for agrarian outrages are derived from the same source. It has occasionally been suggested that police figures for republican party membership might be unreliable, but the county-by-county correlation between these and Sinn Féin's own data on affiliated clubs as of December 1917 is 0.92.
27. Arthur Mitchell, *Labour in Irish Politics, 1890–1930* (New York, 1974), pp.78–103.
28. See Eunan O'Halpin, *The Decline of the Union: British Government in Ireland, 1892–1920* (Dublin, 1987), pp.118–56; Peter Hart, *The IRA and its Enemies: Violence and Community in Cork, 1916–1923* (Oxford, 1998), pp.53–61.
29. Peter Hart, *Mick: The Real Michael Collins* (London, 2005), pp.97–8.
30. See Hart, *The IRA and its Enemies*, pp.204–5.
31. This is not to say that Sinn Féin didn't win a clear majority of seats or nationalist votes in the 1918 general election, but rather that the IRA insisted on their right to act, regardless of the outcome.
32. On the National Aid, see Hart, *Mick*, pp.112–22, and J.J. O'Kelly, 'Report of the Irish National Aid and Volunteer Dependents Fund', *Catholic Bulletin*, August 1919, pp.410–36.
33. O'Kelly, 'Report of the Irish National Aid and Volunteer Dependents Fund', p.416.
34. Ibid., pp.416, 419.
35. For further discussion of this point, see my 'On the Necessity of Violence in the Irish Revolution', in Danine Farquharson and Seán Farrell (eds), *Shadows of the Gunmen* (Cork, 2008).

CHAPTER 2 ENDING WAR IN A 'SPORTSMANLIKE MANNER'

1. Particulars of women attacked by Sinn Féin, Francis Hemming, MS CCC536 QD.2.42, Irish Papers, Bodleian Library; Notes from the *Dundalk Democrat* taken by Rev. Livingstone, 23 April 1921, Marron Collection, 1986:9D9, Monaghan County Museum.
2. Hemming, MS CCC536 QD.2.42, Irish Papers.
3. Ibid.
4. Letter from P. McGrory to Fr Marron (n.d.), Marron Collection, 1986:2G5.
5. Curator, Monaghan County Museum.
6. 'Where there is evidence that a woman is a spy or is doing spy work, the Brigade commandant whose area is involved will set up a court of enquiry to examine the evidence against her … It shall be intimated to her that only consideration of her sex prevents the infliction of the statutory punishment of death.' General Orders, new series, 1920, no. 12 (9 November 1920), University College Dublin Archives (hereafter UCDA), Mulcahy Papers, pp.7a/45.
7. Seamus O'Connor, *Tomorrow Was Another Day* (Tralee, 1970), p.54.
8. 'To members of the IRA', Publicity – Col. Foulkes, The National Archives, London (hereafter TNA), CO 904/168.
9. See examples in the Foulkes Papers, 7/32–7/40, Liddell Hart Centre for Military Archives, King's College London.
10. Maurice Headlam, *Irish Reminiscences* (London, 1947), p.80.

11. Letter to the editor, *The Times*, 14 February 1921.
12. Dublin Castle Statements, November 1920, TNA, CO 904/168.
13. Coroner's inquest, 18 October 1922, County Offaly, National Archives of Ireland (hereafter NAI), Offaly, 1d-16-79.
14. Coroner's inquest, 16 March 1922, County Galway, NAI, Galway, 1d-43-61.
15. Coroner's inquest, 12 March 1923, County Clare, NAI, Clare, 1d-39-113.
16. Notes on the murder of Protestants in Ireland since January 1921, Francis Hemming Papers, Bodleian Library, MS CCC 536, QD.2.42, Irish papers.
17. Ibid.
18. Ibid.
19. Ibid.
20. Ibid.
21. Ibid.
22. Newspaper extracts, Marron Collection, 1986:9D5–6, Monaghan County Museum.
23. Francis Hemming Papers, Bodleian Library, MS CCC 536, QD.2.42, Irish papers.
24. Notes on the murder of Protestants in Ireland since January 1921, ibid.
25. Dublin Castle Statements, November 1920, TNA, CO 904/168.
26. Notes on the murder of Protestants in Ireland since January 1921, Francis Hemming Papers, Bodleian Library, MS CCC 536, QD.2.42, Irish papers.
27. Joanna Bourke, *An Intimate History of Killing: Face-to-Face Killing in Twentieth-Century Warfare* (London, 1999); Samuel Hynes, *The Soldiers' Tale: Bearing Witness to Modern War* (London, 1998).
28. Joanna Bourke, *Dismembering the Male: Men's Bodies, Britain and the Great War* (London, 1999 edn), pp.42–3.
29. J.R.W. Goulden, Bureau of Military History (hereafter BMH), Witness Statement (hereafter WS) 1340.
30. *Irish Times*, 17 January 2004.
31. Quoted in Joe Ambrose, *Dan Breen and the IRA* (Cork, 2006), p.67.
32. John Horgan, *Seán Lemass: The Enigmatic Patriot* (Dublin, 1997), p.17.
33. See for example Donal O'Kelly, 'The Dublin Scene: War Amid the Outward Trappings of Peace', in The Kerryman (ed.), *With the IRA and the Fight for Freedom: 1919 to the Truce* (Tralee, 1950), pp.25–30.
34. Liam Tobin, Ernie O'Malley notebooks, UCDA. p17b/100(111).
35. O'Kelly, 'The Dublin Scene', p.29; Piaras Béaslaí, 'Fourteen British Officers and Agents Executed in Dublin on Bloody Sunday', in The Kerryman (ed.), *With the IRA and the Fight for Freedom*, pp.117–19.
36. Frank Thornton, BMH, WS 615.
37. Quoted in Kevin A. Kearns, *Dublin Tenement Life: An Oral History* (London, 2000 edn), p.85.
38. Joyce M. Nankivell and Sydney Loch, *Ireland in Travail* (London, 1922), p.95.
39. C.S. Andrews, *Dublin Made Me* (Dublin, 1979), p.155.
40. Rex Taylor, *Michael Collins* (London, 1958), p.96.
41. Ibid., p.106.
42. Ibid.
43. Anonymous, *Experiences of an Officer's Wife in Ireland* (London, 1921), p.70.
44. Larry Nugent, BMH, WS 907.
45. 'Account of IRA intelligence during the Anglo–Irish War given by Captain Frank Thornton to Army units', 1940[?], Military Archives, A/0800/IV. He reiterates this exact phrase in his Bureau of Military History statement, WS 615.
46. Ibid.
47. Matty MacDonald, Ernie O'Malley notebooks, UCDA, p17b/105(75).
48. For example, Vinny Byrne recalled that 'one or two men conscientiously objected' when asked to join the Squad, one stating that 'he would have no hesitation in going out to face the enemy in open battle' but not to shoot in cold blood. Vinny Byrne, BMH, WS 423.

49. Frank Saurin, BMH, WS 715.
50. Larry Nugent, BMH, WS 907.
51. Matty MacDonald, Ernie O'Malley notebooks, UCDA, p17b/105(75).
52. Others were said to have attended Mass that morning. Robert Kee, *Ireland: A History* (London, 1995, revised edn), p.187.
53. Andrews, *Dublin Made Me*, pp.151, 153.
54. Charles Dalton, *With the Dublin Brigade* (London, 1929), pp.104–6.
55. Matty MacDonald, Ernie O'Malley notebooks, UCDA, p17b/105(79).
56. Dalton, *Dublin Brigade*, pp.106, 108.
57. Matty MacDonald, Ernie O'Malley notebooks, UCDA, p17b/105(79).
58. Charles Dalton, Ernie O'Malley notebooks, UCDA, p17b/122(23).
59. Charles Dalton, BMH, WS 434.
60. Andrews, *Dublin Made Me*, p.152.
61. Larry Nugent, BMH, WS 907.
62. Ibid.
63. Frank Thornton, BMH, WS 615.
64. Marron Collection, 1986:6D6.
65. Charles Townshend, *The British Campaign in Ireland, 1919–1921* (Oxford, 1975), p.129; Anon., *An Officer's Wife*, p.71.
66. Anon., *An Officer's Wife*, p.71.
67. Edward Kelliher, BMH, WS 477.
68. Seán Smith, Ernie O'Malley notebooks, UCDA, p17b/122(17).
69. Pat McCrea, BMH, WS 413; Idem, Ernie O'Malley notebooks, UCDA, p17b/110(14–15).
70. Andrews, *Dublin Made Me*, p.153.
71. Ibid.
72. Charles Dalton, Ernie O'Malley notebooks, UCDA p17b/122(23).
73. Tim Pat Coogan, *Michael Collins: A Biography* (London, 1990), p.134; Joe Dolan, BMH, WS 663.
74. Vinny Byrne, BMH, WS 423.
75. Joe Leonard, BMH, WS 547.
76. Richard Lloyd George, *Lloyd George* (London, 1960), p.200; Letter from C.S. Markbreiter to Sir Harry Batterbee, 14 April 1931, PRO DO 35/459/9.
77. Bernard Byrne, BMH, WS 631; Paddy Daly, BMH, WS 387.
78. Charles Dalton, Ernie O'Malley notebooks, UCDA, p17b/122(20).
79. Harry Colley, Ernie O'Malley notebooks, UCDA, p17b/97(36).
80. See for example Jim Slattery, Ernie O'Malley notebooks, UCDA, p17b/94(106) and p17b/109(103); Jim Slattery, BMH, WS 445.
81. Éamon Broy, BMH, WS 1,280.
82. James Mackay, *Michael Collins: A Life* (Edinburgh, 1997 edn), p.179.
83. Interview with Robert Kee, *Ireland: A History*; Vinny Byrne, BMH, WS 423.
84. Éamon Broy, BMH, WS 1,280.
85. 'Ignotus', 'Irish realities', *Blackwood's Magazine*, vol. 207 (March 1920), p.349.
86. Vinny Byrne, BMH, WS 423.
87. Quoted in Calton Younger, *Ireland's Civil War* (London, 1968), pp.114–15.
88. Ibid.
89. Charles Dalton, Ernie O'Malley notebooks, UCDA, p17b/122(22).
90. David Neligan, *The Spy in the Castle* (London, 1968), p.71; Coogan, *Michael Collins*, p.77.
91. Bernard Byrne, BMH, WS 631.
92. Éamon Broy, BMH, WS 1,280.
93. Harry Colley, Ernie O'Malley notebooks, UCDA, p17b/97(5).
94. George White, BMH, WS 956.
95. Michael Lynch, O/C Fingal to Adjutant General, 29 March 1921, NAI, Dáil Éireann (DE), 2/517, Portrane Asylum – Incident at dance, 1921.
96. Memo by Seán Ó M, ibid.

97. Evidence of Major General Russell before the army inquiry, 10 May 1924, UCDA, Richard Mulcahy Papers, p7/c/29; Eunan O'Halpin, *Defending Ireland: The Irish State and its Enemies Since 1922* (Oxford, 1999), p.11.

98 Home Affairs returns of serious crime in Ireland with particular reference to responsibility of members of the Army, July–December 1923, NA, D/T s3527.

99. Gerry McCarthy, 'Rebel Hart', *Sunday Times – Culture*, 11 January 2004. Oriel House was headquarters of the new state's Criminal Investigation Department, and was staffed by many of the Squad members and intelligence officers from the 1919–21 period who were fiercely loyal to Collins.

CHAPTER 3 WOMEN'S POLITICAL RHETORIC AND THE IRISH REVOLUTION

1. For an interesting account of the removal of women from the Jacobin Republic, see Joan Landes, *Women and the Public Sphere in the Age of the French Revolution* (New York, 1988). Bolshevik women are discussed in Barbara Evans Clements, *Bolshevik Women* (Cambridge, 1997) and Wendy Z. Goldman, *Women, the State, and Revolution: Soviet Family Policy and Social Life, 1917–1936* (Cambridge, 1993).

2. Peter Hart, *The IRA at War, 1916–1923* (Oxford, 2003), p.16. For women during the Revolution, see Margaret Ward, *Unmanageable Revolutionaries: Women and Irish Nationalism*, rev. ed. (London, 1995); Cal McCarthy, *Cumann na mBan and the Irish Revolution* (Cork, 2007); Ruth Taillon, *When History Was Made: The Women of 1916* (Dublin, 1996).

3. Cumann na mBan Agenda/Notices of Motion for Convention of 28/29 September 1918, c. autumn 1918, Hanna Sheehy-Skeffington Papers, National Library of Ireland (hereafter NLI), 22655.

4. Sinn Féin Standing Committee Minutes, 1918, Sinn Féin Papers, NLI, pos. 3269.

5. 'Third Appeal from Irish Republican Prisoners' Dependents' Fund,' c. Christmas 1920, William O'Brien Papers, NLI, 15703.

6. Kate O'Callaghan, Pamphlet on the Murder of Michael O'Callaghan, c. 1921, Mulcahy Papers, University College Dublin Archives (hereafter UCDA), P7/A/17.

7. Margaret Pearse to Secretary, Ministry of Defence, n.d., Pearse Papers, NLI, 21059 (folder 20).

8. Margaret Pearse to Séamus Moriarty, 28 October 1920, Pearse Papers, Trinity College Dublin Archives (hereafter TCDA), 8265/296.

9. *New York American*, 1 December 1920, Terence MacSwiney Papers, UCDA, P48b/449.

10. Grace Plunkett to Mrs O'Connor, 7 May 1917, Irish National Aid and Volunteer Dependents' Fund Papers, NLI, 24357.

11. Mary McWhorter to Muriel MacSwiney, 4 December 1920, Mary MacSwiney Papers, UCDA, P48a/114(2).

12. *Dáil Debates* (hereafter *DD*), 17 December 1921.

13. Eugene C.P. to Margaret Pearse, Easter 1917, Pearse Papers, TCDA, 8265/25.

14. Margaret Pearse to 'Sir John', 31 May 1917, Pearse Papers, NLI, 21059 (folder 3); Eugene F. Kinkead to Margaret Pearse, 24 December 1928, Pearse Papers, NLI, 21059 (folder 14). Hugh Montague to Eugene F. Kinkead, 8 February 1928, Pearse Papers, NLI, 21059 (folder 15).

15. See, for example, Rev. John P. Monaghan to Mrs Pearse, n.d., Pearse papers, NLI, 21059 (Folder 18).

16. Summary of MacSwiney's 1921 lecture tour, n.d. (but c. late 1921), Mary MacSwiney Papers, UCDA, P48a/160; Mary MacSwiney to Cumann na mBan Headquarters, c. 1921, Mary MacSwiney Papers, UCDA, P48a/9(6).

17. *DD*, 22 December 1921.

18. *DD*, 20 December 1921.

19. *DD*, 14 September 1921. The early debates of the Second Dáil were often recorded in the third person.

20. *DD*, 17 December 1921.

21. Mary MacSwiney to Éamon de Valera, c. October–November 1921, de Valera Papers, UCDA, P150/1444.
22. *DD*, 17 December 1921, 22 December 1921, 4 January 1922.
23. *DD*, 17 December 1921.
24. *DD*, 20 December 1921.
25. *DD*, 17 December 1921.
26. *DD*, 4 January 1922.
27. *DD*, 17 December 1921.
28. Annie MacSwiney to Richard Mulcahy, 23 December 1921, Mulcahy Papers, UCDA, P7a/44.
29. *DD*, 20 December 1921.
30. *DD*, 4 January 1922.
31. Mary MacSwiney to Éamon de Valera, c. autumn 1921, de Valera Papers, UCDA, P150/1444.
32. Pamphlet 'From the Soldiers of the Army of the Republic to their Former Comrades in the Free State Army and Civic Guard', n.d. but c. 1922, Mulcahy Papers, UCDA, P7/B/86.
33. For a synopsis of colonizing rhetoric, see generally Declan Kiberd, *Inventing Ireland: The Literature of the Modern Nation* (London, 1995).
34. *DD*, 20 December 1921.
35. *DD*, 21 December 1921.
36. *DD*, 19 December 1921.
37. *DD*, 19 December 1921.
38. *DD*, 17 December 1921.
39. *DD*, 17 December 1921, 21 December 1921.
40. *DD*, 20 December 1921.
41. Ibid.
42. Batt O'Connor to Máire, 28 December 1921, Batt O'Connor Papers, UCDA, P68/3.
43. *DD*, 20 December 1921.
44. Annie MacSwiney to Éamon de Valera, 29 November 1922, de Valera Papers, UCDA, P150/1442.
45. *DD*, 4 January 1922.
46. Annie MacSwiney to Richard Mulcahy, December 1921, with annotations by Mulcahy c. 1960s, Mulcahy Papers, UCDA, P7/D/1.
47. *DD*, 4 January 1922. The 'brother' in MacCabe's comments is probably Seán MacSwiney, a brother of Terence's who was a fairly silent member of the Second Dáil.
48. *DD*, 21 December 1921.
49. *DD*, 29 November 1922.
50. Kevin O'Higgins, Speech at Dún Laoghaire, 29 October 1923, Mulcahy Papers, UCDA, P7/B/366; *DD*, 8 December 1922.
51. *DD*, 20 September 1922, 27 September 1922.
52. *DD*, 21 May 1924.
53. *DD*, 17 April 1923.
54. *DD*, 20 April 1923.
55. Mary MacSwiney to Director of Intelligence, 15 November 1922, National Archives of Ireland (hereafter NAI), S1369/9; Mary MacSwiney to Archbishop Byrne, 8 November 1922, Mary MacSwiney Papers, UCDA, P48a/194(1).
56. See, for example, Annie MacSwiney to Labour Party members, 27 November 1922, Ernie O'Malley Papers, UCDA, P17a/159. In this letter, Annie also notes: 'she has not her brother's strength.' See also *Freeman's Journal*, 7 November 1922, which covers a Maud Gonne speech that also calls Mary 'the sister of Terence MacSwiney'.
57. De Valera to Mary MacSwiney, 14 November 1922, Mary MacSwiney Papers, TCDA, 7835 (21); de Valera to Mary MacSwiney, 21 November 1922, Mary MacSwiney Papers, UCDA, P48a/115(68).
58. *Poblacht na hÉireann*, 20 November 1922, Mulcahy Papers, UCDA, P7/B/238.

59. The file is in NAI, S 1369/9. The specific letters quoted here are Archbishop Byrne to Cosgrave, 16 November 1922, J.P. Dowdall to Cosgrave, 20 November 1922, George Lyons to Cosgrave, 24 November 1922, and Susan Mitchell to Cosgrave, 16 November 1922.

60. *Straight Talk*, 8 November 1922, de Valera Papers, UCDA, P150/1444.

61. Kevin O'Higgins, Speech at Dún Laoghaire, 29 October 1923, Mulcahy Papers, UCDA, P7/B/366; *DD*, 8 December 1922; George Lyons to Cosgrave, 24 November 1922, NAI, S1369/9.

62. *DD*, 20 April 1923.

63. Cosgrave to Archbishop Byrne, 18 November 1922 and Cosgrave to Cardinal Logue, 15 November 1922, NAI, S1369/9.

64. *DD*, 20 April 1923.

65. Mulcahy to Mary MacSwiney, 10 November 1922, Mulcahy Papers, UCDA, P7a/179; Mulcahy notes, 18 November 1922, Mulcahy Papers, UCDA, P7a/198.

66. *DD*, 2 May 1923.

67. Report of Dr M.H. O'Connor, Prison Medical Officer, 8 November 1922 and Report of Major-General M. Hayes, Director of Medical Services (Mountjoy), c. 10 November 1922, NAI S1369/9.

CHAPTER 4 THE PROBLEM OF EQUALITY

1. For an excellent overview of women in Irish history see Rosemary Cullen Owens, *A Social History of Women in Ireland, 1870–1970* (Dublin, 2005).

2. See Diane Urquhart and Maria Luddy (eds), *The Minutes of the Ulster Women's Unionist Council and Executive Committee, 1911–1940* (Dublin, 2001).

3. Cullen Owens, *Social History of Women*, Chapter 4.

4. Nell Regan, 'Helena Molony (1883–1967)', in Mary Cullen and Maria Luddy (eds), *Female Activists: Irish Women and Change, 1900–1960* (Dublin, 2001), pp.141–68.

5. Maria Luddy, 'Working Women, Trade Unionism and Politics in Ireland, 1830–1945', in Fintan Lane and Donal Ó Drisceoil (eds), *Politics and the Irish Working Class, 1830–1945* (London, 2005), pp.51–3.

6. *Irish Citizen*, January 1918.

7. *Irish Citizen*, October 1917.

8. The Irish Women's Citizen Association (formerly the Irish Women's Suffrage and Local Government Association) was the last organization directly linking nineteenth and twentieth-century suffrage activism. It was incorporated into the Irish Housewives Association in 1949. Also incorporated into the IHA was the Women's Social and Political League formed by Hanna Sheehy Skeffington in 1937.

9. *Irish Times*, 7 April 1970.

10. Cullen Owens, *Social History of Women*, p.314.

11. *Report of the Commission on the Status of Women* (Dublin, 1972).

12. Now known as the National Women's Council of Ireland.

13. For an exception see Isabella M.S. Tod, *On the Education of Girls of the Middle Class* (London, 1874).

14. Article 3 stated that all Irish citizens 'shall within the limits of the jurisdiction of the Irish Free State (Saorstát Éireann) enjoy the privileges and be subject to the obligations of such citizenship'.

15. For recent work on the role of women in politics in these years see Maryann Gialanella Valiulis, 'Power, Gender and Identity in the Irish Free State', *Journal of Women's History*, 6/4–7/1(Winter/Spring 1995), pp.117–36; Mary E. Daly, 'Women in the Irish Free State, 1922–1939: The Interaction Between Economics and Ideology', *Journal of Women's History*, 6/4–7/1 (Winter/Spring 1995), pp.99–116; Caitríona Beaumont, 'Women, Citizenship and Catholicism in the Irish Free State, 1922–1948', *Women's History Review*, 6,4 (1997), pp.563–85.

16. The campaign against the Juries Bill utilized arguments on the rights of citizens and the

significance of phrases from the 1916 Proclamation and the 1922 Constitution. The bill, and the campaign against it, has been definitively addressed in Maryann Gialanella Valiulis, 'Defining Their Role in the New State: Irishwomen's Protest against the Juries Act of 1927', *Canadian Journal of Irish Studies*, 18,1 (July 1992), pp.43–60.

17. See http://www.irishstatutebook.ie/1924/en/act/pub/0005/index.html for the act.
18. Memorandum circulated to the Executive Council by the minister for finance, December 1924, 'Civil Service, Exclusion of Women to Open Competitive Examinations', Department of Taoiseach File, S4195, National Archives of Ireland, Dublin [hereafter DT, NAI]19. *Irish Independent*, 24 November 1925.
20. Copy letter from the Attorney General, S. Ua Broin, to Mr Boland, Department of Finance, 15 December 1924, in 'Civil Service, Exclusion of Women to Open Competitive Examinations', DT, S 4195, NAI.
21. *Dáil Debates* (hereafter *DD*), 18 November 1925, vol. 13, col. 503.
22. *Seanad Debates* (hereafter *SD*), 17 December 1925, vol. 6, col. 246.
23. *SD*, 17 December 1925, vol. 6, col. 247.
24. *DD*, 25 November 1925, vol. 13, col. 863.
25. *DD*, 18 November 1925, vol. 13, col. 513.
26. Ibid., col. 514.
27. Ibid., col. 510.
28. Ibid., col. 527.
29. See, for instance, Deputy Johnson's remarks in ibid., cols 515–58.
30. Ibid., col. 519.
31. *DD*, 1 November 1925, vol. 13, col. 522.
32. Ibid., col. 524.
33. *DD*, 2 December 1925, vol. 13, col. 1093.
34. *DD*, 1 November 1925, vol. 13, col. 524.
35. *DD*, 18 November 1925, vol. 13, col. 515.
36. Collins O'Driscoll accepted the minister's comment that since women were a majority in the electorate, the power granted under the bill would eventually be determined by the 'general trend of events in the outside world'. *DD*, 17 November 1925, vol. 13, col. 536.
37. *SD*, 17 December 1925, vol. 6, col. 245.
38. Ibid.
39. Ibid., col. 246.
40. Ibid., col. 259. Wyse Power had noted that while there were 451 men at the junior executive level of the civil service, only four women occupied such posts. No women occupied administrative grades.
41. *SD*, 17 December 1925, vol. 6, col. 257.
42. *Irish Independent*, 24 November 1925.
43. *Irish Independent*, 18 November 1925.
44. Ibid.
45. *Irish Independent*, 25 March 1925.
46. *Irish Independent*, 16 December 1925.
47. This meant in practice that the bill could not be enacted for 270 days.
48. Memorandum to the Executive Council from the Department of Finance, 7 November 1934, 'Equal pay for men and women' (1) the Civil Service (2) International Labour Conference Report, DT, S 6834A, NAI.
49. Circular from the Department of Finance, 5 December 1925, Finance Circulars 1925, DT, S 4235, NAI.
50. Circular letter from H.S. Murphy sent to Louie Bennett and others, 21 November 1927. Committee on Unemployment, Setting up of Committee, DT, S 5553A, NAI.
51. Copy letter from Louie Bennett, Secretary, Irish Women Workers' Union, to the Minister of Industry and Commerce, 25 November 1927, Committee on Unemployment, Setting up of Committee, DT, S 5553A, NAI.
52. Cited in Beaumont, 'Women, Citizenship and Catholicism in the Irish Free State', p.578.

53. *SD*, 17 December 1925, vol. 6, col. 248.
54. Saorstát Éireann, Census of Population, 1926, vol. 2, Occupations, available at www.cso.ie/census/census_1926_volume_2.htm. In 1936 the female population above the age of 14 was 1,072,204. Of that number 351,367 were in employment. Just over 30 per cent (106,723) were employed in agriculture and 31 per cent (108,951) were in domestic service of some kind. Interestingly, given the debate on women in the civil service, there were 3,985 women working in that sphere while there were more than twice that number of women who had joined religious orders or congregations (9,228), perhaps revealing the limits of gainful employment for middle-class women at this time.
55. W.E. Vaughan and A.J. Fitzpatrick (eds), *Irish Historical Statistics: Population 1821–1971* (Dublin, 1978).
56. Regulations by Minister of Finance under Section 9 of the Civil Service Regulation Act (1924), 26 April 1924. See memo to the editor of *Iris Oifigiúil*, 15 October 1923, Civil Service, Civil Service Regulation Act, Regulations, DT, S 3345A, NAI.
57. *Commission of Inquiry into the Civil Service, 1932–35* (Dublin, 1935), R54/2: Addendum C, 185.
58. *Irish School Weekly*, 4 June 1932; *Irish Times*, 9, 16 January, 13 February, 28 May 1932.
59. Memorandum circulated by the Office of National Education to members of the Executive Council, 18 March 1932. 'Women national teachers (1) Question of compulsory retirement on marriage (2) Special measures to meet scarcity, 1953, (3) Rules for recognition', DT, S 6231A, NAI.
60. See *Irish School Weekly*, 17 June 1933, 14 October 1933.
61. By July of 1933 it was noted that the INTO campaign on the issue had been considerably scaled back. Commentary in the *Irish School Weekly* could not decide whether it was 'the fault of the men leaders of the INTO or because the women's section of the Organisation had lost hope', *Irish School Weekly*, 22 July 1933.
62. *Irish Times*, 12 June 1935.
63. Memorandum from the Department of Industry and Commerce to members of the Executive Council, October 2, 1933, Conditions of Employment Act, 1936, DT, S 6462A, NAI.
64. *DD*, 17 May 1935, vol. 56, col. 1264.
65. This phrase, 'the invasion of women into industry' was used on a number of occasions during the debate. Of the 351,367 females aged 14 and over in employment in 1936 just over 10 per cent (36,532) were in what were termed 'industrial employment'. This included textile work and 'makers of food, drink and tobacco'. In 1926, 9.4 per cent of employed women were in 'industrial employment'. Saorstát Éireann, Census of Population, 1926, vol. 2, Occupations, available at www.cso.ie/census/census_1926_volume_2.htm.
66. *DD*, 26 June 1935, vol. 57, col. 1073.
67. *DD*, 17 May 1935, vol. 56, col. 1281.
68. *DD*, 26 June 1935, vol. 57, col. 1071.
69. Ibid., col. 1072.
70. *DD*, 27 June 1935, vol. 57, col. 1207.
71. *SD*, 27 November, 1935, vol. 20, cols 1247–8.
72. Ibid., col. 1247.
73. Ibid., cols 1257–8.
74. *SD*, 11 December 1935, vol. 20, col. 1398.
75. Aodh de Blacam in an article in the *Irish Press*, 18 November 1936. He argued that women's 'sensitive constitutions wither' with industrial work.
76. *Irish Times*, 9 May 1935.
77. *The Right to Work But Not For Women*, pamphlet published by the IWWU (Dublin, 1935).
78. Extracts from the memo were reported in the *Irish Times*, 11 July 1935.
79. *Irish Press*, 9 May 1935.
80. *Irish Times*, 9 May 1935.

81. Irish Trade Union Congress, Annual Report, 1935.
82. Ibid. Cited in Rosemary Cullen Owens, *Louie Bennett* (Cork, 2001), pp.84–5.
83. For the act, see www.irishstatutebook.ie/1936/en/act/pub/0002/index.html.
84. *Irish Independent*, 6 May 1937.
85. *Irish Independent*, 7 May 1937.
86. *Irish Times*, 11 May 1937.
87. Ibid. The letter was published in all of the national newspapers.
88. *DD*, 2 June 1937, vol. 67, col. 1587.
89. Ibid., cols 1594–5.
90. Ibid., col. 1594.
91. *DD*, 12 May 1937, vol. 67, cols 241–7.
92. The letter was published in the *Irish Press*, 12 May 1937.
93. Ibid.
94. *Irish Independent*, 26 June 1937.

CHAPTER 5 NUANCED NEUTRALITY AND IRISH IDENTITY

1. Ronan Fanning, 'Irish Neutrality: An Historical Review', *Irish Studies in International Affairs*, vol. 1 (1982), p.28; see also John A. Murphy, 'Irish Neutrality in Historical Perspective', in Brian Girvin and Gregory Roberts (eds), *Ireland and the Second World War: Politics, Society and Remembrance* (Dublin, 2000), pp.9–10.
2. Fanning, 'Irish Neutrality: An Historical Review', pp.28–9. He especially notes how Irish nationalism prior to the First World War emphasized Irish distinctiveness, but also recognized Ireland's economic dependence on Britain.
3. See, for example, issues from *Irish Times, Cork Examiner, Freeman's Journal* between 1910 and 1920, or more regional publications like the *Cork Free Press* during that same period.
4. *Westminster Gazette*, 7 February 1920. De Valera was clearly unaware of the provision in the Platt Amendment which read: 'That the government of Cuba consents that the United States may exercise the right to intervene [in Cuban affairs] for the preservation of Cuban independence.'
5. Winston S. Churchill, *The Gathering Storm* (Boston, 1948), p.276.
6. Nicholas Mansergh, *The Unresolved Question: The Anglo-Irish Settlement and its Undoing, 1912–1972* (New Haven, 1991), pp.182–3.
7. Michael Kennedy, *Ireland and the League of Nations, 1919–1946: International Relations, Diplomacy and Politics* (Dublin, 1996), p.35.
8. *Documents on Irish Foreign Policy: Vol. II, 1923–1926* (Dublin, 2000), no. 145.
9. As early as October 1922 Kevin O'Higgins had made it clear that Article 48 of the Free State Constitution precluded the country from entering any war without the Irish parliament's consent, thus rendering redundant the then proposed referendum to ensure such neutrality.
   Dáil Debates, 5 October 1922, vol. 1.
10. Deputies Desmond FitzGerald, Éamon de Valera and T.J. O'Connell were the principal participants in this exchange. *Dáil Debates*, 16 November 1927, vol. 21.
11. Patrick Keatinge, *A Singular Stance: Irish Neutrality in the 1980s* (Dublin, 1984), pp. 13–14.
12. Michael Kennedy, 'The Irish Free State and the League of Nations, 1922–1932: The Wider Implication', *Irish Studies in International Affairs*, vol. 3 (1992), p.23. For further treatment of Irish foreign policy relating to the League and the Commonwealth during this period, see Kennedy, *Ireland and the League of Nations, 1919–1946*, and David Harkness, *The Restless Dominion: The Irish Free State and the British Commonwealth of Nations, 1921–1931* (New York, 1970).
13. Martha Kavanagh, 'The Irish Free State and Collective Security, 1930–6', *Irish Studies in International Affairs*, vol. 15 (2004), pp.120–1.
14. See, for example, *Irish Times, Irish Independent* and *Cork Examiner*, as well as *Dáil*

Debates for the period from 1923 to 1935; see also *Documents on Irish Foreign Policy*, vols.1–3 for this same period.

15. With the all too apparent collapse of collective security, de Valera declared, during a Dáil debate in June of that year: 'we want to be neutral.' *Dáil Debates*, 14 June 1936, vol. 62. Yet he also contemplated the possibility of a defensive Anglo-Irish military alliance at about this same point in time; see John Bowman, *De Valera and the Ulster Question, 1917–1973* (Oxford, 1982), pp.119–20.

16. The degree to which de Valera personally helped to craft the Irish Constitution of 1937, and subsequently promote its ratification in a national referendum, is definitively examined in Dermot Keogh and Andrew McCarthy, *The Making of the Irish Constitution* (Cork, 2007).

17. For an excellent analysis of this transformation see Deirdre McMahon, *Republicans and Imperialists: Anglo-Irish Relations in the 1930s* (London, 1984). Of course, under the provisions of the 1931 Statute of Westminster, Ireland, as well as all other dominions, had the implicit legal right to secede from the Commonwealth.

18. Constitution of Ireland [Bunreacht na hÉireann], Articles 2 and 3.

19. Fanning, 'Irish Neutrality: An Historical Review', p.30; see also Robert Fisk, *In Time of War: Ireland, Ulster and the Price of Neutrality, 1939–1945* (Dublin, 1982), p.552.

20. Clair Wills, *That Neutral Island* (London, 2007), p.7.

21. Neal G. Jesse, 'Contemporary Irish Neutrality: Still a Singular Stance', *New Hibernia Review*, 11, 1 (Spring 2007), p.77.

22. *Documents on Irish Foreign Policy, vol. IV, 1939–1941*, no. 221. Joseph Walshe served as secretary to the Department of External Affairs from 1922 to 1946, a civil servant whose twenty-four-year tenure even eclipsed the sixteen consecutive years [1932–48] that de Valera served as taoiseach in this same general time frame.

23. Conor Cruise O'Brien, *Memoir: My Life and Times* (New York, 2000), p.117.

24. Donald Kenson, *The United States and Ireland* (Cambridge, 1973), p.255.

25. Thomas E. Hachey, 'The Neutrality Issue in Anglo-Irish Relations During World War II', *South Atlantic Quarterly*, 78, 2 (Spring 1979), pp.159–60.

26. David Gray was highly unpopular with the Dublin government as early as 1940 owing to his imprudent criticism of Irish neutrality to de Valera and others. *Documents on Irish Foreign Policy, vol. VI, 1939–1941* (Dublin, 2008), no. 359. Even after the end of the war in Europe, in June 1945, the Irish government sought to have Gray recalled by the US Department of State. Tim Pat Coogan, *Éamon de Valera* (New York, 1993), p.613.

27. Eunan O'Halpin, *Spying in Ireland: British Intelligence and Irish Neutrality During the Second World War* (Oxford, 2008), pp.153, 163.

28. PRO, Foreign Office, 371/36602. Dominion Secretary Clement Attlee to Foreign Secretary Anthony Eden, memorandum of 3 March 1943.

29. John Colville, *The Fringes of Power: 10 Downing Street Diaries, 1939–1945* (New York, 1985), p.306.

30. O'Halpin, *Spying on Ireland*, pp.300–4.

31. Fisk, *In Time of War*, pp.530–2 and T. Ryle Dwyer, *Irish Neutrality and the USA, 1939–1947* (Dublin, 1977), pp.184–6.

32. Murphy, 'Irish Neutrality in Historical Perspective', p.14.

33. As early as 1931, in a speech before the House of Commons, Churchill warned that the Statute of Westminster would negate the restrictions on Ireland's status as intended under the Anglo-Irish Agreement of 1921. Robert Rhodes James (ed.), *Winston S. Churchill: His Complete Speeches, 1897–1963* (London, 1974), vol. 5, p.5106.

34. O'Halpin, *Spying on Ireland*, p.305. O'Halpin further notes how Churchill displayed no similar animus toward Sweden, Switzerland or Spain despite the fact that all three of those wartime neutrals provided significant intelligence assistance and concessions to Germany.

35. Churchill had remarked, as early as 1941, that 'Southern Ireland is not a Dominion, it has never accepted that position. It is a state based upon a treaty, which treaty has been completely demolished. Southern Ireland, therefore, becomes a state which is an un-

defined and unclassified anomaly. No one knows what its juridical and international rights are.'Winston S. Churchill, *Blood, Sweat, and Tears* (New York, 1941), p.13.

36. Diarmaid Ferriter, *Judging Dev* (Dublin, 2007), p.263.
37. *The Times*, 3 May 1945; *New York Herald Tribune*, 4 May 1945. For further detail regarding the BBC broadcast, see Martin Gilbert, *Never Despair: Winston S. Churchill, 1945–1965* (London, 1988), p.12.
38. Maurice Moynihan (ed.), *Speeches and Statements by Éamon de Valera: volume I, 1917–73,* (Dublin, 1990), pp.474–5.
39. Murphy, 'Irish Neutrality in Historical Perspective', p.13.
40. R.J. Raymond is representative of those who do see another development. Indeed, he contends that neutrality has always been a major element in Irish republican thinking. See Raymond James Raymond, 'Irish Neutrality: Ideology or Pragmatism', *International Affairs*, vol. 60 (Winter, 1983), p.31.
41. Trevor Salmon, *Unneutral Ireland* (Oxford, 1989), p.118.
42. Ibid.
43. Garret FitzGerald, 'The Origins, Development and Present Status of Irish "Neutrality"', *Irish Studies in International Affairs*, vol. 9 (1998), pp.13–14.
44. Brian Girvin, *The Emergency: Neutral Ireland, 1939–45* (London, 2006), p.18.
45. T. Ryle Dwyer, *Behind the Green Curtain: Ireland's Phoney Neutrality During World War II* (Dublin, 2009), p.18.
46. Ernie O'Malley, 'No. 7 Renaissance', *La France Libre*, 13, 74 (December 1946/January 1947) [supplement on Ireland], pp.138–43.
47. Eunan O'Halpin, *Defending Ireland: The Irish State and its Enemies Since 1922* (Oxford, 1999), p.254.
48. Determined to remain unaligned from any military alliance, some have viewed Ireland's policy not as principled neutrality but as unprincipled non-belligerency since the country made no effort to maintain a credible defence force. See Roisin Doherty, *Ireland, Neutrality and European Security Integration* (Burlington, VT, 2002), p.17.
49. Ronan Fanning, 'Anglo–Irish Relations: Partition and the British Dimension in Historical Perspective', *Irish Studies in International Affairs*, vol. 2 (1985), p.15.
50. Garret FitzGerald, 'The Origins, Development and Present Status of Irish "Neutrality"', *Irish Studies in International Affairs*, vol. 9 (1998), p.15. FitzGerald further notes how the Americans also declined a 1950 proposal by Irish foreign minister Seán McBride for an Irish–US defence pact. Ibid.
51. *Irish Times*, 22 March 1949.
52. Kris Braun, 'Ireland's Foreign Policy 1951–5', *Irish Studies in International Affairs*, vol. 10 (1999), p.118.
53. Joseph M. Skelly, 'Ireland, the Department of External affairs, and the United Nations, 1946–55: A New Look', *Irish Studies in International Affairs*, vol. 7 (1996), p.78.
54. Ronan Fanning, *Independent Ireland* (Dublin, 1983), p.202.
55. O'Halpin, *Defending Ireland*, p.271.
56. For a comprehensive analysis of this period, see John Horgan, *Seán Lemass: The Enigmatic Patriot* (Dublin, 1999).
57. Paula L. Wylie, *Ireland and the Cold War: Diplomacy and Recognition, 1949–63* (Dublin, 2006), pp.38–9.
58. For a detailed and thorough account of these proceedings, see D.J. Maher, *The Torturous Path: The Course of Ireland's Entry into the EEC, 1948–1973* (Dublin, 1986), pp.118–19.
59. Dermot Keogh, 'Irish Neutrality and the First Application for Membership of the EEC, 1961–63', in Michael Kennedy and Joseph M. Skelly (eds), *Irish Foreign Policy, 1919–1996: From Independence to Internationalism* (Dublin, 2000), p.277.
60. Maher, *The Torturous Path*, pp.156–7.
61. Keogh, 'Irish Neutrality and the First Application for Membership of the EEC', p.266.
62. Horgan, *Seán Lemass*, p.227.
63. Maher, *The Torturous Path*, p.152.

64. *Irish Press*, 2 December 1970.
65. Jesse, 'Contemporary Irish Neutrality', p.79.
66. For more expansive coverage on this point, see Brian Girvin, 'National Interests, Irish Neutrality and the Limits of Ideology', in Michael Gehler and Rolf Steininger (eds), *The Neutrals and European Integration, 1945–1995* (Vienna, 2000), pp.87–112.
67. An authoritative and expansive analysis of Irish neutrality is provided in Joseph Lee, *Ireland, 1912–1985: Politics and Society* (Cambridge, 1989), pp.258–70.
68. Patrick Keatinge, *A Singular Stance*, p.30.
69. *Dáil Debates*, 11 March 1981, vol. 327, col. 1466.
70. *Dáil Debates*, 11 March 1981, vol. 327, col. 1398.
71. *Dáil Debates*, 11 March 1981, vol. 327, col. 1420.
72. FitzGerald would later write: 'Of course, as a realistic politician … I had no alternative but to accept the status quo. But my own personal beliefs on this matter have never changed since the North Atlantic Alliance was established in 1949.' FitzGerald, 'The Origins, Development and Present Status of Irish "Neutrality"', p.19.
73. *Dáil Debates*, 11 March 1981, vol. 327, col. 1466.
74. Salmon, *Unneutral Ireland*, pp.306, 310.
75. See *Irish Times*, 15 January and 8 July 1985 for the reaction of the Workers' Party and the Labour Party, respectively, regarding their misgivings about it being an ominous compromise regarding Irish neutrality.
76. Salmon, *Unneutral Ireland*, pp.270–1.
77. So pervasive was the scramble to curry public favour on this subject that one political commentator referred to it as the 'neutrality season'. *Irish Times*, 8 May 1985.
78. *Irish Times*, 29 April 1985. A survey taken in 1988 reported that 60 per cent of the Irish people supported neutrality, while others indicated support as high as 80 per cent. Garret FitzGerald, while readily acknowledging the popularity of that policy with the electorate, attributes the disparity in those returns to the different ways in which questions were posed in the respective pollings. FitzGerald, 'The Origins, Development and Present Status of Irish "Neutrality"', pp.17–18.
79. Patrick Keatinge, 'Ireland and European Security: Continuity and Change', *Irish Studies in International Affairs*, vol. 9 (1978), p.32.
80. Doherty, *Ireland, Neutrality and European Security Integration*, pp.220–1.
81. For the full text of PANA's political positions, see www.pana.ie.
82. Nicholas Rees, 'Ireland's Foreign Relations in 1997', *Irish Studies in International Affairs*, vol. 9 (1998), pp.143–4.
83. Brian Cowen, 'State of the Union', delivered at the Institute of European Affairs, Dublin, on 19 December 2001.
84. Michael J. O'Sullivan, *Ireland and the Global Question* (Cork, 2006), p.744.
85. Daniel Sweeney, 'Irish Security Policy, 1973–2003: The Influence of European Union Security Integration and the Limits Imposed by Domestic Political Factors', unpublished PhD dissertation, Cambridge University, 2005.
86. Jesse, 'Contemporary Irish Neutrality', p.81.
87. *Observer*, 13 September 2009.
88. Sweeney, 'Irish Security Policy, 1973–2003', pp.319–24.
89. *Irish Times*, 1 February 2005.
90. Sweeney, 'Irish Security Policy, 1973–2003', pp.325–7.
91. Jesse, 'Contemporary Irish Neutrality', p.90.
92. See Karin Gilland, 'Ireland: Neutrality and the International Use of Force', in Philip Everts and Pierangelo Isernia (eds), *Public Opinion and the International Use of Force* (New York, 2001), and Pat Lyons, 'Public Opinion and the Republic of Ireland – 2001', *Irish Political Studies Data Yearbook 2002–3*, vol. 17 [supplement], pp.4–16.
93. Neal Jesse, who identifies a different source (Doherty, *Ireland, Neutrality and European Security Integration*, p.223) for this survey, provides an excellent synopsis of the distinguishing characteristics in each of the principal European neutral nations, illustrating how Ireland's neutrality was, and is, distinctly different. See Jesse, 'Contemporary Irish Neutrality', pp.74–95.

94. Keatinge, *A Singular Stance*, p.100.
95. O'Sullivan, *Ireland and the Global Question*, pp.130–43.
96. In 1979, Ireland dramatically underscored that reality when the government chose to break from the British sterling standard, electing instead to align with the European Monetary System (EMS).
97. Fanning, 'Small States, Large Neighbours: Ireland and the United Kingdom', *Irish Studies in International Affairs*, vol. 9 (1998), p.25.

CHAPTER 6 MODERNITY, THE PAST AND POLITICS IN POST-WAR IRELAND

1. Liam Downey, *Ireland in the Year 2000: The Perspectives and Challenges* (Dublin, 1982), p.5, quoted in Joseph Lee, 'Reflections on the Study of Irish Values', in Michael Fogarty, Liam Ryan and Joseph Lee, *Irish Values and Attitudes: The Irish Report of the European Values Systems Study* (Dublin, 1984), p.107.
2. Michael Bannon, *Planning: The Irish Experience, 1920–1988* (Dublin, 1989), pp.132–3.
3. For an original and as yet unsurpassed sociological analysis of these social forces, see Michel Peillon, *Contemporary Irish Society: An Introduction* (Dublin, 1982).
4. The most recent examination of which is Diarmaid Ferriter, *The Transformation of Ireland, 1900–2000* (London, 2004).
5. For a lively and characteristically perceptive assessment of the contemporary era, see R.F. Foster, *Luck and the Irish: A Brief History of Change, 1970–2000* (London, 2007).
6. See, for instance, the discussion contained in Joe Cleary, 'Introduction: Ireland and Modernity', in Joe Cleary and Claire Connolly (eds), *The Cambridge Companion to Modern Irish Culture* (Cambridge, 2005), pp.1–21. A good overview can be found in Stuart Hall, 'Introduction', in Stuart Hall and Bram Gieben (eds), *Formations of Modernity* (Cambridge, 1992), pp.1–17.
7. Perry Anderson, 'Modernity and Revolution', *New Left Review*, no. 144 (1984), pp.96–113; Marshall Berman, *All That Is Solid Melts Into Air: The Experience of Modernity* (New York, 1982); Anthony Giddens, *The Consequences of Modernity* (Cambridge, 1990); Anthony Giddens, *Modernity and Self-Identity: Self and Society in the Late Modern Age* (Cambridge, 1991); Jürgen Habermas, *The Philosophical Discourse of Modernity: Twelve Lectures* (Cambridge, 1987); Zygmunt Bauman, *Modernity and Ambivalence* (Cambridge, 1991); Zygmunt Bauman, *Liquid Modernity* (Cambridge, 2000); Charles Taylor, *Modern Social Imaginaries* (Durham, NC, 2004); Charles Taylor, *A Secular Age* (Cambridge, MA, 2007). See also Mica Nava and Alan O'Shea (eds), *Modern Times: Reflections on a Century of English Modernity* (London, 1996) for an application of the concept to nineteenth- and twentieth-century England.
8. Anderson, 'Modernity and Revolution', p.97.
9. Peter Osborne, 'Modernity is a Qualitative, Not a Chronological, Category', *New Left Review*, no. 192 (1992), pp.65–84; Hall, 'Introduction', pp.8–10.
10. Dipesh Chakrabarty, *Provincializing Europe: Postcolonial Thought and Historical Difference* (Princeton, NJ, 2000).
11. See Luke Gibbons, *Transformations in Irish Culture* (Cork, 1996); David Lloyd, *Irish Times: Temporalities of Modernity* (Dublin, 2008).
12. See, for example, Cleary, 'Introduction: Ireland and Modernity'; Séamus Deane, *Strange Country: Modernity and Nationhood in Irish Writing Since 1790* (Oxford, 1997); Declan Kiberd, *Inventing Ireland* (London, 1995); Diarmuid Ó Giolláin, *Locating Irish Folklore: Tradition, Modernity, Identity* (Cork, 2000).
13. Eviatar Zerubavel, *Time Maps: Collective Memory and the Social Shape of the Past* (Chicago, IL, 2003), pp.18–19.
14. J.J. Lee, *Ireland, 1912–1985* (Cambridge, 1989), pp.271–328; Terence Brown, *Ireland: A Social and Cultural History, 1922–2002* (London, 2004, 2nd edn), pp.199–226.
15. Fergal Tobin, *The Best of Decades: Ireland in the 1960s* (Dublin, 1984).
16. Joseph Lee and Gearóid Ó Tuathaigh, *The Age of de Valera* (Dublin, 1982); Brian Girvin and Gary Murphy (eds), *The Lemass Era: Politics and Society in the Ireland of Seán Lemass* (Dublin, 2005).

17. J.J. Lee, 'Seán Lemass', in idem (ed.), *Ireland, 1945–70* (Dublin, 1979), p.25.
18. R.F. Foster, *Modern Ireland, 1600–1972* (London, 1988), p.569.
19. Alvin Jackson, *Ireland, 1798–1998: Politics and War* (Oxford, 1999).
20. Foster, *Modern Ireland*, p.569.
21. Tobin, *The Best of Decades*, p.8.
22. Mary E. Daly, *The Slow Failure: Population Decline and Independent Ireland, 1922–1973* (Madison, WN, 2006), pp.21–74; Mary E. Daly, 'The Modernization of Rural Ireland, c.1920–c.1960', in David Dickson and Cormac Ó Gráda (eds), *Refiguring Ireland: Essays in Honour of L.M. Cullen* (Dublin, 2003), pp.356–69; Enda Delaney, *Demography, State and Society: Irish Migration to Britain, 1921–1971* (Kingston/Montreal and Liverpool, 2000), pp.234–48; Brian Girvin, *From Union to Union: Nationalism, Democracy and Religion in Ireland* (2002), pp.136–68; Damian F. Hannan, *Rural Exodus* (London, 1970); Damian F. Hannan, 'Peasant Models and the Understanding of Social and Cultural Change in RuralIreland', in P.J. Drudy (ed.), *Ireland: Land, Politics and People* (Cambridge, 1985) (Irish studies 2), pp.153–61.
23. Enda Delaney, *The Irish in Post-War Britain* (Oxford, 2007), pp.24–44.
24. Damian F. Hannan, 'Irish Emigration Since the War', unpublished TS of RTÉ Thomas Davis Lecture [1973], p.8.
25. R.S. Devane, SJ, *The Imported Press: A National Menace – Some Remedies* (Dublin, 1950), pp.8, 23; for more information about Devane and his views, see Michael Adams, *Censorship: The Irish Experience* (Dublin, 1968), pp.162–4; Louise Fuller, *Irish Catholicism Since 1950: The Undoing of a Culture* (Dublin, 2002), p.38.
26. K.G. Forecast, 'Radio Éireann Listener Research Inquiries, 1953–1955', *Journal of the Statistical and Social Inquiry Society of Ireland*, vol. 19 (1955–6), pp.10–12.
27. Kevin Rockett, 'Protecting the Family and the Nation: The Official Censorship of American Cinema in Ireland, 1923–1954', *Historical Journal of Film, Radio and Television*, vol. 20, 3 (2000), p.283.
28. Gabriel Fallon, 'Celluloid Menace', in *The Capuchin Annual, 1938* (Dublin, 1937), p.249, citing statistics presented in Thekla J. Beere, 'Cinema Statistics in Saorstát Éireann', *Journal of the Statistical and Social Inquiry Society of Ireland*, 89th session (1935–6), p.97.
29. Ibid.
30. Cited in Fuller, *Irish Catholicism Since 1950*, p.40.
31. Kevin Rockett, *Irish Film Censorship: A Cultural Journey from Silent Cinema to Internet Pornography* (Dublin, 2004), p.26.
32. On censorship of film, see Rockett, *Irish Film Censorship*, chps. 3–7 and Donal Ó Drisceoil, *Censorship in Ireland, 1939–1945* (Cork, 1996), pp.30–58. The best available treatment of the censorship of publications still remains Adams, *Censorship*.
33. B.G. MacCarthy, 'The Cinema as a Social Factor', *Studies*, vol. 33 (1944) p.46, also partly quoted in Rockett, *Irish Film Censorship*, p.26, and Ferriter, *The Transformation of Ireland*, p.429.
34. S.5, Rural Survey of Clonmel, Arklow and Wexford, prepared by W. A. Honohan, Sept. 1948, Marsh Papers, Trinity College Dublin (TCD), MS 8306.
35. See Ross McKibbin, *Classes and Cultures: England, 1918–1951* (Oxford, 1998), pp.431–2, 434.
36. Fuller, *Irish Catholicism Since 1950*.
37. Brown, *Ireland: A Social and Cultural History*, pp.186–93.
38. This material draws on the account in John Cooney, *John Charles McQuaid: The Ruler of Catholic Ireland* (Dublin, 1999) pp.160–1; see also J.C. Heenan, *Not the Whole Truth* (London, 1971), pp.242–3.
39. Cooney, *John Charles McQuaid*, pp.160–1.
40. Ibid.
41. See Mary E. Daly and Margaret O'Callaghan (eds), *1916 in 1966: Commemorating the Easter Rising* (Dublin, 2007).
42. Pierre Nora, 'The Era of Commemoration', in idem (ed.), *Realms of Memory: The Construction of the French Past, vol. iii* (New York, 1998), pp.609–37.

43. *Cuimhneachán 1916–1966: A Record of Ireland's Commemoration of the 1916 Rising* (Dublin, 1966), p.11.
44. Quoted in John Horgan, *Seán Lemass: The Enigmatic Patriot* (Dublin, 1997), p.328.
45. Quoted in Brian Farrell, *Seán Lemass* (Dublin, 1991), p.98.
46. J.H. Whyte, *Church and State in Modern Ireland, 1923–1979* (Dublin, 1980, 2nd edn), p.314.
47. William J. Philbin, *Patriotism* (Dublin, 1958), p.13f.
48. Quoted in Ronan Fanning, *Independent Ireland* (Dublin, 1983). p.192.
49. T.H. Marshall, *Citizenship and Social Class* (Cambridge, 1950).
50. Tom Garvin, 'The Destiny of the Soldiers: Tradition and Modernity in the Politics of de Valera's Ireland', *Political Studies*, vol. 26 (1978), pp.328–47.
51. Farrell, *Seán Lemass*, p.100.
52. Mary E. Daly, 'Nationalism, Sentiment, and Economics: Relations between Ireland and Irish-America in the Post-War years', *Éire–Ireland*, vol. 37, 1–2 (2002), pp.74–92.
53. Quoted in ibid., p.84.
54. Paul Keating, Irish Consul-General in New York, quoted in ibid.
55. Kevin O'Connor, *The Irish in Britain* (London, 1972), p.119.
56. Anne O'Grady, *Irish Migration to London in the 1940s and 1950s* (London, 1988), p.14.
57. O'Connor, *The Irish in Britain*, p.92.
58. See Robert J. Savage, *Irish Television: The Political and Social Origins* (Cork, 1996); idem, 'Introducing Television in the Age of Lemass', in Brian Girvin and Gary Murphy (eds), *The Lemass Era: Politics and Society in the Ireland of Seán Lemass* (Dublin, 2005), pp.191–214.
59. Quoted in Fuller, *Irish Catholicism Since 1950*, p.128.
60. Ibid.
61. See Ferriter, *Transformation of Ireland*, pp.569–76, and Brown, *Ireland: A Social and Cultural History*, pp.254–96.
62. Tom Garvin, 'Priests and Patriots: Irish Separatism and Fear of the Modern, 1890–1914', *Irish Historical Studies*, vol. 25 (1986), pp.67–81; idem, *Nationalist Revolutionaries in Ireland, 1858–1928* (Oxford, 1987), Ch. 4.
63. Quoted in Daly, *The Slow Failure*, p.30.
64. See Delaney, *Demography, State and Society*, pp.193–4.
65. Ferriter, *Transformation of Ireland*, p.6.
66. John Healy, *The Death of an Irish Town* (Cork, 1968).
67. Originally called the Economic Research Institute; for more details, see Lee, *Ireland, 1912–1985*, p.581.
68. Delaney, *Demography, State and Society*, pp.234–47.
69. John A. Jackson, *Report on the Skibbereen Social Survey* (Dublin, 1967).
70. Whyte, *Church and State in Modern Ireland*, p.332.
71. F.X. Martin, 'The Thomas Davis Lectures, 1953–67', *Irish Historical Studies*, vol. 15, 59 (1967), p.277.
72. See Ciarán Brady, '"Constructivist and Instrumental": The Dilemma of Ireland's First "New" Historians', in idem (ed.), *Interpreting Irish History: The Debate on Historical Revisionism* (Dublin, 1994), pp.3–6.
73. Martin, 'The Thomas Davis Lectures', p.281
74. Brown, *Ireland: A Social and Cultural History*, p.274; Francis Shaw, 'The Canon of Irish History: A Challenge', *Studies*, vol. 61 (1972), pp.11–157.
75. Becky Conekin, Frank Mort and Chris Waters 'Introduction' in idem(eds), *Moments of Modernity: Reconstructing Britain, 1945–1964* (London, 1998), p.15.
76. Ibid.
77. Lee, *Ireland, 1912–1985*, pp.562–643.
78. Liam O'Dowd (ed.), *On Intellectuals and Intellectual Life in Ireland* (Belfast, 1996). For the earlier period, see Nicholas Mansergh, *The Irish Question, 1840–1921* (London, 1965).

79. The classic analysis of this issue in an international context is Michael Mann, *The Sources of Social Power, II: The Rise of Classes and Nation-States, 1760–1914* (Cambridge, 1993).

CHAPTER 7 'IRELAND IS AN UNUSUAL PLACE'

* The author wishes to gratefully acknowledge the support of the Arts and Humanities Research Board, British Academy and Leverhulme Trust that enabled the research to be undertaken for this work, and the Center for Irish Programs, Boston College, where this paper was written while a Visting Professor.

1. For the most recent detailed narrative of Kennedy's visit see James Robert Carroll, *One of Ourselves: John Fitzgerald Kennedy in Ireland* (Boston, MA, 2003).
2. For a discussion of Clinton's role in Irish politics see Conor O'Clery, *The Greening of the White House* (Dublin, 1997) and Thomas Hennessey, *The Northern Ireland Peace Process* (London, 2001).
3. J.H. Whyte, 'Economic Crisis and Political Cold War, 1949–57', in J.R. Hill (ed.), *A New History of Ireland VII: Ireland, 1921–84* (Oxford, 2003), p.304.
4. For a discussion of Lemass in office and his modernization of Ireland see Paul Bew and Henry Patterson, *Seán Lemass and the Making of Modern Ireland* (Dublin, 1982), William G. Shade, 'Strains of Modernization: The Republic of Ireland under Lemass and Lynch', *Éire-Ireland*, 14, 1 (1979), pp.26–46, and Robert Savage, *Seán Lemass: Life and Times* (Dublin, 1999).
5. Dermot Keogh, *Twentieth-Century Ireland: Nation and State* (Dublin, 1994), p.252.
6. Fergal Tobin, *The Best of Decades: Ireland in the Nineteen Sixties* (Dublin, 1984), pp.91–2.
7. Jian Wang and Tsan-Kuo Chang, 'Strategic Public Diplomacy and Local Press: How a High-Profile 'Head-of-State' Visit was Covered in America's Heartland', *Public Relations Review*, vol. 30 (2004), p.11.
8. See James Loughlin, 'Allegiance and Illusion: Queen Victoria's Irish Visit of 1849', *History*, vol. 87 (2002), pp.491–513, and Senia Paseta, 'Nationalist Responses to Two Royal Visits to Ireland, 1900 and 1903', *Irish Historical Studies*, 31, 124 (1999), pp.488–504.
9. See J.B. Manheim, *Strategic Public Diplomacy and American Foreign Policy: The Evolution of Influence* (New York, 1994), p.3.
10. Wiang and Chang, 'Strategic Public Diplomacy and Local Press', p.13.
11. This process has been explained in terms of visibility and valence in Wiang and Chang, 'Strategic Public Diplomacy and Local Press', p.15, and Manheim, *Strategic Public Diplomacy and American Foreign Policy*, p.131.
12. Titus Ensink, 'The Footing of a Royal Address: An Analysis of Representativeness in Political Speech, Exemplified in Queen Beatrix's Address to the Knesset on March 28, 1995', *Current Issues in Language and Society*, 3, 3 (1996), p.207.
13. For a brief discussion of the importance of Berlin and Cold War politics to the Kennedy administration see Gregory Nicholson, 'The Berlin Crisis During the Kennedy Administration', *Towson State Journal of International Affairs*, 17, 2 (1983), pp.81–92.
14. See Ensink, 'The Footing of a Royal Address', p.211 for discussion of the expected roles and functions of dignitaries during such visits.
15. Letter from Embassy of Ireland, Washington, to Secretary, Department of External Affairs, Dublin, 27 March 1962, Department of the Taoiseach, S17401A/63, National Archives of Ireland (hereafter NAI).
16. Letter from Embassy of Ireland, Washington, to Secretary, Department of External Affairs, Dublin, 14 May 1962, Department of the Taoiseach, S17401A/63, NAI.
17. Letter of invitation from de Valera to Kennedy, 27 March 1963, Department of the Taoiseach, S17401A/63, NAI.

18. Decoded cable sent from Kennedy to de Valera, 12 April 1963, Department of the Taoiseach, S17401A/63, NAI.
19. See, for example, *Evening Herald*, 16 and 17 April 1963, pp.1 and 8.
20. See *Irish Press*, 6 May 1963, p.1 and *Irish Times*, 8 May 1963, p.4.
21. The size and scale of the Eucharistic Congress in many ways outstrips that of the Kennedy visit, although the differing roles of the Irish Catholic hierarchy at the heart of each event is revealing of how Ireland was changing by the early 1960s. For an explanation of the Congress see David Holmes, 'The Eucharistic Congress of 1932 and Irish Identity', *New Hibernia Review*, 4, 1 (2000), pp.55–78.
22. For minutes of the inter-departmental committee and the planning of the visit, see Department of the Taoiseach, S17401A/63, NAI.
23. CIA report on the presidential visit to Ireland, quoted in Keogh, *Twentieth-Century Ireland*, p.251.
24. *Sunday Press*, 9 June 1963, p.5.
25. *Irish Press*, 6 June 1963, p.5.
26. *New York Times*, 17 June 1963, p.39.
27. *New York Times*, 28 June 1963, p.1.
28. The rejection of American-produced stereotypical images of the Irish were of a key concern to the Department of Foreign Affairs during the 1960s, and was much evidenced in reports and complaints relating to American-organized St Patrick's Day celebrations. For details see Mike Cronin and Daryl Adair, *The Wearing of the Green: A History of St Patrick's Day* (London, 2002), Chapter 6.
29. *Irish Independent*, 15 May 1962, p.8.
30. For details of the stereotyping of the Irish in American film and television during this period, see William Dowling, 'John Ford's Festive Comedy: Ireland Imagined in the Quiet', *Éire-Ireland*, 36, 3–4 (2001), pp.190–211, and Robert Savage, 'Constructing/Deconstructing the Image of Seán Lemass' Ireland: The Tear and the Smile', in Film Institute of Ireland, *Nationalism: Visions and Revisions* (Dublin, 1999), pp.15–23.
31. For an examination of Ireland under the Marshall Plan see Bernadette Whelan, 'Ireland and the Marshall Plan', *Irish Economic and Social History*, vol. 19 (1992), pp.49–70, and Bernadette Whelan, *Ireland and the Marshall Plan, 1947–57* (Dublin, 2000).
32. For a discussion of many aspects of this period see Dermot Keogh and Carmel Quinlan (eds), *Ireland in the 1950s: The Lost Decade?* (Cork, 2004).
33. Ronan Fanning, *Independent Ireland* (Dublin, 1983), p.203.
34. *Irish Press*, 26 June 1963, p.1.
35. *New York Times*, 26 June 1963, p.17.
36. *New York Times*, 27 June 1963, p.13.
37. *Irish Press*, 27 June 1963, p.1.
38. Ibid., p.4.
39. Ibid., p.4.
40. *New York Times*, 23 June 1963, p.7.
41. *New York Times,* 28 June 1963, p.1.
42. Ibid., p.3. The Albatross Company was a fertilizer factory, and John V. Kelly the local auctioneer.
43. *Irish Press*, 28 June 1963, p.6.
44. *New York Times*, 23 June 1963, p.7.
45. *Irish Press*, 28 June 1963, p.1.
46. Ibid., p.6.
47. Ibid., p.7.
48. *Dáil Debates*, 22 May 1963, vol. 203, col. 78.
49. Memo to the Taoiseach, 31 May 1963, Department of the Taoiseach, S17401A/63, NAI.
50. *Northern Whig and Belfast Post*, 26 June 1963, p.1.
51. *Irish Press*, 23 May 1963, p.3
52. Letter from the Attorney-General to the Taoiseach, 4 May 1963, Department of the Taoiseach, S17401A/63, NAI.

53. *Irish Press*, 29 June 1963, p.1.
54. *New York Times*, 29 June 1963, p.1.
55. See *Irish Press*, 29 June 1963, pp.3 and 7 for details.
56. *New York Times*, 30 June 1963, p.3.
57. Ibid.
58. *Irish Press*, 29 June 1963, p.10.
59. *New York Times*, 30 June 1963, p.10.
60. *New York Times*, 27 June 1963, p.13.
61. Minutes of meeting between Kennedy and Lemass, 27 June 1963, Department of the Taoiseach, S17401C/63.
62. Note from the Irish Embassy, Washington, to the Taoiseach, 4 June 1963, Department of the Taoiseach, S17401A/63, NAI.
63. See, for example, *A Memory of John Fitzgerald Kennedy's Visit to Ireland, 26–29 June 1963* (Dublin, 1964) and Maurice Hennessy, *I'll Come Back in the Springtime: John F. Kennedy and the Irish* (London, 1966). The Irish state broadcaster also screened a film after the visit, *Welcome Mr President: Highlights of President Kennedy's Visit to Ireland* (Dublin, 1963).
64. Tony Gray, *The Irish Answer: An Anatomy of Modern Ireland* (London, 1966), and Donald Connery, *The Irish* (London, 1968).

CHAPTER 8 SEX AND THE ARCHBISHOP

1. John Banville, 'The Ireland of de Valera and O'Faolain', *Irish Review*, nos. 17–18 (Winter 1995), pp.142–53.
2. Diarmaid Ferriter, *What If? Alternative Views of Twentieth-Century Ireland* (Dublin, 2006), pp.40–52. See also John Cooney, *John Charles McQuaid: Ruler of Catholic Ireland* (Dublin, 1999).
3. Ibid.
4. Deirdre McMahon, 'John Charles McQuaid: Archbishop of Dublin, 1940–1972', in James Kelly and Daire Keogh (eds), *A History of the Catholic Diocese of Dublin* (Dublin, 2000), pp.331–44.
5. Ibid., p.333.
6. Tom Garvin, *Preventing the Future: Why Was Ireland So Poor For So Long?* (Dublin, 2004), p.56.
7. Ibid., p.57.
8. Ibid., p.160.
9. John Cooney, 'McQuaid Has Been Betrayed By his Own Voluminous Archive', *Irish Times*, 7 April 2003, and Cooney, *John Charles McQuaid*.
10. *Irish Times*, 7 April 2003.
11, Ibid.
12. See *Irish Times*, 26 November 1999.
13. Catriona Crowe, 'On the Ferns Report', *Dublin Review*, no. 22 (Spring 2006).
14. Quoted in McMahon, 'John Charles McQuaid'.
15. John O'Brien (ed.), *The Vanishing Irish* (London, 1954), p.113.
16. June Levine, *Sisters: The Personal Story of an Irish Feminist* (Dublin, 1982).
17. Garvin, *Preventing the Future*, p.57.
18. Dublin Diocesan Archives (hereafter DDA), Papers of Archbishop John Charles McQuaid, Diocesan Press Office (hereafter DPO), AB8/B/xxxx/ic, McQuaid to Dowling, 6 March 1970.
19. DDA, DPO, McQuaid to Dowling, 27 April 1965.
20. Ibid.
21. DDA, DPO, 1968–1970, AB8/B/xxxxic, 22 November 1968.
22. DDA, DPO, AB8/B/xxxx, 8 August 1967.
23. Angela Bourke, 'Rocks in the Road', *Dublin Review*, no. 21 (Winter 2005–6), pp.102–12.
24. Angela McNamara, *Yours Sincerely* (Dublin, 2003), p.69.

25. *Hibernia Fortnightly Review*, 24 April 1969.
26. *Irish Press* article by Richard Grogan on family planning, 9 September 1966.
27. DDA, Catholic Social Welfare Bureau (hereafter CSWB) Box 6, AB/8/B/xix, 'Marriage Counselling Service, 1966–1971', McQuaid address to Our Lady's School, Templeogue, 3 March 1968.
28. DDA, CSWB, 'Marriage Section, 1955–71', 5 October 1956.
29. Ibid., 2 November 1967.
30. Ibid., memorandum by Fr Michael Browne, 19 April 1970.
31. Ibid., Joan Devitt and Bernard Duff to McQuaid, 30 November 1971.
32. DDA, CSWB, Box 5, 'Family Welfare Section', AB/8/Bxix, 20 October 1967.
33. DDA, CSWB, Box 5, 'Family Welfare Section', 3 December 1968.
34. DDA, CSWB, Box 2, 'Annual Reports for Emigrant Section', 1963.
35. Ibid.
36. Ibid., McQuaid to Cecil Barrett, 12 November 1963.
37. *Irish Times*, 18 November 1963, and DDA, CSWB, Box 3, AB8/B/xix, Barrett to McQuaid and McQuaid's reply, 23 March 1964.
38. Ibid., McQuaid to Barrett, 3 March 1963.
39. DDA, CSWB, BOX 2, AB8/B/xix, Henry Gray to McQuaid, 14 June 1943.
40. Ibid., CSWB, Box 3, McQuaid to William Gidfrey, 12 May 1960.
41. DDA, CSWB, Box 3, Hubert Daly to McQuaid, 16 August 1954.
42. *The Standard*, 11 December 1953.
43. National Archives of Ireland (NAI), Department of the Taoiseach (DT), 'Irish Labour Emigration', S11582, July 1953.
44. DDA, 'Report of the Catholic Television Interim Committee', AB8/B/xxx Iq, June 1962.
45. Ibid., Report of June 1965.
46. DDA, 'Communications: Radharc, 1963–9', AB/8/B/xxxx, Dunn to McQuaid 26 July 1968 and his reply, 31 July 1968.
47. DDA, 'Communications: Television, RTÉ, 1960–62', AB/8/B/xxvi, Dermot O'Flynn to McQuaid, 7 March 1962.
48. Ibid. Roth to McQuaid 20 January 1962.
49. Ibid., Gearoid Kelly to McQuaid, 21 November 1966.
50. Ibid., McQuaid's reply, 30 November 1966.
51. Ibid., McCourt to McQuaid, 15 February 1966.
52. DDA, 'Evil Literature, 1956–61', AB8/xviii/13, Coyne to McQuaid 5 April 1960.
53. DDA, Government Box 3, Department of Justice, AB8/xviii/10, 10 December 1964.
54. DDA, 'Communications: Television: RTÉ 1960–6', McQuaid to James MacMahon, 18 August 1960.
55. DDA, DPO, April–May 1965.
56. DDA, DPO, 1966–7, McQuaid to James Reidy, 6 October 1966.
57. DDA, DPO, AB8/Bxxxxic, 11 April 1967.
58. DDA, DPO, 1965, AB8/B/xxxxic, Dowling to MacMahon, 6 July 1965 and 12 July 1965.
59. DDA, 'Evil Literature: 1967–71', MacMahon to McQuaid, 21 December 1967 and file: 'Evil Literature, 1967–71', October 1971.
60. DDA, DPO, 1971, AB8/B/xxxxic, Dowling to McQuaid, 23 January 1971.
61. Ferriter, *What If?* pp.140–52.
62. Ibid.
63. Ibid.

CHAPTER 9 TURMOIL IN THE SEA OF FAITH

1. An early version of the argument in this paper appeared in my *Preventing the Future: Why Was Ireland So Poor For So Long?* (Dublin, 2004), pp.199–232.
2. B.F. Biever, *Religions, Culture and Values: A Cross-Cultural Analysis of Motivational Factors in Native Irish and American-Irish Catholicism* (New York, 1976).

3. Ibid., pp.270–1, 306, 397.
4. Ibid., pp.226–7, passim.
5. AD UCD/LA/56 James Meenan Papers, 18 February, 1944.
6. See references in *Preventing the Future*, pp.258–9.
7. Tom Inglis, *Moral Monopoly* (Dublin, 1997).
8. Harry Eckstein, *Division and Cohesion in Democracy: A Study of Norway* (Princeton, NJ, 1966), pp.225–88.

CHAPTER 10 THE IRISH CATHOLIC NARRATIVE

1. Emmet Larkin, 'Church, State and Nation in Modern Ireland', in *The Historical Dimensions of Irish Catholicism* (New York, 1976), pp.1268–70.
2. Patrick Murray, *Oracles of God: The Roman Catholic Church and Irish Politics, 1922–37* (Dublin, 2000), p.7.
3. Larkin, 'Church, State and Nation in Modern Ireland', pp.1271–2.
4. See text of bishops' pastoral letter in *Irish Times*, 11 October 1922, p.5.
5. Louise Fuller, *Irish Catholicism Since 1950: The Undoing of a Culture* (Dublin, 2002), pp.6–7.
6. *Dáil Debates*, 12 April 1951, vol. 125, col. 668.
7. *Irish Catholic Directory, 1952*, p.709.
8. *Irish Times*, 13 April 1955.
9. T.K. Whitaker, *Economic Development* (Dublin, 1958).
10. Department of Finance, *Programme for Economic Expansion* (Dublin, 1958). See Ronan Fanning, *The Irish Department of Finance, 1922–58* (Dublin, 1978), pp.518–19.
11. Archbishop D'Alton, 'The Furrow and its Programme', *The Furrow*, 1, 1 (February 1950), p.6.
12. *Dáil Debates*, 19 July 1956, vol. 159, col. 1494.
13. See *Report of the Council of Education on (1) The Function of the Primary School, (2) The Curriculum to be Pursued in the Primary School* (Dublin, 1954), paras 195, 196, pp.130, 132.
14. See *Report of the Council of Education on the Curriculum of the Secondary School* (Dublin, 1962), paras 150, 164, pp.80, 88.
15. See John J. O'Meara, *Reform in Education* (Dublin, 1958), p.16.
16. *Sunday Press*, 4 October 1959.
17. *Investment in Education: Report of the Survey Team* (Dublin, 1966).
18. Sean O'Connor, 'Post-Primary Education: Now and in the Future', *Studies*, vol. LVII (Dublin, 1968), p.233.
19. See the Executive Council of the Teaching Brothers' Association's response to Sean O'Connor in *Studies*, vol. LVII (Dublin, 1968), pp.281–3.
20. See Robert J. Savage, *Irish Television: The Political and Social Origins* (Cork, 1996), p.208.
21. See Fuller, *Irish Catholicism Since 1950*, p.14.
22. 'Statement of the Irish Hierarchy on forthcoming Irish TV network, Maynooth, October 1961', *The Furrow*, 12, 11 (November 1961), pp.695–7.
23. President de Valera's address at the launch of Telefís Éireann, 31 December 1961 in Martin McLoone and John MacMahon (eds), *Television and Irish Society: Twenty-One Years of Irish TV* (Dublin, 1984), Appendix 1, p.149.
24. Incident recalled by Gay Byrne in *To Whom it Concerns* (Dublin, 1972), pp.71–4.
25. Ibid., pp.86–91.
26. *Irish Times*, 29 March 1966, p.9.
27. *Encyclical Letter of His Holiness Pope Paul VI, Humanae Vitae: On the Regulation of Births*, 21 July 1968, in *The Furrow*, 19, 9 (September 1968), pp.542–56.
28. *Report of the Committee on the Constitution* (Dublin, 1967), pp.43–8.
29. *Irish Times*, 22 September 1969, pp.1, 11.
30. Ibid., 23 September 1969, p.1.

31. See *Irish Times*, 24 May 1971, pp.1, 13.

32. *Report of the Commission on the Status of Women* (Dublin, 1972), pp.223–5.

33. See *Irish Times*, 20 December 1973.

34. *Health (Family Planning) Act, 1979*, no. 20 in public statutes of the oireachtas, 1979.

35. Statement of the Irish Episcopal Conference, 25 November 1973, *Irish Times*, 26 November 1973, pp.1, 16.

36. Ibid.

37. See *Declaration on Religious Freedom*, 7 December 1965 in Walter M. Abbott, SJ (ed.), *The Documents of Vatican II* (Dublin, 1966).

38. See *Irish Times*, 1 June 1976.

39. Kevin McNamara, 'Church and State', *Doctrine and Life*, 30, 3–4 (March–April 1979), p.141.

40. See *The Pope in Ireland: Addresses and Homilies* (Dublin, 1979).

41. Garret FitzGerald, *All in a Life: An Autobiography* (Dublin, 1992), p.378.

42. Statement by the Irish Episcopal Conference, 22 August 1983, *Irish Times*, 23 August 1983, p.5.

43. See *Irish Times*, 9 September 1983. See also Tom Hesketh, *The Second Partitioning of Ireland: The Abortion Referendum of 1983* (Dublin, 1990), p.364.

44. *New Ireland Forum Report, No. 12*, Public Session, Thursday, 9 February 1984, Dublin Castle (Dublin, 1984), p.2.

45. *Irish Times*, 28 June 1986, p.1.

46. Laurence Ryan, 'Some Post-Referendum Reflections', *The Furrow*, 37, 8 (August 1986), p.492.

47. Health (Family Planning) (Amendment) Act, 1992, no. 20 in public statutes of the oireachtas, 1992.

48. *Irish Times*, 6 March 1992.

49. See European Court of Human Rights, *Case of Norris v. Ireland, Judgement of 26 October 1988 (Series A, no. 142)*, Effects of Judgements or Cases, 1959–98.

50. Criminal Law (Sexual Offences) Act, 1993, no. 20 in public statutes of the oireachtas, 1993.

51. *Irish Times*, 7 May 1992. See Joe Broderick, *Fall from Grace* (Dingle, 1992).

52. See advertisement by Commission to Inquire into Child Abuse, inviting persons to give evidence, *Irish Times*, 3 July 2000, p.5. See *Report of the Commission to Inquire into Child Abuse* (Ryan Report) published in May, 2009.

53. *Irish Times*, 27 November 1995.

54. Fuller, *Irish Catholicism Since 1950*, pp.193–5.

55. Ibid., p.195.

56. *Irish Times*, 6 March 1992.

57. *Irish Times*, 26 November 1992. See also Ailbhe Smyth (ed.), *The Abortion Papers* (Dublin, 1992).

58. See *Use Your Vote: Twenty-Fifth Amendment of the Constitution (Protection of Human Life in Pregnancy) Bill, 2001*, an explanatory booklet published by the Referendum Commission (Dublin, 2002). See also *Statement for the Information of Voters on the Twenty-Fifth Amendment of the Constitution (Protection of Human Life in Pregnancy) Bill, 2001*.

59. See *Statement of the Irish Episcopal Conference on the Proposed Abortion Referendum*, press release issued by the Catholic Communications Office, 12 December 2001.

60. *Irish Times*, 8 March 2002.

61. Reaction by Fr Martin Clarke, spokesperson for the bishops, when questioned by Charlie Bird, chief news correspondent, RTÉ, on 'Six One News', RTÉ, 7 March 2002.

CHAPTER 11 SOME FITTING AND ADEQUATE RECOGNITION

1. Marcia Pointon, *Hanging the Head: Portraiture and Social Formation in Eighteenth-Century England* (London, 1993), p.13.

2. Ibid., p.27.
3. See John Beckett, *City Status in the British Isles, 1830–2002* (Hants, 2005) for an analysis of the process by which Belfast became a city, and in doing so set a precedent for the rest of the British Isles.
4. See author's own *Belfast City Hall: One Hundred Years* (Belfast, 2006).
5. Kate Hill, '"Thoroughly Imbued with the Spirit of Ancient Greece": Symbolism and Space in Victorian Civic Culture', in Alan Kidd and David Nicholls (eds), *Gender, Civic Culture and Consumerism: Middle-Class Identity in Britain, 1800–1940* (Manchester, 1999), p.106.
6. Simon Gunn, *Public Culture of the Victorian Middle Class* (Manchester, 2000) p.163.
7. See, for comparative examples of other cities and towns, Gunn, *Public Culture*; Beckett, *City Status*; James Vernon, *Politics and the People: A Study in English Political Culture, c.1815–1867* (Cambridge, 1993); Tristram Hunt, *Building Jerusalem* (London, 2004); Patrick Joyce, *Work, Society and Politics: The Culture of the Factory in Later Victorian England* (Sussex, 1980).
8. Gunn, *Public Culture*, p.163.
9. W.A. Maguire, *Belfast* (Staffordshire, 1993), p.92.
10. Beckett, *City Status*, pp.47–8.
11. Gerard Slater, 'Belfast Politics, 1798–1868', unpublished PhD, University of Ulster, 1982, p.267.
12. Maguire, *Belfast*, p.48.
13. Ibid., p.98.
14. Beckett, *City Status*, p.49.
15. Gunn, *Public Culture*, p.163.
16. Ian Budge and Cornelius O'Leary, *Belfast: Approach to Crisis. A Study of Belfast Politics, 1613–1970* (London, 1973), p.64.
17. Gunn, *Public Culture*, p.169.
18. *Belfast Newsletter*, 23 October 1874.
19. Pointon, *Hanging the Head*, p.24.
20. *Belfast Street Directory*, 1884, pp.16–17.
21. *Belfast Street Directory*, 1895, p.lxv.
22. Ibid.
23. Of the latter, those extant depict Sir William G. Johnston, mayor in 1849 (by Richard Hooke); Sir William Ewart, MP, mayor in 1859 and 1860 (by Sir Thomas A. Jones); Sir Edward Coey, mayor in 1861 (by Sir Thomas A. Jones); John Lytle, mayor in three successive years (1863–64–65) (by Sir Thomas A. Jones); William Mullan, mayor in 1866 (by Philip R. Morris); and Sir David Taylor, mayor in 1867 (and again in 1883 and 1884) (by Richard Hooke). There is also a portrait of Samuel McCausland, mayor in 1868. These portraits now all hang in Belfast City Hall.
24. By 1895 there seemed to be no room left in the Town Hall for civic portraits, the *Belfast Street Directory*, 1895 noting that portraits 'for which there is not room in the Chamber, are hung on the walls of the principal hall and staircase'. In 1899 a portrait of Sir James Henderson was presented to the council and was hung in the Robing Room. Sir Otto Jaffe's civic portrait was presented 'by the Corporation and some friends' to the Art Gallery of the Free Public Library in 1900. A portrait of Charles C. Connor, JP (mayor in 1889–90–91) was also presented and hung in the Free Public Library (*Belfast Street Directory*, 1901). Thus the Free Public Library, in the decade before the opening of the City Hall, provided a temporary space where the city's civic portraits could be hung.
25. Beckett, *City Status*, p.49. 'In July 1864, William Dunville, a wealthy local liberal merchant, surveyed the political scene in Belfast and Ulster: Roman Catholics and Protestant Liberals were divided (he blamed the former); there was division over the Chancery suit; no Liberal candidate had a chance in the town; elsewhere in the province, the Presbyterians identified themselves with the "ultra Tory or Orange party".' Slater, 'Belfast Politics', p.163.
26. Slater, 'Belfast Politics', p.334.

27. Pointon, *Hanging the Head*, p.141.
28. Slater, 'Belfast Politics', p.417.
29. Sir John Preston's portrait was unveiled on 14 April 1887.
30. In 1868 twenty-eight members of the corporation were merchants and manufacturers, three were gentlemen, two doctors, three solicitors, one ship owner, two architects, two jewellers. Slater, 'Belfast Politics', Appendix 1.
31. Louis Purbrick, 'The Bourgeois Body: Civic Portraiture, Public Men and the Appearance of Class Power in Manchester, 1832–50', in Alan Kidd and David Nicholls (eds), *Gender, Civic Culture and Consumerism: Middle-Class Identity in Britain, 1800–1940* (Manchester, 1999), p.84.
32. Pointon, *Hanging the Head*, p.13.
33. In its first decade six civic portraits were presented to Belfast Town Hall – they were Samuel McCausland, JP, mayor in 1868 (by R. Hooke); Dr Samuel Browne, RN, JP, mayor in 1870, the gift of 'some of his past pupils' at the Royal Hospital (by R. Hooke); Philip Johnston, JP, mayor in 1871 (by R. Hooke); Sir John Savage, JP, mayor in 1872 (by R. Hooke); James Alex Henderson, JP, mayor in 1874 (by Sir T.A. Jones); Sir Robert Boag, mayor in 1876 (by Sir T.A. Jones); and John Browne, JP, mayor 1879 and 1880 (by R. Hooke). The portrait of Philip Johnston was unveiled in 1874, James Alex Henderson's was unveiled in 1876, Sir Robert Boag's was unveiled in July 1877, Dr Samuel Browne's was also placed in the chamber in 1877, Sir John Savage's was placed in the chamber in 1880 and both John Browne's and Samuel McCausland's were unveiled in 1882. Eileen Black, *Art in Belfast, 1760–1888* (Dublin, 2006), p.255. Philip Johnston died 23 September 1882, Sir John Savage died 15 June 1883, John Browne died 16 September 1893, Samuel McCausland died 22 April 1895.
34. *Belfast Newsletter*, 25 September 1882.
35. There appears to be no portrait of Thomas G. Lindsay.
36. Eileen Black, *Paintings, Sculptures and Bronzes in the Collection of the Belfast Harbour Commissioners* (Belfast Harbour Commissioners, 1983), p.23.
37. Jones was commissioned to execute portraits of Belfast's earlier mayors, such as Edward Coey, mayor in 1861, John Lytle, mayor in 1863, 1864, 1865, William Ewart, MP, mayor in 1859 and 1860. Lytle's is a very elaborate portrait; he is depicted wearing the mayoral robe, an elaborately embroidered waistcoat, sword and mayoral chain. By way of contrast, Ewart's portrait depicts him soberly and darkly dressed, seated wearing the mayoral chain, with the mayoral robe on a table next to him, and paper in his hand. Thomas A. Jones joined the Royal Hibernian Academy (RHA) in 1860 and became president in 1869. He was knighted in 1880, by the lord lieutenant, Duke of Marlborough. A successful portraitist, he completed portraits of Lady Randolph Churchill, Sir Edward Harland and the Duke of Cambridge. He died 10 May 1893.
38. Samuel Browne was Presbyterian.
39. John Browne was Presbyterian (and supporter of Rev. Dr Henry Cooke) and a Conservative. A councillor for eighteen years, he was chair of the Improvement Committee. Obit., *Belfast Newsletter*, 18 September 1893.
40. Budge and O'Leary, *Belfast: Approach to Crisis*, p.73. Philip Johnston was born into the Church of Ireland, but on being orphaned was brought up as a Moravian. As a young man he became a Wesleyan, and was a prominent member of the Donegall Street Church. A senior partner in Brookfield Linen Company, he later joined his sons in Jennymount Mill where he remained until his death. He began his career in the wholesale tea trade, before becoming a linen merchant and then a flax merchant. A Conservative, he was a councillor for thirty years, and held the honour of being the first mayor to preside in the new Town Hall. He was one of the original members of the new municipal body established in 1842. His portrait was presented to the corporation 'by his friends'. Obit., *Belfast Newsletter*, 25 September 1882. A Methodist and a Conservative who became a Presbyterian in later life, Sir John Savage was proprietor of John Savage & Co. flax spinners; he became a councillor in 1855 for St Anne's Ward, and in 1861 for St George's Ward. He was knighted in 1872 (along with Sir James Hamilton) during the

visit of the Earl of Spencer, the lord lieutenant, to Belfast to open a basin named in his honour. Obit., *Belfast Newsletter*, 16 June 1883. Alderman John Preston, JP, of Preston, Smyth & Co. (who succeeded Robert Boag and was later knighted) was a linen merchant, bleacher and cambric handkerchief manufacturer. James Alex Henderson was succeeded as mayor by James Lindsay, of James Lindsay & Co. general drapers, linen merchants and carpet warehousemen.

41. *Oxford Dictionary of National Biography*. See author's 'Symbolizing the Civic Ideal: The Civic Portraits in Belfast's Town Hall', *Urban History*, 35, 3 (2008), pp.363–81 for a consideration of the controversy surrounding Sir Robert Boag's portrait.

42. The British Association for the Advancement of Science held its annual conference in Belfast in 1852, 1874, 1902 and 1952.

43. Philip Johnston (1871) left £17,156 8s 1d; Thos. G Lindsay (1875) left £89,362 16s 10d; Sir John Preston (1877 & 1878) left £94,086 9s 7d; John Browne (1879 & 1880) left £58,723 17s 10d. Public Record Office of Northern Ireland (hereafter PRONI) Online wills.

44. The new mayoral chain, designed and manufactured by William Gibson (goldsmith and jeweller of Donegall Place who would later make the ornamental key presented to the lord lieutenant on the laying of the foundation stone for the new City Hall) cost £180, and was a particular point of civic pride. The chain bore the arms and crests of each mayor, with the name and year of office engraved on the back. The largest badge bore the arms of the borough and on the back was engraved: 'This chain and badge were purchased by the Corporation of Belfast, in the year 1874, during the mayoralty of Jas. Alex Henderson, Esq., JP. The shields were presented by the mayors and ex-mayors or their representatives.' Report of General Purposes Committee, 1 January 1875. PRONI LA/7/2EA/11.

45. The council also thought it appropriate to spend £200 on 'providing a more suitable chair for the Mayor than the present one'. Minutes of the General Purposes Committee, 1 April 1874. PRONI LA/7/2EA/11.

46. *Belfast Newsletter*, 23 October 1874.

47. Ibid.

48. Meeting of the Town Hall committee, 25 September 1868. LA/7/16AB/3/2, PRONI.

49. He was also the brother-in-law of Robert Lindsay, who later became the Conservative leader of the corporation. Frank Wright, *Two Lands on One Soil: Ulster Politics Before Home Rule* (Dublin, 1996), p.217.

50. Slater, 'Belfast Politics', p.258.

51. Their numbers were twenty in 1860, twelve in 1863 and eight in 1868.

52. Wright, *Two Lands on One Soil*, pp.217, 260.

53. Slater, 'Belfast Politics', p.282.

54. *Belfast Newsletter*, 23 October 1874.

55. Ibid.

56. Ibid.

57. Mullan's portrait is now in the City Hall.

58. *Belfast Newsletter*, 23 October 1874.

59. Ibid.

60. Ibid.

61. Ibid.

62. Ibid.

63. Vernon, *Politics and the People*, p.49.

64. See author's *Belfast City Hall* for more on the portrait statuary of the City Hall.

65. There was one exception, when in 1986 Lord Mayor Sammy Wilson chose to commission a photographic portrait of himself and his lady mayoress.

CHAPTER 12 THE ORIGINS OF THE PEACE PROCESS

1. Brooke–Mayhew Talks Papers: SDLP, 11 May 1992; UUP, 11 May 1992; DUP, 11 May

1992; IG, 28 August 1992.
2. Linen Hall Library (hereafter LHL), Northern Ireland Political Collection (hereafter NIPC), Messages Between the IRA and the Government: British Message sent 26 February 1993; Message from the Leadership of the Provisional Movement, 5 March 1993; British Message sent 11 March 1993; British Nine-Paragraph Note sent 19 March 1993; Message from the Leadership of the Republican Movement, 22 March 1993. 'Setting the Record Straight': Sinn Féin's 'April' Document – Sinn Féin's Basis for Entering Dialogue.
3. Éamon Mallie and David McKittrick, *The Fight for Peace: The Secret Story Behind the Irish Peace Process* (London, 1996), pp.375–6.
4. Ibid., pp.176–7.
5. Joint Declaration by An Taoiseach, Mr Albert Reynolds, TD and the British Prime Minister, the Rt. Hon. John Major, MP, 15 December 1993 (Dublin, 1993).
6. LHL, NIPC, Frameworks for the Future Cmmd. 2964 (London, 1995).
7. LHL, NIPC, Frameworks for the Future Cmmd. 2964; 'We Reject the Governments' "Frameworks" Proposals as the Basis for Negotiations' (Ulster Unionist Party, 1995); Response to 'Frameworks for the Future' (Ulster Unionist Party, n.d.); Report of the International Body, 22 January 1996.
8. Alastair Campbell and Richard Stott (eds), *The Blair Years: Extracts from the Alastair Campbell Diaries* (London, 2007), p.288.
9. Jonathan Powell, *Great Hatred, Little Room: Making Peace in Northern Ireland* (London, 2008), p.93.
10. Ibid., p.95.
11. Campbell and Stott, *The Blair Years*, p.290.
12. Powell, *Great Hatred, Little Room*, pp.95–6.
13. Campbell and Stott, *The Blair Years*, p.289.
14. Ibid., p.96.
15. Ibid., pp.295–6.
16. Powell, *Great Hatred, Little Room*, pp.100–1.
17. Campbell and Stott, *The Blair Years*, p.296.
18. Powell, *Great Hatred, Little Room*, p.101.
19. Ibid., pp.103–4.
20. Ibid., p.105.
21. Belfast Agreement: Strand 1, Paragraphs 1–33.
22. Belfast Agreement: Strand 2, Paragraphs 1–19 and Annex.
23. Belfast Agreement: Strand 3, British–Irish Council, Paragraphs 1–12.
24. Belfast Agreement: Strand 3, British–Irish Intergovernmental Conference, Paragraphs 1–10.
25. Belfast Agreement: 'Constitutional Issues', Paragraph 1; Annex A; Schedule 1; Annex B.
26. Northern Ireland Constitution Act, 1998, Clause 43.
27. Belfast Agreement: Rights, Safeguards and Equality of Opportunity, Paragraphs 1–10.
28. Belfast Agreement: Security, Paragraphs 1–5; Policing and Justice, Paragraphs 1–5.
29. Belfast Agreement: Prisoners, Paragraphs 1–2.
30. Belfast Agreement: Decommissioning, Paragraphs 1–6.

Other Sources

Bunreacht na hÉireann (Constitution of Ireland)

Ireland Act, 1949

Northern Ireland Constitution Act, 1973

Agreement Between the Government of the United Kingdom of Great Britain and Northern Ireland and the Government of the Republic of Ireland, 1985 Joint Declaration by An Taoiseach, Mr Albert Reynolds TD and the British Prime Minister, the Rt. Hon. John Major, MP, 15 December 1993 (Dublin, 1993) *Frameworks for the Future* (London, 1995)

Report of the International Body, 22 January 1996 (London, 1996) *The Belfast Agreement, 1998* (London, 1998)

Linen Hall Library, Northern Ireland Political Collection

Brooke-Mayhew Talks Papers

'Agreeing New Political Structures': A Submission by the SDLP to the Inter-Party Talks, 11 May 1992

'Arrangements for the Internal Government and Administration of Northern Ireland': A Submission by the Ulster Unionist Party, 11 May 1992

'A Sure Advance': A Paper Submitted by the Democratic Unionist Party, 11 May 1992 'Constitutional Issues': A Paper Submitted by the Irish Government Delegation, 28 August 1992

Miscellaneous

Messages Between the IRA and the Government (British Government, 1993)

Response to 'Frameworks for the Future' (Ulster Unionist Party, nd)

'Setting the Record Straight' (Sinn Féin, 1993)

'We Reject the Governments' "Frameworks" Proposals as the Basis for Negotiations (Ulster Unionist Party, 1995)

Multi-Party Talks Papers

Propositions on Heads of Agreement, 12 January 1998

'Freedom, Justice, Democracy, Equality: Nature, Form and Extent of New Arrangements': A Sinn Féin Submission to Strands 1 and 2 of the Peace Talks

Strand 1 Meeting, 4 March 1998

Stand 2 Meetings, 28 February 1998, 3 March 1998, 10 March 1998

The Legal Basis of Proposed North-South Institutions, Irish Government, 1 April 1998

Index